LEARNING FROM
TRI-CIPROCAL CITIES: THE TIME, THE PLACE, THE PEOPLE

2011–12 BI-CITY BIENNALE OF URBANISM\ARCHITECTURE (HONG KONG)

EDITED BY
GENE KWANG-YU KING
ANDERSON LEE

ORO
EDITIONS

CONTENTS

005 COMMENT CARDS

006 Sponsors' Forewords
018 Preface
022 Curator's Statement by Anderson LEE
026 Curator's Statement by Gene Kwang-Yu KING
030 About the Biennale

034 DIALOGUES
(Q&A 001–

EXHIBITS

PAVILION 1
038 Hong Kong Exhibits
(EXH 001–012)

PAVILION 2
106 Shenzhen and Other Mainland Cities Exhibits
(EXH 013–024)

174 PAVILION 3
Taipei Exhibits
(EXH 025–030)

210 PAVILION 4
Asian Urban Portraits Exhibits
(EXH 031–033)

230 PAVILION 5
World Exhibits
(EXH 034–054)

346 OUTDOOR INSTALLATIONS
Kowloon Park and Beyond
(EXH 055–060)

Q&A 016)
378 DIALOGUES

382 Public Events & Symposium Excerpts
398 Index of Exhibits and Dialogues
406 Acknowledgments
410 About the Curators
414 Afterlife

417 COMMENT CARDS

Hong Kong
is
a
Hectic City!

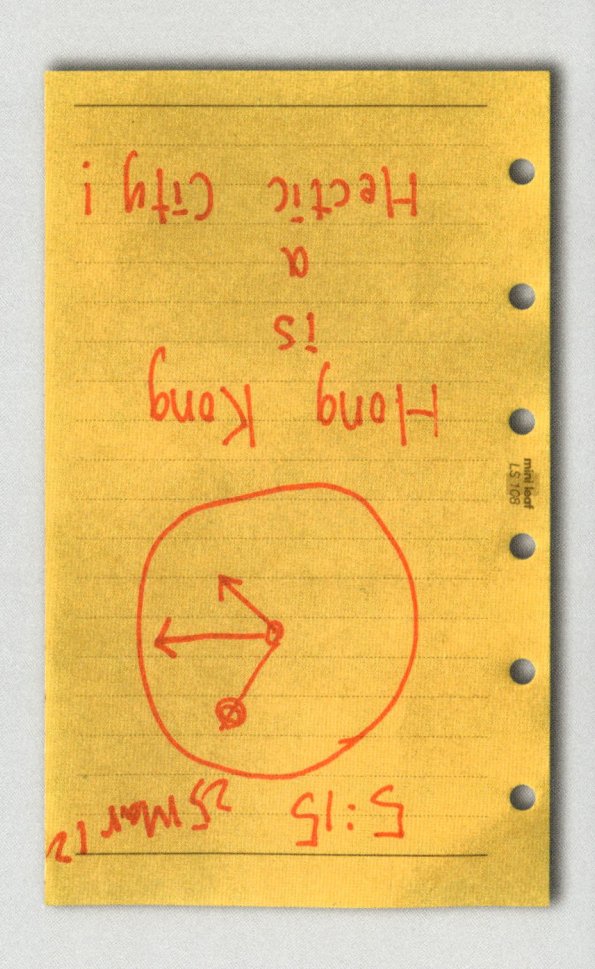

5:15 25 Mar 15

SPONSOR FOREWORD

Since its debut in 2007, the Hong Kong & Shenzhen Bi-City Biennale (now renamed as 'Bi-City Biennale of Urbanism\Architecture in 2013') co-organized by the two neighboring cities of Hong Kong and Shenzhen, has been regarded as a prominent platform in the Asia-pacific region and worldwide to present creative responses to city development and aspect of architecture, urban planning and design.

Themed 'Tri-ciprocal Cities: The Time, The Place, The People,' the 2011 Hong Kong & Shenzhen Bi-City Biennale of Urbanism\Architecture (HKSZ2011) has struck a deep chord between the public and professional practitioners by presenting thematic stories of Hong Kong, Mainland China and Taiwan as part of a delicate picture woven by architecture, history and human beings. We are proud to have hosted around 150,000 visitors to the exhibition during the three-month showing in Kowloon Park, Hong Kong, which was a significant record that almost went neck-to-neck with the Venice Biennale International Architecture Exhibition in Italy 2010. HKIA, as the leading organizer, is honoured to have this commemorative publication produced as a significant record of the marvelous exhibition.

The exhibition was therefore not only a tribute to all artists, visitors, partners, and supporting organizations, but also to the behind-the-scenes curatorial team led by Mr. Gene K King, Mr. Anderson Lee, Ms. Julia Lau and Ms. Tristance Kee, who were an essential part of making the HKSZ2011 and this commemorative publication a success.

I hope you enjoy reading and will be inspired by the vitality and creativity of the Biennale.

Ada FUNG, JP, FHKIA, RA
President
The Hong Kong Institute of Architects

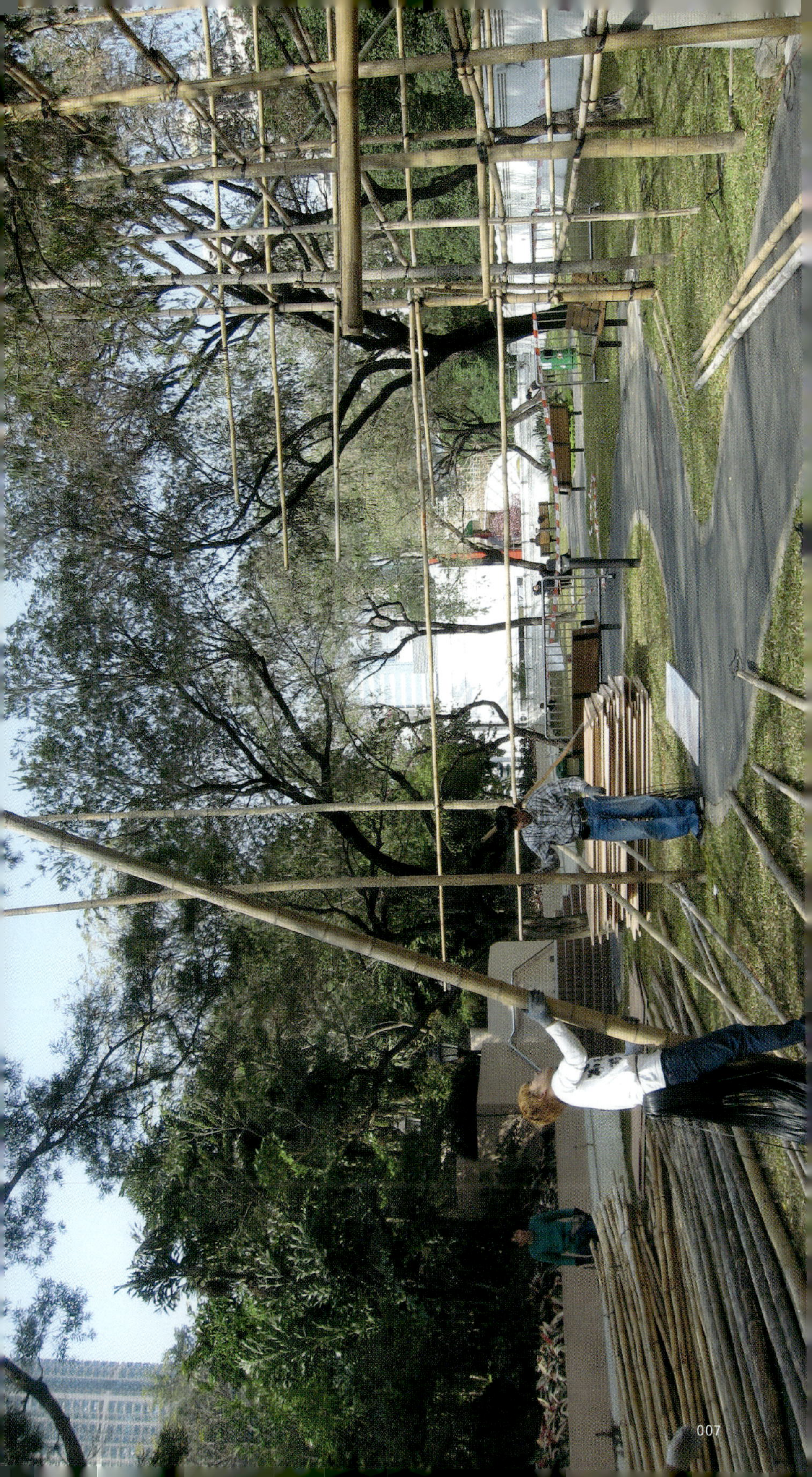

008

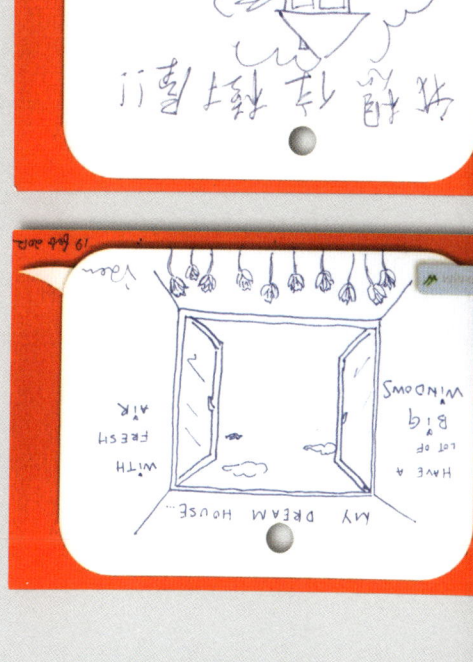

I want to have a house that I design. It doesn't have to be big, but it must have enough private space for my family.

我想有樣有個房子!!

MY DREAM HOUSE.

HAVE A LOT OF BIG WINDOWS

WITH FRESH AIR

SPONSOR FOREWORD

Hong Kong-Shenzhen Bi-city Biennale 2011–12 was an unequivocal success, with attendance of approximately 150,000, which almost doubled the figure of the previous Biennale and was the highest among all previous Biennales. The Hong Kong Institute of Planners is honored to have organized the 2011–12 Biennale together with Hong Kong Institute of Architects and Hong Kong Designers Association. It was successful in arousing public awareness on the diversity and creativity of architects, planners and designers in responding to the social and cultural values underpinning the metamorphosis of our urban environment.

The Biennale provided a platform for practitioners to showcase their new concepts and gave visitors an opportunity to be engaged and reflect on their aspirations and relationship with the ever-evolving city. The venue at Kowloon Park was a perfect location for providing easy access as well as a living example of adaptive reuse, heritage preservation, sustainable development and green living, which are important concepts affecting the city. It all matched well with the theme of the Biennale – 'Tri-ciprocal Cities: The Time, The Place, The People.'

I would like to take this opportunity again to congratulate the curatorial team for putting together such a group of remarkable and engaging exhibits. We are also grateful to our sponsors for their generosity. The 2011–12 Biennale was not just an occasion to showcase our creativity and innovation but also provided an opportunity for us to be inspired and stimulated to make changes and positive impacts to the continuous transformation of our beloved city.

Raymond LEE
President
Hong Kong Institute of Planners

011

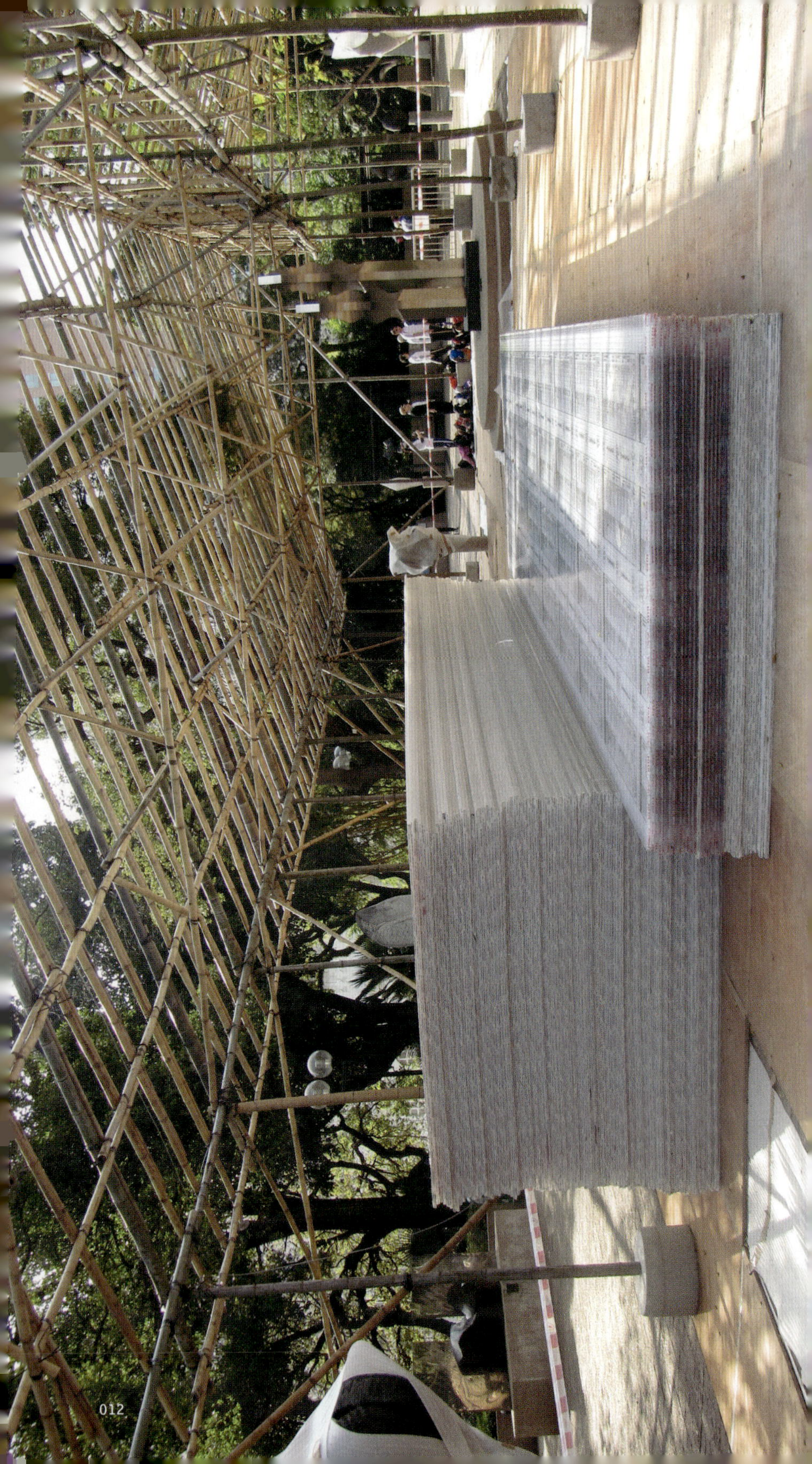

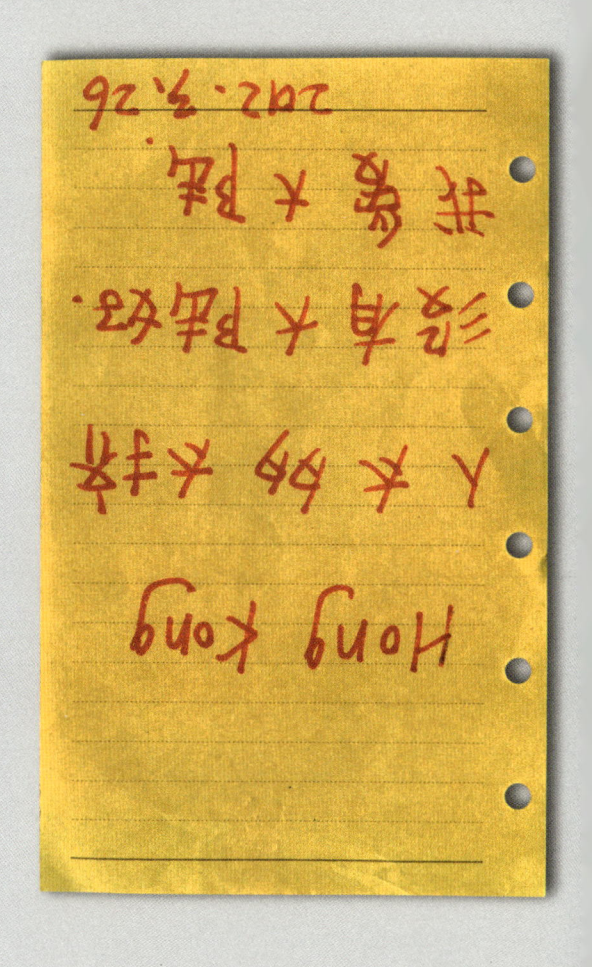

Hong Kong

人 大 的 大 好美

没有 大 跟好。

老婆 大 跟美。

2142. 9. 26

SPONSOR FOREWORD

I am much honored to have the chance to participate in the Hong Kong & Shenzhen Bi-City Biennale of Urbanism\Architecture. This is one of the most important, if not to say indispensable, exhibitions for the people of the neighboring cities, and even people elsewhere in the world who are living in highly urbanized places. With the efforts of the curators, the 2011 biennale is the fourth of a series of joint exhibitions of the city planners, architects, designers and all the people concerned with ways to pursue a perfect life style or even a philosophy, a wisdom of modern living. The theme of 'Tri-ciprocal Cities: The Time, The Place, The People' is exactly focused on shaping a new form of urbanism.

In the past century one of the most important issues of global development was the speed of urbanization, with modern mega cities rising one by one: Chicago, New York, London, Tokyo, Hong Kong, Shanghai, and Beijing... High rises, mass transportation, chain stores, super shopping malls, densely populated houses, highly electronic controlled life components... these not only change the shapes of our cities, but also they have completely changed our way of living: we are a different kind of human from a hundred years ago. The designers and architects have played an important role there.

On the other hand, many problems follow the comfort and the pleasurable, convenience of modern living: pollution, financial fluctuations, unemployment, and homelessness, conflicting human relationships, unbalanced wealth distribution, monotony and stressful life. These are certainly the most unwanted by-products. So it will be a trend in the future to help to solve these problems, as well as to develop a new face of urbanization.

The 2011 exhibition made very impressive insights to the problem, and with no doubt, I am expecting the Hong Kong & Shenzhen Bi-City Biennale of Urbanism\Architecture in 2013 will promote more innovative ideas about the future of urban living.

Francis York Wah LEE
Chairman
Hong Kong Designers Association

015

016

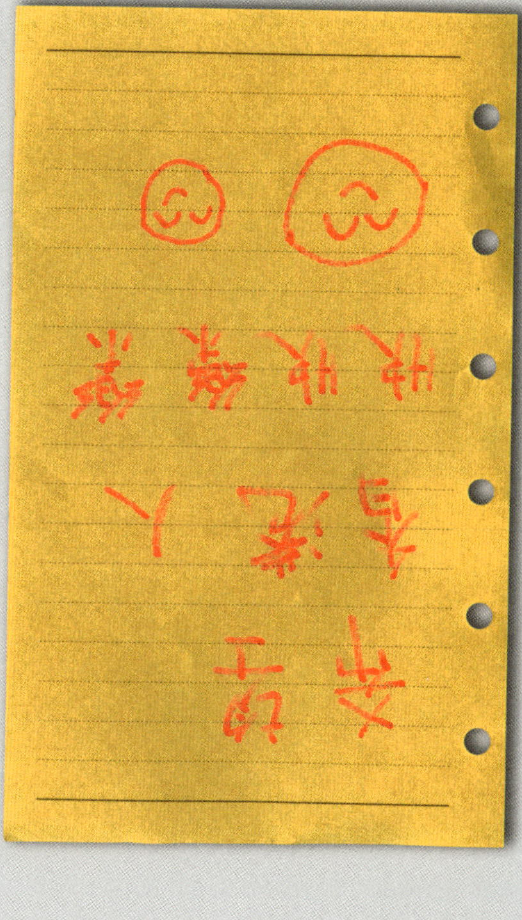
希望
香港人
快快樂樂

PREFACE

On the Count of Three: Tri-ciprocal Cities Revisited

One faces a dilemma when trying to put together a publication such as this one. How to reveal and document an event that lasted for over four months and included over 25 symposiums, guided tours and workshops? The task seems even more insurmountable when the event in question happened over eighteen months ago.

Because of the time lapse, the curators strongly felt that this publication should be more than just a book to record what took place from December 2011 to April 2012. Instead, we wanted to treat the project as a continuation of the theme we developed in the Biennale: 'Tri-ciprocal Cities: The Time, The Place, The People.' In a sense, we see the book as the final participant/exhibitor of the Biennale, though it comes as a belated entry 18 months after the main event. The book-making reflects the idea of a 'triciprocal' relationship, acting as a device to interact with the readers. Its design is loosely organized into three parts – the **PAST**, the **PRESENT**, and the **FUTURE** – in a somewhat hybridized, if not random, order, and it can be read in three different orientations.

As with most publications of a similar nature, this project functions like a Catalogue and attempts to capture the **PAST** in order to give readers an atmospheric sense of presence at the Biennale. In the span of 69 days, the Biennale took place in locations in Kowloon Park, Wanchai Visual Archive, Oasis Gallery, and Hong Kong Art Center, with over 150,000 people involved (including organizing committee members, special guests of honor, 60 exhibitors, 65 symposium speakers and public visitors).

This publication is also a Dialogue. This project gave us, the curators, an opportunity to acknowledge the **PRESENT** by furthering discussions on the Biennale's theme. We have corresponded with various exhibitors and symposium speakers to share current thoughts and views on 'Tri-ciprocal Cities: The Time, The Place, The People.' The publication illustrates the continuum of time which is vital to the development of any architectural work and urban transformation. A few exhibitors shared the present state of work that was shown during the biennale, and we were delighted to learn that some pieces transformed themselves and became permanent marks in the city, while others continue to metamorphose into other projects. The textual contents generated from these correspondences form a second layer of reading throughout the design of the book, acting as an interlude to the graphic and visually dominant nature of the Catalogue.

Finally this publication is an Epilogue. The third part of the publication represents a selection of post-it notes and comment cards collected from the general public during the four-month period of the show. These materials are both visual and textual, and they represent the diversified **FUTURE** visions of each visitor's imagined city.

So on the count of three: the book has no specific order and there is no correct way to read it. It is a catalogue, dialogue and epilogue, which loosely corresponds to the past, the present and the future. It is designed to be used in at least three different orientations. For this love triangle continues to reinforce our conviction and believe that Architecture and the City are a continuous recognition, acknowledgement and interaction of the time, the place and the people.

Anderson LEE & Gene Kwang-Yu KING
November 28, 2013
Hong Kong

019

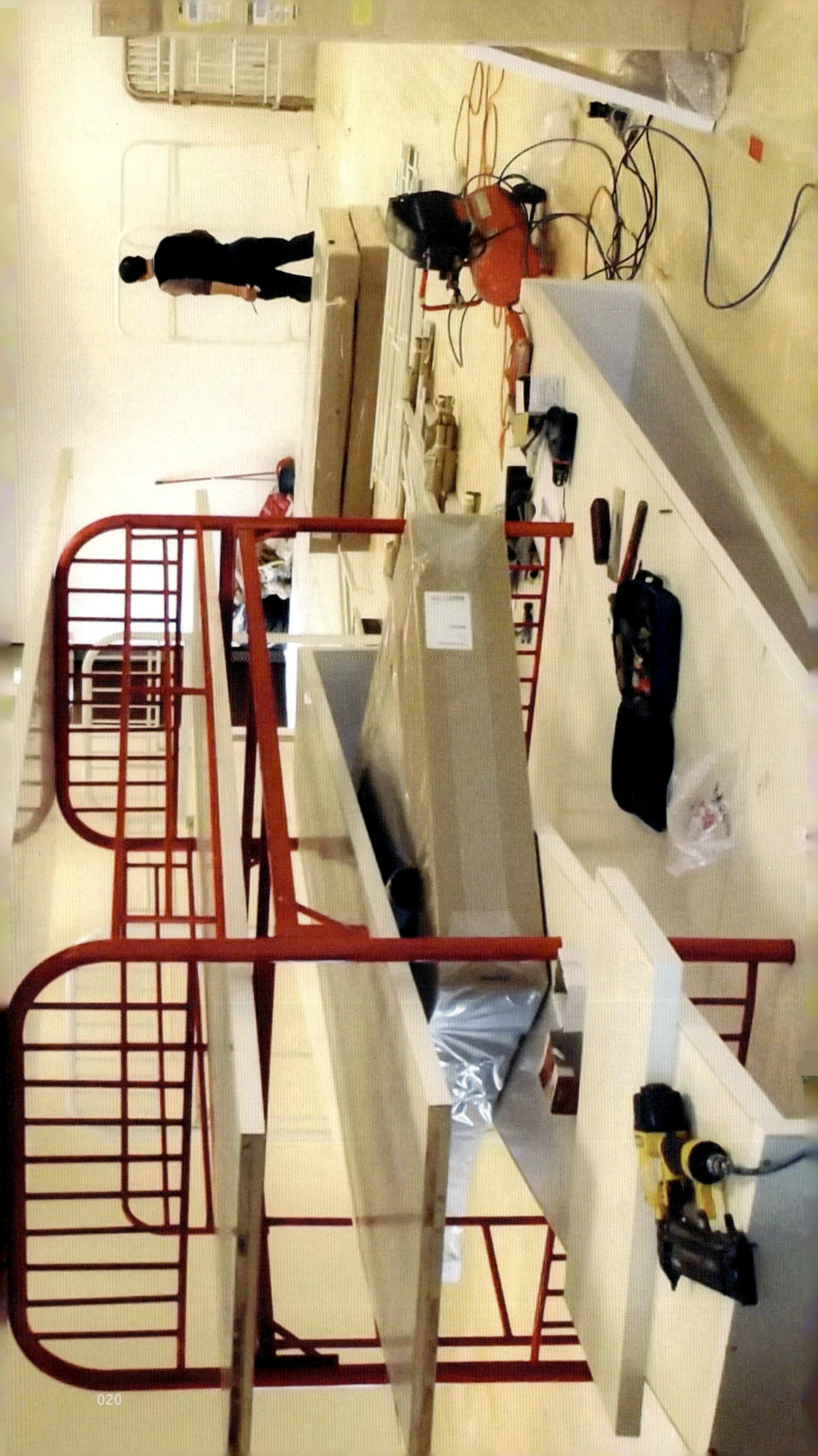

花費一個1.36代吃太貴。

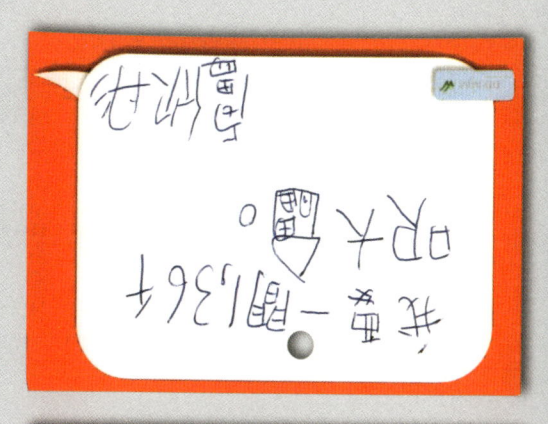

包廂大小

一樓四口 F1OOR
atrium
目 room

CURATOR'S STATEMENT

A Parallel of Time and Space, with People: A 'Retrospective' on the Idea of Tri-ciprocal Cities

It has long been the expected role of a biennale to predict or project the future. This fascination with the future is inextricably linked to the idea of a linear time/space continuum. The curatorial theme, 'Tri-ciprocal Cities: The Time, The Place, The People,' aims to explore the intertwining relationships of these three fundamental elements that inform different stages of a city's development and its architecture.

Drawing a parallel between individual biological development and urban development, we categorized cities into various stages, labeling them as young cities, middle-aged cities in crisis, or mature cities at their zenith. Exhibitors responded to our curatorial theme with projects from their respective cities. The contents and theoretical bases of their entries (which we called 'city stories') went far beyond our expected methods. More often than not, we began to find that each city could have traces of all three life-stages coexisting simultaneously.

The best biological analogy I can find between a city and a human body is that the city is made up of thousands of individual cells that come together to form something like the organs in a body. In other words, the body is physical 'hardware' not unlike the infrastructure and built fabric of our cities. To take it one step further, the body is ultimately built to house a person's soul or personality, which is similar to the particular characteristics and charms of a city. Therefore, it becomes possible to argue that each city might embody young, mid-life, and mature characteristics at the same time. This led me to think of the time/space continuum as no longer a linear progression but rather a cyclical phenomenon.

If aging is considered to be a linear process moving from youth to mid-life and maturity, then by contrast the idea of cyclical time means that maturity can be followed by youth and mid-life again, in a continuous looping process without end. Thus it is possible to imagine a city, or any of its parts, undergoing transformation, rejuvenation, and revitalization at different paces, making the coexistence of all three biological stages possible. Conceptually this recalls Italo Calvino's poetic urban descriptions in 'Invisible Cities,' which plausibly collapse time, space and place.

The recent Taiwanese movie, 'You Are the Apple of My Eye,' also made use of this idea of parallel universes. I found it particularly fascinating in the context of this Biennale, because comparing cities in different stages of development is almost like comparing alternate realities. The fact is that most European cities started the urbanization process in the eighteenth/nineteenth centuries, followed by American cities in the nineteenth/twentieth centuries, and now by Asian cities in the twentieth/twenty-first centuries.

This passage of time undeniably sets up a tempting framework of linear development, where one city can act as predecessor for the others. But if we are to think of each city as predecessor and successor while learning from each other's wisdom and mistakes, we will soon discover that our cities, irrespective of physical age, have the ability to absorb the past and project into the future while inhabiting the present fully. Any city should be able to offer the energy possessed by the young, the skepticism and experience accumulated by the middle-aged, and the wisdom and grace found in the mature. It is through the intertwining of these three states that its inhabitants can truly create dream cities of their own.

Anderson LEE, AIA

023

024

jjj

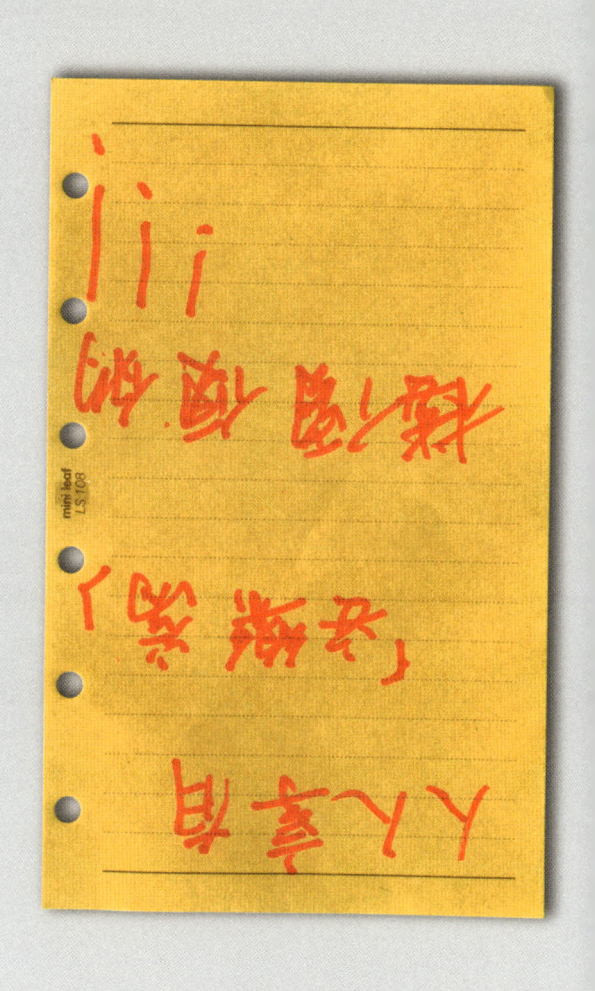

新歌 昌小琳

〔紫海鸥〕

丫丫幸甚

CURATOR'S STATEMENT

Hardware, Software, People, and the Disposition of a City

After the closing of the 2011–12 Hong Kong & Shenzhen Bi-City Biennale of Urbanism\Architecture, I had the opportunity to co-teach a design studio, titled 'Inventing the Immemorial,' with my wife and partner, Erin C. Shih.

We selected three sites in Taipei located in an areas developed during the Qing Dynasty, Japanese colonization, and KMT-control periods. We asked the students to look into the context of each site, examining elements tangible and intangible, physical and cultural, as well as present and past. The students were expected to compile the context they gathered for future use as inspiration for their designs.

The title is an extension of the theme 'Tri-ciprocal Cities: The Time, The Place, The People' in the sense that although physical planning and architecture do not entail living beings, the city's design creates an ambiance and character that makes a city unique. It enables cities, just as a living creature, to change and grow with the passage of time. In this ever-evolving world, we observe that there are perpetual fluctuations among 'constants' and 'variables.' These constants in life are continually changing while new variables are integrated as constants. This happens in hardware (city planning, infrastructure, and buildings), software (policy, private sector development and operation), as well as people (management and attitudes towards life) – again, tri-ciprocally, everything is unceasingly re-defined.

Traditional Chinese epics (Romance of Three Kingdoms, Adventure of the Monkey, Outlaws of the Marshes, etc.) differ from Western theories in their notions toward literary creation. These stories have endured the erosion of generations and undergone countless revisions until they were eventually organized into the popularized versions we know today, retaining the essence of each retelling. This creative evolution corresponds to the urban development process, and we architects and designers are no more nor less than the storytellers that pass the stories down with our own interpretations. A master is one who can see through the extraneous fluff and consolidate everything into an undying theme.

During the Biennale and the semester at HKU, I mostly stayed at Robert Black College, the University guest house located in the Mid-Levels on the western side of Hong Kong Island. Whenever possible, I got up early and hiked the nearby mountain trail and usually ended my trip at the Peak. Despite the incessant waves of development through the years, there are many things about the island that remain just like the day the British fleet dropped its anchor for the Opium War. The city has a stubborn resilience that has allowed its incessant changes to coexist with its past, even when the difference between the two is as distant as the peak and Victoria bay. The ability to hold onto the basics in spite of its quest for a new identity – be it Chinese or cosmopolitan – is the key to the city's uniqueness.

Gene Kwang-Yu KING

027

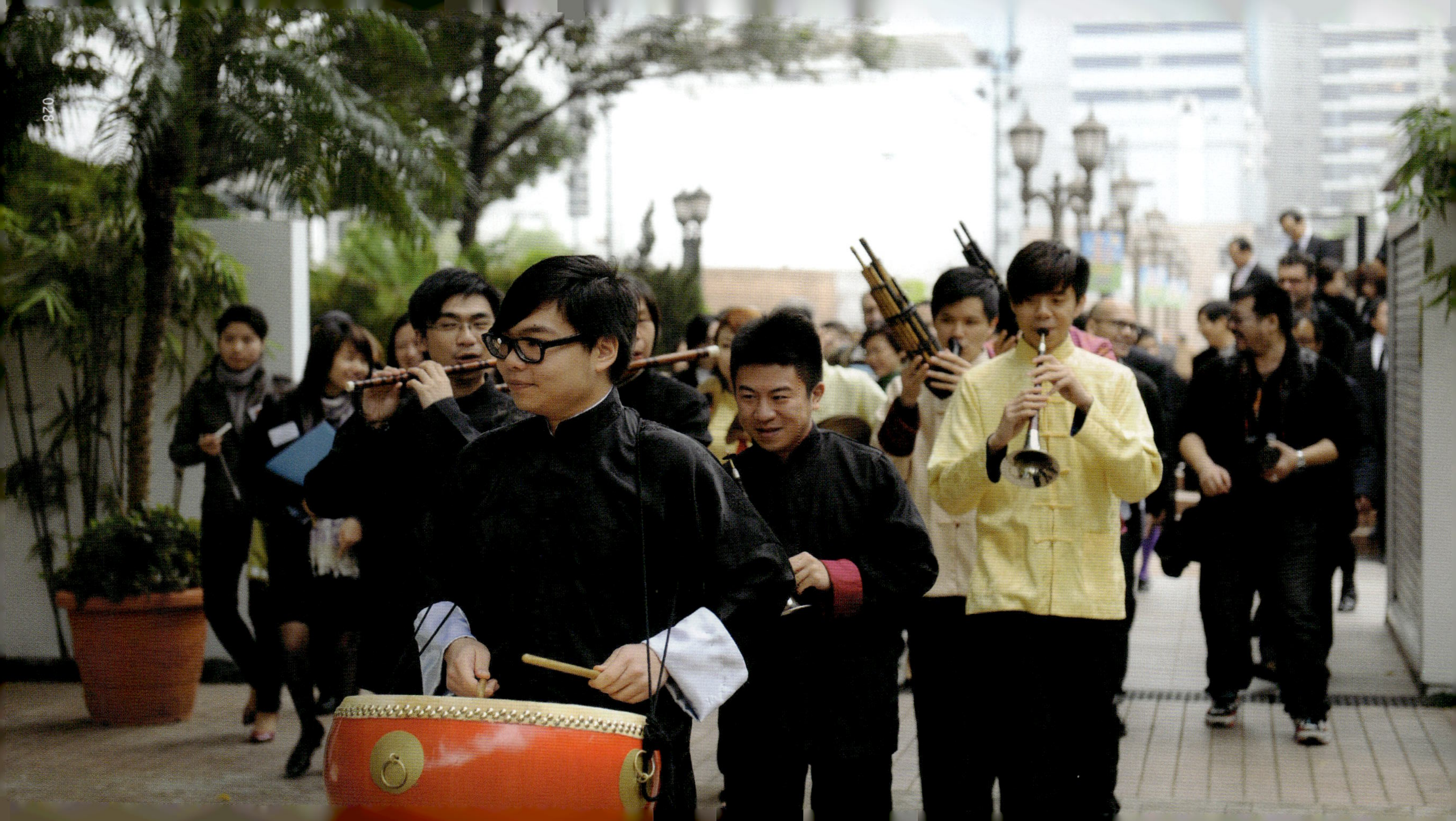

用知吧

About the Biennale

The Hong Kong side of the 2011–12 Hong Kong & Shenzhen Bi-City Biennale of Urbanism\Architecture was held at Kowloon Park in Tsim Sha Tsui (TST). The exhibition injected a new kind of energy to the park and expanded the interaction with visitors of diverse backgrounds – locals and tourists.

'Tri-ciprocal' – a word derived from 'reciprocal' – emphasizes the interplay of time, place, and people; each of these elements significantly shapes the essence and quality of a city. In Chinese the theme of the biennale, if translated directly, means 'three-phased cities: time, place, people.' It is followed, however, by the character 間 (jian), which means 'realm' or 'dimension' but might also mean 'in-between,' indicating an abstract and intangible relationship. The Biennale drew an analogy between the development of a city and the biological time of a person, and wished to render comparative representations of cities at their different biological times in order to provide valuable mutual references.

Five pavilions reflected the thematic consistency of 'Tri-ciprocal Cities':

1. Pavilion for Hong Kong Exhibits
2. Pavilion for Shenzhen and Other Mainland Cities Exhibits
3. Pavilion for Taipei Exhibits
4. Pavilion for Asian Urban Portraits Exhibits
5. Pavilion for World Exhibits (inside the Hong Kong Heritage Discovery Centre)

There were also outdoor installations in Kowloon Park as well as two Satellite Venues (Central Oasis Gallery and Wanchai Visual Archive) to showcase the works.

The biennale employed the 'bunk bed' as a basic unit for the exhibitors to react against. The bunk bed concept was not only inspired by the high-density housing prevalent in Hong Kong, but was also a practical response to the limitation of suitable indoor exhibition space within Kowloon Park. It aimed to provoke an overwhelming sense of collective memory of the Hong Konger and further reflection on the colonial past of the site as a former military barracks filled with bunk beds occupied by military personnel.

The exhibition and its related cultural programs and community events were held at various other venues in the city. Guided heritage walks originated within Kowloon Park and stretched towards the Miramar Shopping Centre and Knutsford Terrace to the east and the China Hong Kong City to the west, informing visitors of the site's historical past. The far-reaching extent of the activities echoed the curatorial theme of 'Public Realm' of the cities in different stages of development. The hope was to show that a dream city, no matter of what age, is like a person who has the compassion and wisdom of the old, sophistication and practicality of the middle-aged, and purity and vitality of the young.

031

032

033

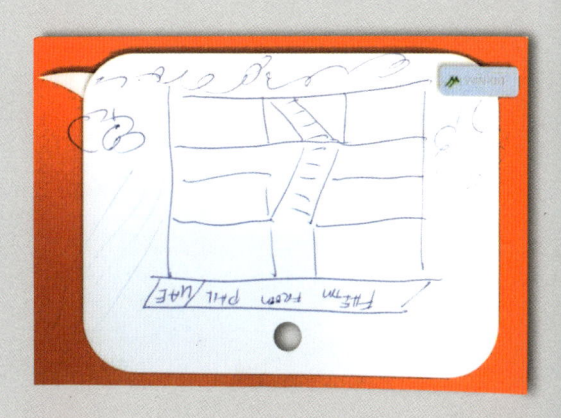

DIALOGUES

Email Q&A conducted August–October 2013 with various Biennale participants

FROM: Anderson Lee, Gene King
TO: Aaron Betsky; Joshua Bolchover; Felix Claus; Kristof Crolla; Norihiko Dan; Tris Kee; Shu-Chang Kung; Julia Lau; Ulf Meyer; Jesse Reiser & Nanako Umemoto; Terence Riley; Nasrine Seraji; Weijen Wang; Kacey Wong; Kim Yao; Rocco Yim
SENT: 05 August 2013 14:53
SUBJECT: 2011–12 HKSZ Biennale Tri-ciprocal Cities Dialogue/publication

Dear Friends and Colleagues,

We hope this email finds you well and in good spirits! A pair of voices from a (not so) distant past… We are putting together a publication (tentatively) entitled 'Learning from(for) Tri-ciprocal Cities: a continuum of time, place and people.' The book is not a usual catalog to recap what had happened 18 months ago during our biennale, but also a beginning of a new dialogue to reflect, ponder, postulate on what 'Tri-ciprocal Cities' means to all of us, now and present. We are honored to have had you take part in the biennale, and hope you can find some time to contribute to a set of Q&As that we will send out shortly to each one of you. It is a set of tailored questions from us and, with your kind permission, we will put your responses into the publication, which is scheduled to be launched right before the upcoming biennale 2013 (yes, time has passed so very quickly). There is no specific word count requirement. As you might know, we are on a tight schedule (yup, Hong Kong speed again!), so we would appreciate your utmost cooperation in our endeavors.

Looking forward to hearing from you,
Gene and Anderson

Q&A 001

DIALOGUE WITH
Aaron Betsky

TO: Aaron Betsky
FROM: Gene King, Anderson Lee

As I mentioned in Tokyo, we are finally going to publish the book on HK Biennale, even though it is almost a year and a half since it was closed. Anderson has a good idea, which is that since it is so long ago, we might well have a dialogue and reflection about the topic again I think it will make a much more readable book. Your words will mean a lot for us.

TO: Gene
FROM: Aaron

It was great to see you. It seems like I spent most of the time on the plane, but that is the way it is. As to your questions, I would be happy to answer, but have to counter-question:
I am not sure how the question at the end of the first paragraph follows from the preceding. Are you saying that we should step back from defining architecture in broader terms, either philosophically or in terms of scale, and concentrate on what 'real' licensed architects do? I hope not, because then my answer would be a simple no. It would be boring and of little use. That is what technical manuals are for. Case in point the most recent Venice biennale.
As to the second, do you think I am qualified to opine about Chinese cities? I really have

035

036

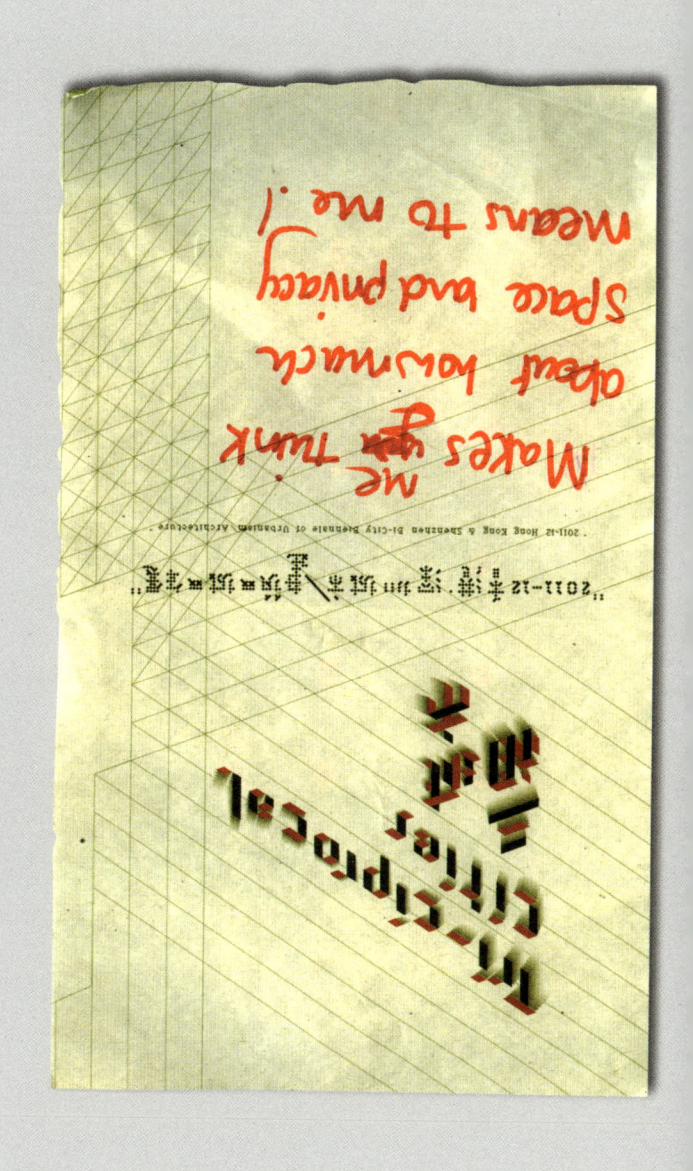

Makes me think about how much space and privacy means to me.!

"2011-12 香港 & 深圳 城市\建筑 双城双年展."

2011-12 Hong Kong & Shenzhen bi-city Biennale of Urbanism\Architecture

互惠
城市
Reciprocal
Cities

PAVILION 1
Hong Kong Exhibits

The pavilion for Hong Kong Exhibits was anchored by two case studies examining architecture's response to changing social and economic conditions, reflecting the curatorial theme of time, place and people. One showed the evolution of local school typologies, tracing a path from the missionary schools of the colonial settlement to the overcrowded rooftop classrooms of the mid-twentieth century to the more recent standardized schools and private schools. As birth rates go up or down, and as the role of education changes in society, schools must evolve and change to respond. The second case study focused on East Kowloon's history and development. As a hub of manufacturing in the 1960s and 70s, the area saw the construction of many industrial buildings, and high-rise residential towers were built to house the workforce needed to sustain the industry. As more and more manufacturing has moved to Mainland China, and especially after the relocation of the airport to Lantau Island, this area has become a new void in the city. Planners and designers are currently in the process of reimagining this neighborhood as an embodiment of the new part of Hong Kong.

Alongside these case studies, the pavilion also showed the work of individual exhibitors with subject matter ranging from growing seeds in street sidewalks to the literal melting of iconic Hong Kong historical buildings.

ABOUT THE PAVILION
The Pavilion was designed by a local Bamboo Master, who employed traditional wisdom to make the most of bamboo's inherent tensile strength and flexibility. This kind of structure is usually built as a temporary outdoor pavilion for the performance of Chinese Opera. Unlike those traditional pavilions, which use galvanized sheet metal as cladding, this pavilion was clad in polycarbonate panels to allow light to filter into the space.

HONG KONG EXHIBITS 039

040 HONG KONG EXHIBITS

我的臨筆 My Sharing

The ever changing Education
system in HK is making
the children's life hard.
a teacher ;

我的臨筆 My Sharing

大學 final year 要兼顧一個
Sem 讀 3 個係一切 hw, 仲
有 3 份功課要係埋成個月
搞, 甚至一月, 真的好辛苦!!

甚至!!

EXH 001

PAVILION:

Hong Kong Exhibits

PROJECT:

Changing Face of Kowloon East

DESCRIPTION:

The places we used to call Kwun Tong Industrial Area and Kowloon Bay Industrial Area have been strongholds of the manufacturing industry since its emergence through reclamation in the 50s and 60s. The Changing Face of Kowloon East took visitors through the decades of this area's development, changes in its urban landscape along with the relocation of the Kai Tak Airport and the transformation of Hong Kong's economy, and brought forth a vision of a vibrant node for business, leisure, recreation, entertainment and tourism.

EXHIBITOR:

Hong Kong SAR Planning Department

The Planning Department (PlanD) of HKSAR Government is responsible for the preparation of various types of town plans to guide the proper use and development of land with the objective of making Hong Kong a better place to live and work in.

ORIGIN:

Hong Kong

HONG KONG EXHIBITS 043

Past and Present

50 60 70 80 90

CONCEPTUAL MASTER PLAN
CBD²

044 HONG KONG/EXHIBITS

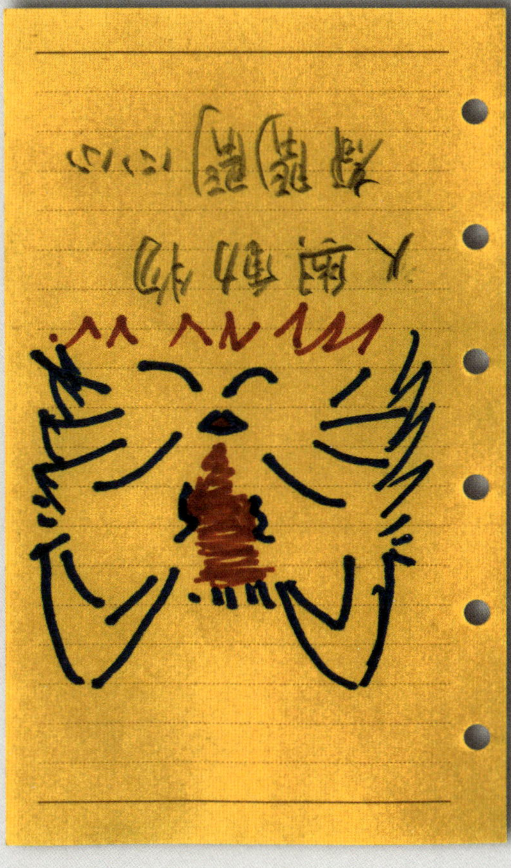

EXH 002

PAVILION:
Hong Kong Exhibits

PROJECT:
A Bed of Life

DESCRIPTION:
This exhibition captured beds of different types of housing, from subsidized 'cage' housing to mediocre private properties to luxurious dwellings to create a thought-provoking spatial experience questioning how urban spaces should be organized in Hong Kong.

EXHIBITOR:
Hong Kong Institute of Planners, Young Planners Group Committee

HKIP Young Planners Group Committee was formed by a group of energetic and forward-thinking young planners who are passionate about planning a better future for Hong Kong, and additionally aim to promote professional development for young practitioners.

ORIGIN:
Hong Kong

Caged House 籠屋
1 Bed 床位 一張單人床
十八平方呎 / 0.34 Bed/person
一人享有面積三十四平方呎
3ft. by 6ft.
每月七百三十二元
HK$1300/month
床位一千三百元半月一

Small Units 小單位

A BED of LIFE

HONG KONG EXHIBITS 047

Caged House 籠屋

1 Bed 18 sq.ft. 三呎乘六呎 0.34 Bed/person 一張床
一人享有零點三四張床 3 ft. by 6 ft. 72 sq ft/month床
HKD$1300/month 月租一千三百元 月租一
床位一千三百元 HKD1300/bed

Please Don't Climb 請勿攀爬

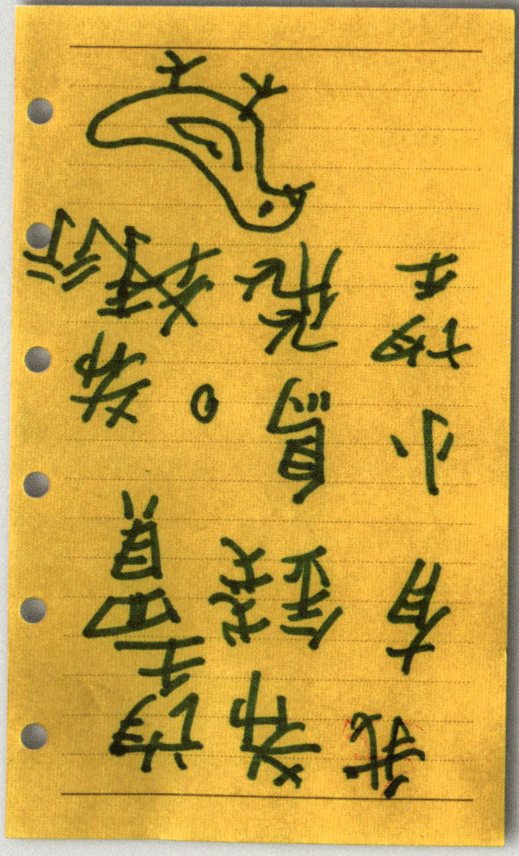

EXH 003

PAVILION:

Hong Kong Exhibits

PROJECT:

BioShell (Biodegradable Vacuum-formed Modularized Shelter) [©]

DESCRIPTION:

This exhibit was created with BioShell which is a biodegradable, ultra-lightweight structure as well as spatial art; a patent-filed and innovative architectural structure that creates all-new space for work, play, and living with nature. It is environmentally friendly, modular, packable, reusable, flexible, easy to set up and light to transport. Ideal for temporary constructions such as booths, parties, greenhouses, playrooms, and disaster relief shelters, it can be dismantled easily after use without burdening the environment.

EXHIBITOR:

Shinya OKUDA

Shinya Okuda is an registered architect in the Netherlands and Japan, currently Assistant Professor at the National University of Singapore. He has received multiple international awards including the Advanced Architecture Competition in Barcelona in 2008 and HKDA Excellence Awards in Hong Kong in 2009.

ORIGIN:

Japan / Singapore

HONG KONG EXHIBITS 051

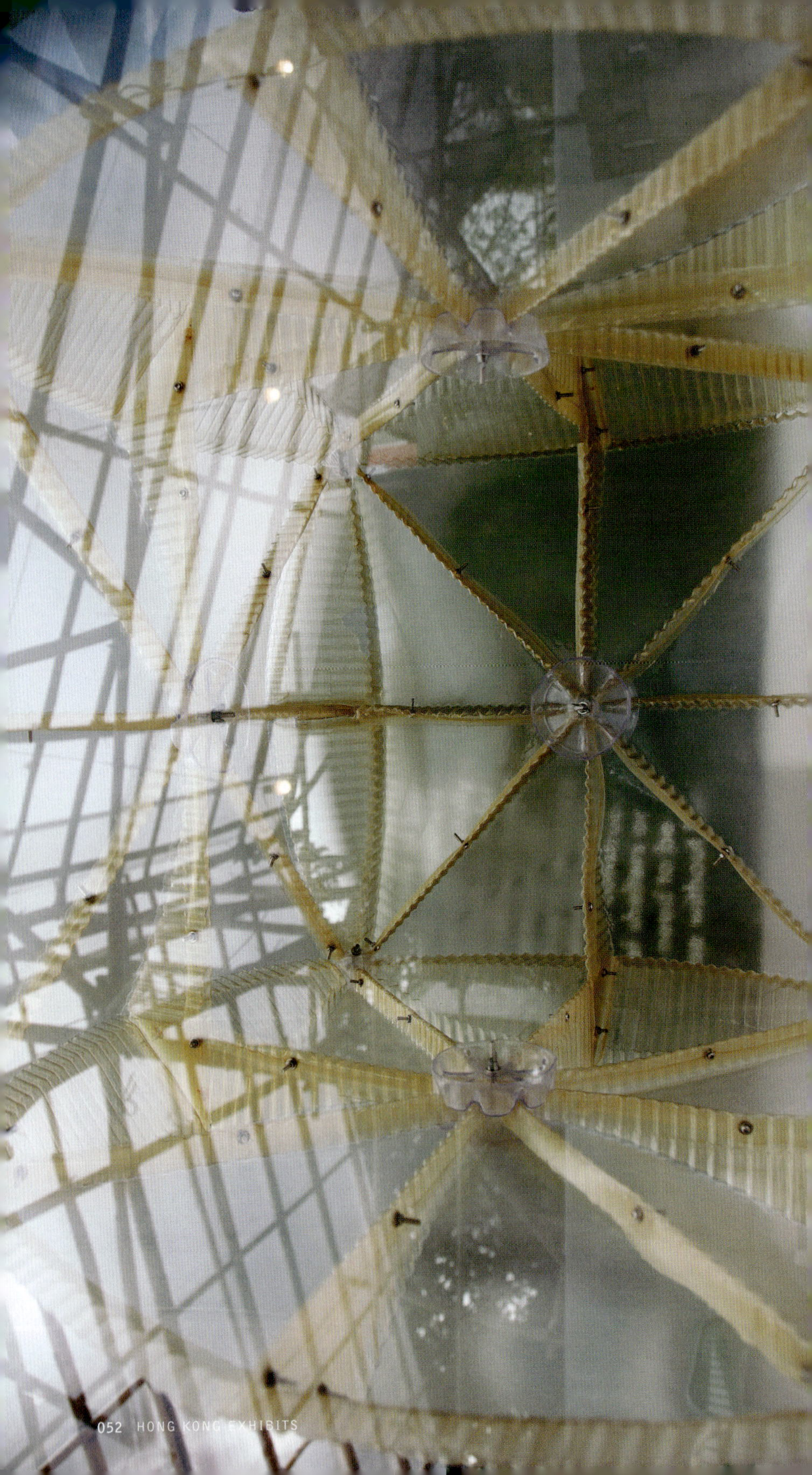

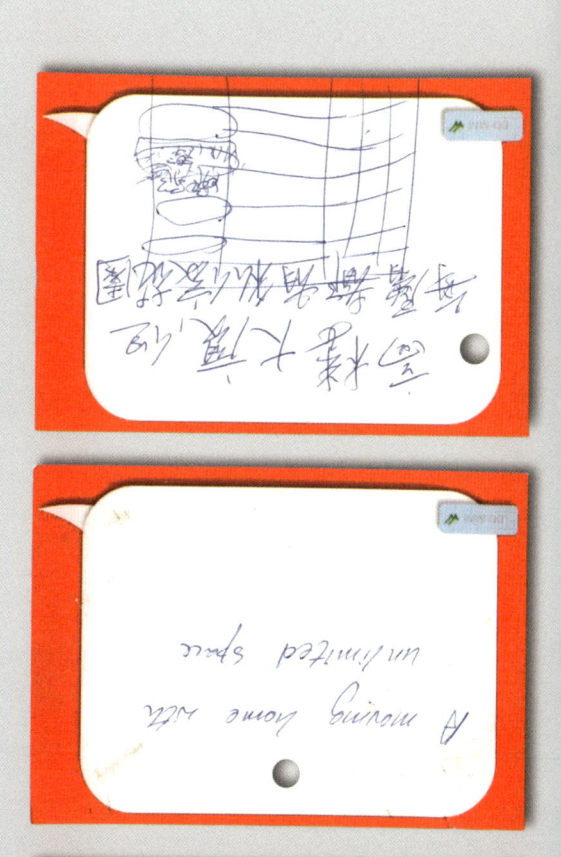

会稀某大道.163
每座寄居城市的缩图

A moving home with
unlimited space

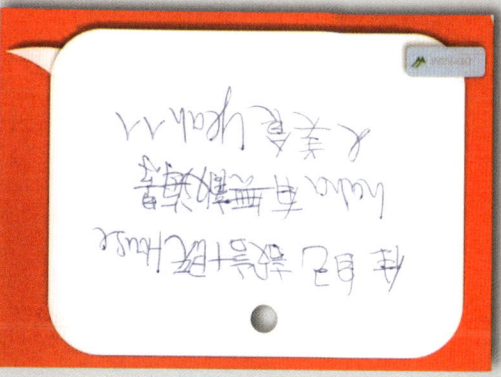

每日日移至十区House
lulu 有無限英間
人类居住的小人

053

only a dilettante's knowledge of either their current state or their history. Of course none of us like what we see in most places, and are, as always, encouraged by isolated experiments. But am I looking at these situations with eyes that are too Western? I do not know.

TO: Aaron
FROM: Gene

Of course not going back to technical manuals, but also I think there are too much emphasis on starchitects' grand, expensive buildings with display of forms while so little attention is paid to other aspects of architecture, namely spaces, relationship to cities or landscape, possibilities for alternate uses, etc. I understand your rigorous definition among building and architecture, I only think current architectural scene is not exactly what you define architecture either. I just hope to get your view upon what an event like the Biennale can do for architecture.

Chinese cities are such a myth, nobody knows what they are any way. Even you look at Chinese cities with Western viewpoint, it is a true Western, unlike most Chinese just try to pretend Western. Additionally, you have traveled far and wide, and you can't be too Western any way. I really enjoy what you said about the sexiness of Japanese men and women, it is so true and quintessential of Japanese psyche. Your viewpoint on Chinese or Asian cities must be very inspirational also.

TO: Gene
FROM: Aaron

Chinese cities are both completely recognizable to us coming from the West, and very alien. They have all the components of modern cities and the parts that have been redone in the last twenty years — which is almost all of them — are to a large part indistinguishable from other cities in the rest of the world. This is true not just in the urban cores, but also in the outskirts, where sprawl has taken over: I recently drove between Hangzhou and Shanghai without ever leaving an urbanized area.

What is different to us is the signage and the general graphic material. This might sound trivial, but it is the only thing that gives these places their own character. The very exotic nature of this layer of signification makes them fascinating to us.

What is also different is the density of these cities, but that might be a question of time. With development comes wealth, and with wealth a demand for larger personal space. In most cities, that leads to a de-densification over time. We should remember that large parts of Manhattan had the same density a hundred years ago.

Finally, there are remnants of the old that remain, hidden behind the tall buildings or stretched out between isolated exurban housing developments. These ruins might be, as such remains always can be, the building blocks for some for of urbanism that might be Chinese. I am not enough of an expert to know what these might be, but I find in work as disparate as that of Amateur Architects and Ai Wei Wei hints of what kind of materiality, elements, and coherence they might have.

It would seem to me that a skin of modern Chinese identity on the bones of what remains, stretched out over the technology- and profit-driven grid that is everywhere the same, might be the appropriate future for a Chinese urbanism.

Q&A 002

DIALOGUE WITH
Joshua Bolchover

TO: Joshua Bolchover
FROM: Anderson Lee, Gene King

Your installation at the Biennale dealt with the border/boundary conditions between Hong

055

056

Congratulations!

"2011-12 深圳·香港城市\建筑双城双年展"

Keep up the amazing thinking for better society!

Jaslikshing! From someone living in South Africa with so much space it is educative to see how can be done in ultra high-density living. Une also have to expanded geographically now struggle to provide affordable services!

EXH 004

PAVILION:

Hong Kong Exhibits

PROJECT:

Romus Domus: Porcelain Cities

DESCRIPTION:

Giovanni Paolo Panini's masterful painting 'Galleria di vedute di Roma moderna' (1759) unfurls all of the important views of that city in a picture gallery under one roof, or one dome. This diorama installation consisted of over 700 monotone porcelain bowls, a most utilitarian of domestic objects, arranged into a single hemisphere with selected bowls acting as stages for speculative characters that occupied these hollows and migrated across a landscape of mass consumption and collective work.

EXHIBITOR:

Thomas TSANG

Thomas Tsang graduated from the Cooper Union and was the recipient of the Rome Prize in Architecture. Currently he is an Assistant Professor in Architecture at the University of Hong Kong.

ORIGIN:

Hong Kong

HONG KONG EXHIBITS 059

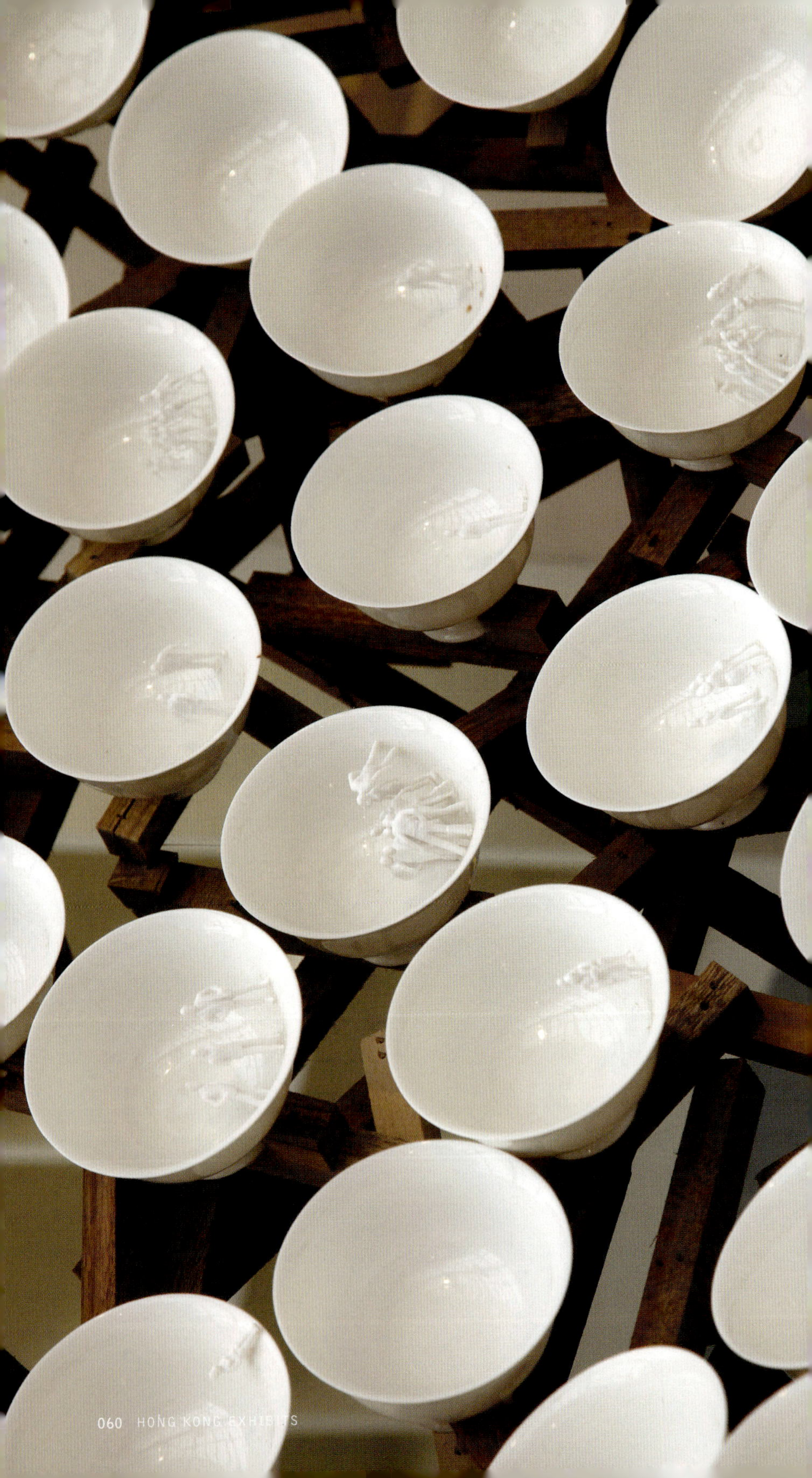

朝，「夢
賺鑊
藝術家
華子大夢
華華

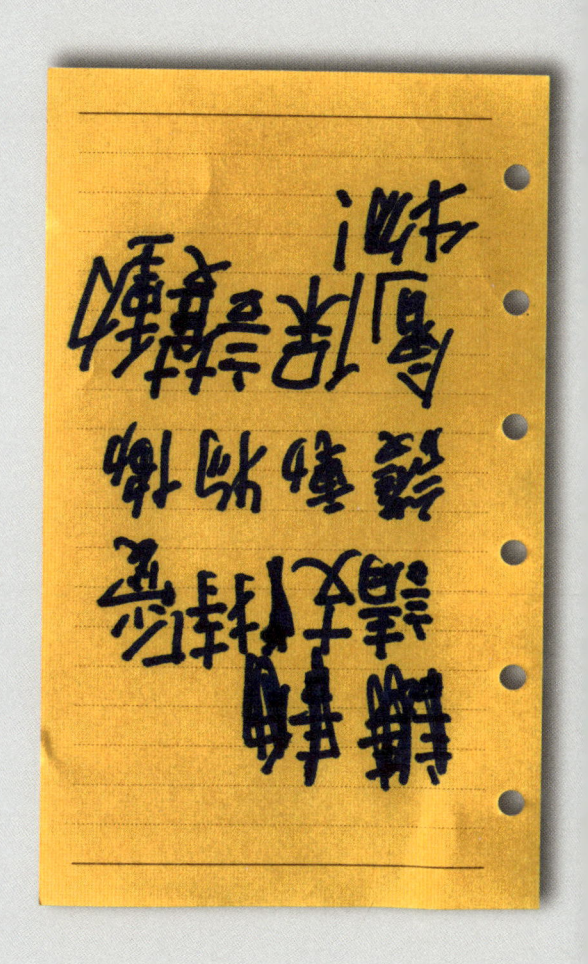

EXH 005

PAVILION:

Hong Kong Exhibits

PROJECT:

Evolving Schools

DESCRIPTION:

This exhibition reviewed the transformation of school architecture in Hong Kong, from prewar and rooftop schools to standard designs driven by education policy shifts and individualized designs oriented to specific school users and stakeholders. It recognized the architects' contribution to the education community, working together to shape various school types to meet the needs and aspirations of the community at large.

CURATOR:

Chinese University of Hong Kong, School of Architecture; Traces Limited

CUHK team: Thomas CHUNG, Allen POON, Dave CHEUNG, Jimmy HO, Robert JIANG, Prudence LAU, Jim LAU, Eric NG, Kai Hung NG, Sarah NG, Alan TSE, Sam WONG, Yvonne WONG

Traces Ltd. team: Julia LAU, Edwin TANG

ORIGIN:

Hong Kong

EVOLVING SCHOOLS 學舍春秋

HONG KONG EXHIBITS 063

064 HONG KONG EXHIBITS

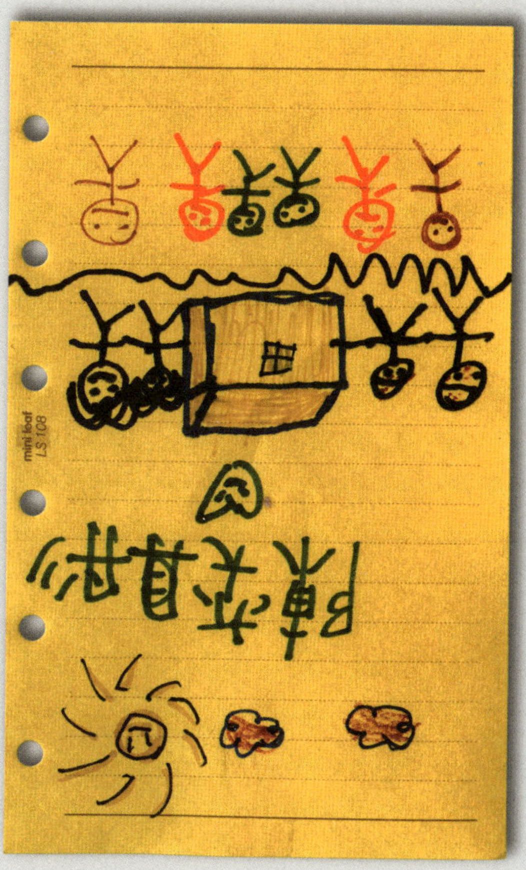

EXH 006

PAVILION:

Hong Kong Exhibits

PROJECT:

Inside the Blue House

DESCRIPTION:

The Blue House is a historic landmark of Wan Chai, an example of how people interpret and modify architecture to create their own unique spaces over the past 90 years. By opening the Blue House's doors, the team hoped to inspire discussion about the real heritage value embedded in vernacular buildings. How should Hong Kong's urban renewal be carried out in the future?

EXHIBITOR:

LWK & Partners (HK) Limited

LWK & Partners is a Hong Kong-based architectural practice founded in 1986 committed to the pursuit of excellence in architectural design and aims to improve people's quality of life. The firm was awarded the BCI Asia Top Ten Architects Award in 2011. The project contributors include Bosco Kwan, Eric C.M. Lee, Ho Chung Chan, Hanny Ng, Haynie Sze, Lydia Yeung, Terence Ho, and Wilson Chan.

ORIGIN:

Hong Kong

HONG KONG EXHIBITS 067

068 HONG KONG EXHIBITS

069

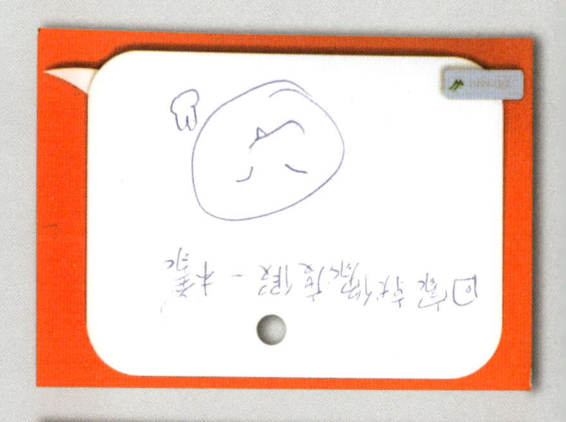

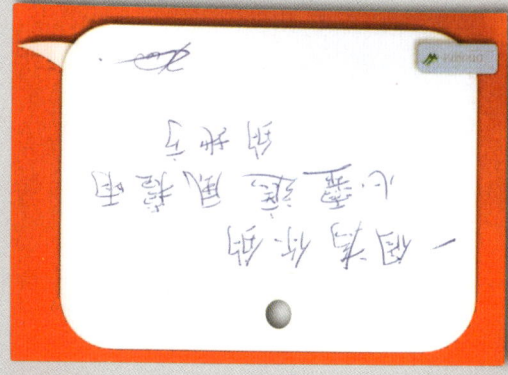

Kong and Shenzhen. This restricted area, also known as the Frontier Closed Area (FCA) was, in our opinion, the most appropriate issue to explore the potential and possibilities within this 'comfort' or rather 'discomfort' zone between a young energetic city like Shenzhen versus Hong Kong, of which we used the term 'mid-life crisis' city to describe it during the biennale. Almost two years have passed and I knew you have been continuing your research in the FCA. Would you mind shedding some light on your latest research development?

>TO: Anderson, Gene
>FROM: Joshua

The Berlin Wall, well known as an iconic demarcation between two ideologies, divided a city that formerly was united. In a reunified Germany, it was commonly said that the true reunification would have to overcome the wall in people's minds. Similar borders exist today in many locations cutting places, peoples and geographies into very different realities. The Hong Kong-Shenzhen border is clearly different in many ways from the Berlin Wall, but it also shares many similarities. Like the Berlin Wall, the HK-SZ border area is a highly unique and complex environment. It is a place of considerable tension and contrast where a hybrid mix of natural system, human settlement and highly urbanized environments coexist, separating ideologies, cultures, new and old, rich and poor.

Many people do not perceive the HK-SZ border in this context or associate it as a legacy from the post-WWII colonial era. As a register of Hong Kong's collective and open history, there is a need to comprehensively understand and make public the specific conditions found within the Frontier Closed Area. Our research aims to document and archive its distinct status for future generations, given that it is highly likely that this area will fundamentally change in the foreseeable future. How it will change and the role it will play given its strategic position between the two cities will be critical in shaping the future of the region.

Our preliminary research prior to 2011 identified, classified and analyzed the FCA in various ways. Our current work, including the work exhibited in the Biennale, began to understand the continuous evolution of the border region as metabolic system, a continual process of change and transformation that is part man made and part natural, a symbiosis of the two. Therefore for our continuing research we came to the point of view that it is necessary to understand the border region as an integral part of a larger urban ecology existing between the cities of Hong Kong and Shenzhen, both as a spatial phenomenon and as a broad based cultural issue with its various levels of complexity, and on the level of the interrelations of both. By examining the specific urbanization processes and the forces at work in the border area as a metabolic system, this research can be well positioned to contribute its findings in ways that can have a public presence and participate in public and academic discourse on the future of the border.

Q&A 003

DIALOGUE WITH
Felix Claus

>TO: Felix Claus
>FROM: Anderson Lee, Gene King

Hope this email finds you well. Gene might have mentioned this to you, we are compiling a publication for the biennale and would like to send a few questions via email and perhaps you can contribute a few words? Below is the email we sent earlier to various exhibitors. Looking forward to your kind participation.

071

072

I LOVE GREEN HOME INDONESIA. SAT Tide Holly.

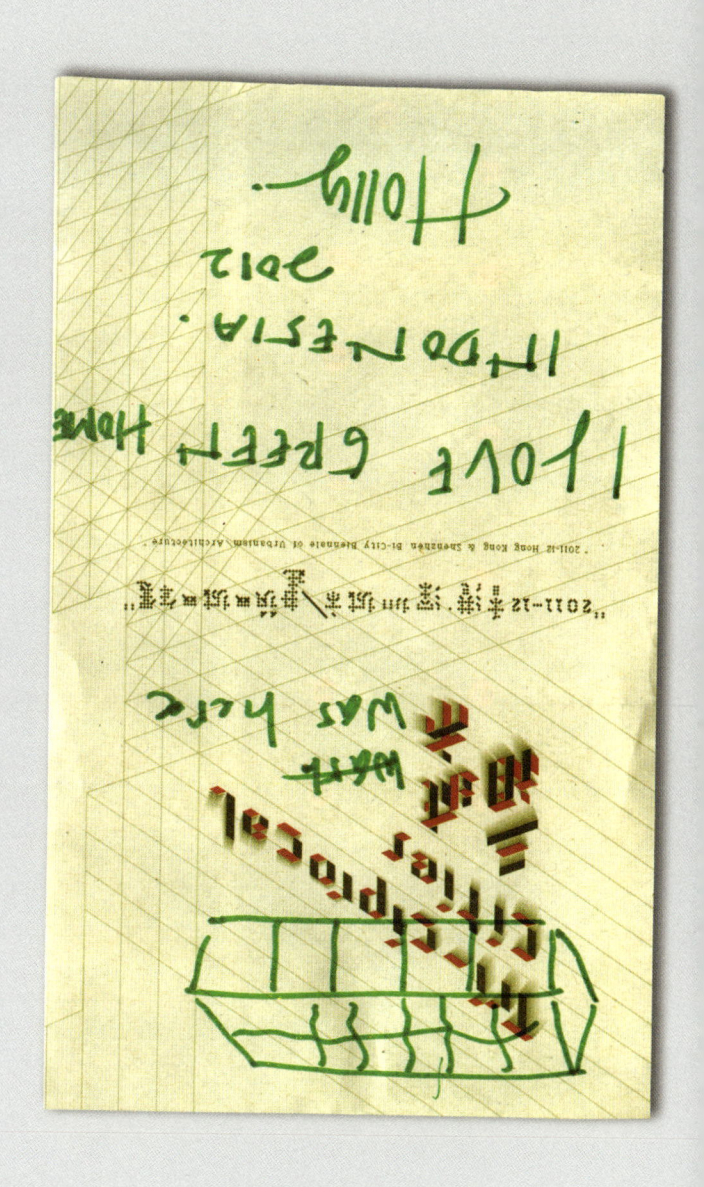

"2011-12 香港 · 深圳城市\建筑双城双年展"
2011-12 Hong Kong & Shenzhen Bi-city Biennale of Urbanism\Architecture.

我： was here

Areciprocal cities

EXH 007

PAVILION:

Hong Kong Exhibits

PROJECT:

The Cultivation of Urban Cracks

DESCRIPTION:

The city and its built environment grow and wither as time goes by, and the image of the city we witness today is nothing but a momentary fragment within the infinity of time. The Cultivation of Urban Cracks was a series of installations. Each projected a time-lapse model of one part of the city fabric, and at the same time produced a number of mnemonic devices that concretize the memory of our city.

EXHIBITOR:

ArChoi Kit Wang CHOI, Ruby Wai Yue LAW, Bill Yiu Kwan CHAN, William Wing Fung LAI, Juliana Yat Shun KEI

ArChoi Kit Wang Choi, Ruby Wai Yue Law, Bill Yiu Kwan Chan, and William Wing Fung Lai are recent graduates from the Department of Architecture at the University of Hong Kong. Juliana Yat Shun Kei is a recent graduate with a master of architecture from GSAPP, Columbia University. She currently works at Urbanus Hong Kong.

ORIGIN:

Hong Kong

HONG KONG EXHIBITS 075

076 HONG KONG EXHIBITS

#Home is where
all the people you
love are. There's
no place like
Home.

EXH 008

PAVILION:

Hong Kong Exhibits

PROJECT:

Eco-Pod

DESCRIPTION:

The exhibit was made of an Eco-Pod, which is a temporary and modular algae bioreactor for urban sites. The fine-grained modularity of the structure allows it to occupy a variety of sites, while its pre-fabricated and pre-cycled logic allows it to be erected and dismantled quickly to fit within the available time windows of site vacancy. The bioreactor program allows for on-site urban power generation through bio-fuel production. An on-site robotic armature is designed to reconfigure the modules to maximize algae growth conditions. As an open and reconfigurable structure, the voids between pods form a network of vertical public parks and botanical gardens housing unique plant species.

EXHIBITOR:

Höweler + Yoon Architecture LLP; Squared Design Lab

Höweler + Yoon Architecture specializes in the integration of architecture, new technologies, and public space. Eric Höweler is an Assistant Professor at Harvard Design School. Meejin Yoon is an Associate Professor in the Department of Architecture at MIT.

Squared is a digital design laboratory in architecture, industrial design, online interactivity, and film. Co-founders Josh Barandon and Franco Vairani graduated from MIT with degrees in Architecture, Design, and Computation.

ORIGIN:

United States

HONG KONG EXHIBITS 079

1:CUT 2:FOLD 3:TAB 4:STACK

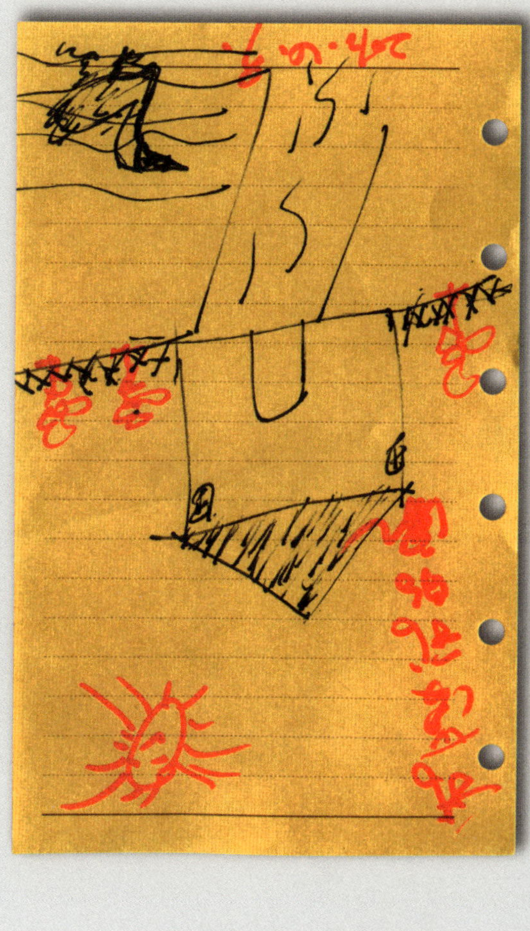

EXH 009

PAVILION:
Hong Kong Exhibits

PROJECT:
Sugar Treasure

DESCRIPTION:
Sugar recalls sweetness and childhood; it is impermanent, fragile and dissolvable. In this project, sugar cubes were used as building blocks to recreate the vanished buildings of twentieth-century Hong Kong, along with water droplets that fell slowly from a device above. The sugar melted, slowly revealing objects inside the buildings. Participants were invited to play with the device and enter into this time journey to the memorable past with us.

EXHIBITOR:
Kwok Kin SO, Stanley Kwok Kin SIU, Calvin Chi Hoi LEUNG, Winnie Yuen Lai CHAN

Kwok Kin So, Stanley Siu, and Calvin Leung are practicing architects and designers. Winnie Chan is a doctoral student at Oxford University researching the history of Chinese gardens and landscape art. Their works explore the social-historical aspects of architecture and the urban landscape as manifested in art.

ORIGIN:
Hong Kong

HONG KONG EXHIBITS

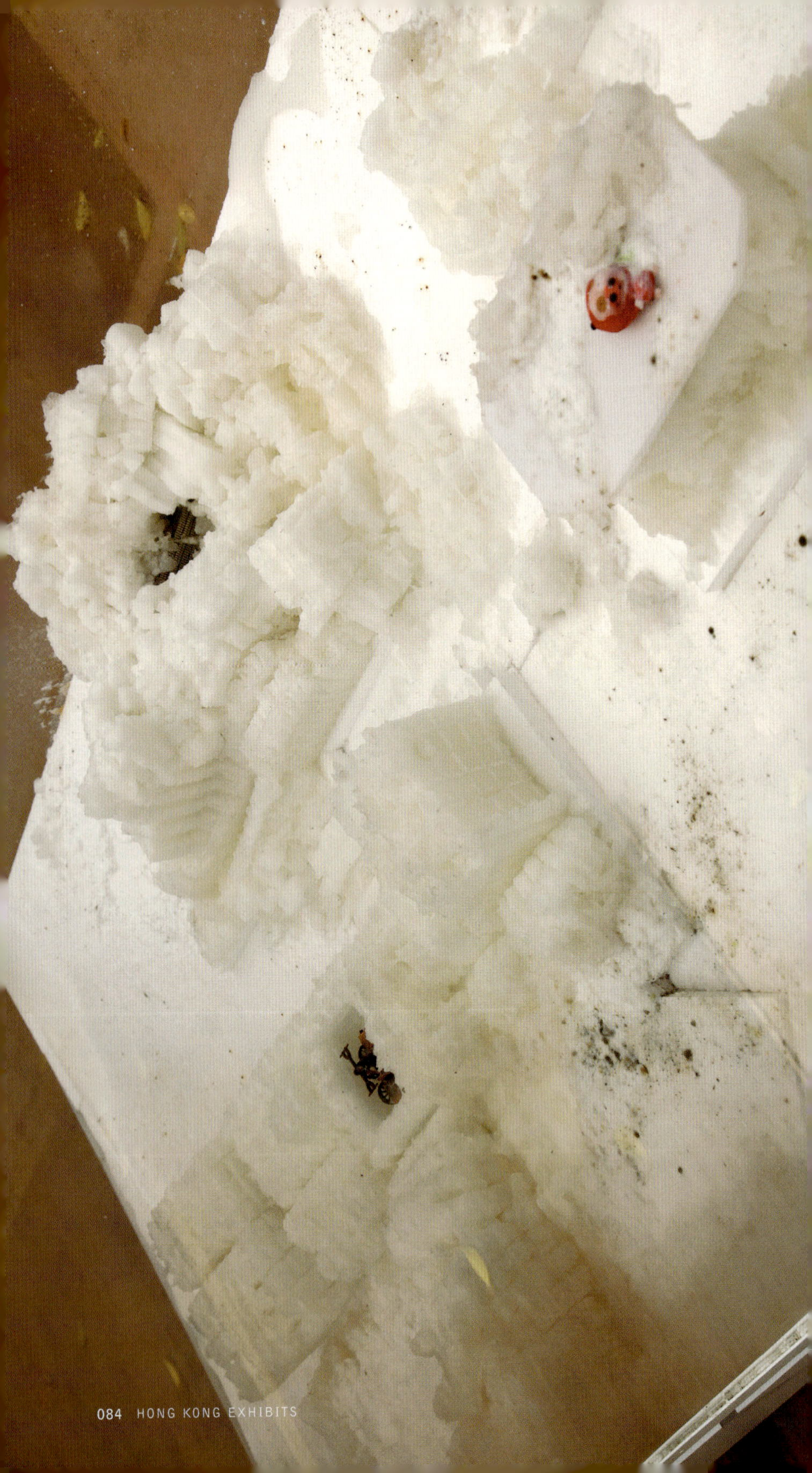

085

TO: Anderson
FROM: Felix

No problem, good idea! I have to dig in my archives, I wrote something about it last year will check over the weekend.

TO: Felix
FROM: Anderson

Thanks for your kind reply.

You mentioned that Tokyo is a city traditionally with almost no urban planning since the law does authorize expropriating land (land is a sacred right) while Amsterdam started with total planning since people may die if they didn't coordinate on water management. As you have homes in both cities, how do you see the charm and limitations of them?

As we visited your house in Aoyama, Tokyo, I was amazed by this 5-story single house, with site area of about 50 square meters and one room for every floor. Norihiko mentioned that he used to think this kind of development results in buildings with no elevations, but even he was amazed by the quietness and self-contentedness of each house among the interior of a city block. It was almost both urban and rural, and everyone has ground below their feet and sky above their head. In your film, you also mentioned that people almost never tear down old buildings to build new ones in Amsterdam, the City just diverts new development in new area and remains a low-rise, low-density condition. Do you see similarity among the two cities in that aspect? People just insist on a lifestyle and probably refuse that of New York and Hong Kong?

When you visited Hong Kong University before the Biennale, you mentioned that 30 Western Street is an outstanding building. It used to be a school building and now a community center with some small offices while keeping its circulation, a monumental stair, and its classical facade. What do you see out of it? Does it fit into your title for the exhibit at Biennale 'Great form has no shape'?

TO: Anderson, Gene
FROM: Felix

OK Guys, Three questions:

First: Japanese Law does NOT authorize expropriation. The charm of the planned city lies in the carefully elaborated public space. This public space is the result of an orchestrated effort, and as such always referential to an intention, be it rationalist (as in the case of the Dutch city of the 17th century), be it triumphalist (as in the French examples: Paris, Bordeaux, Nancy). This offers a common quality that is more important than the quality of the individual architecture. There exists a notion of communal appreciation to which the individual is subjugated, perfectly in line with the republican belief of civility or even equality. For the architect this means adaptation or conflict.

The Japanese city is a combination of free market and built-up infrastructure, without any requirements as to material or form. Obviously this comes as a relief for any architect from the former habitat, being able to project purely on basis of rational data (zoning etc.) But this practical pleasure only lasts within the solitude of the project, both on site and in time. Since the project has absolutely no reference nor value as a building. As soon as the programme becomes obsolete, the building disappears.

Second: I don't think people in metropolises like HK, NY, London, Paris or Tokyo are free to choose a lifestyle. It is a perversity of contemporary reality that the center areas of these cities become un-attainable for people with normal and even high-paying jobs. It is just rich foreigners collecting trophy-homes and occupying them for only a few weeks per year, in this way undermining the neighbourhood structure. At the same time these cities keep attracting people due to their economic strength, resulting in a zombie center and a dense and dependent outside. In Tokyo perhaps not as strong as NY, London or Paris but, for young professionals, living within the Yamanote Line is just impossible.

087

088

"2011-12香港·深圳城市\建筑双城双年展"

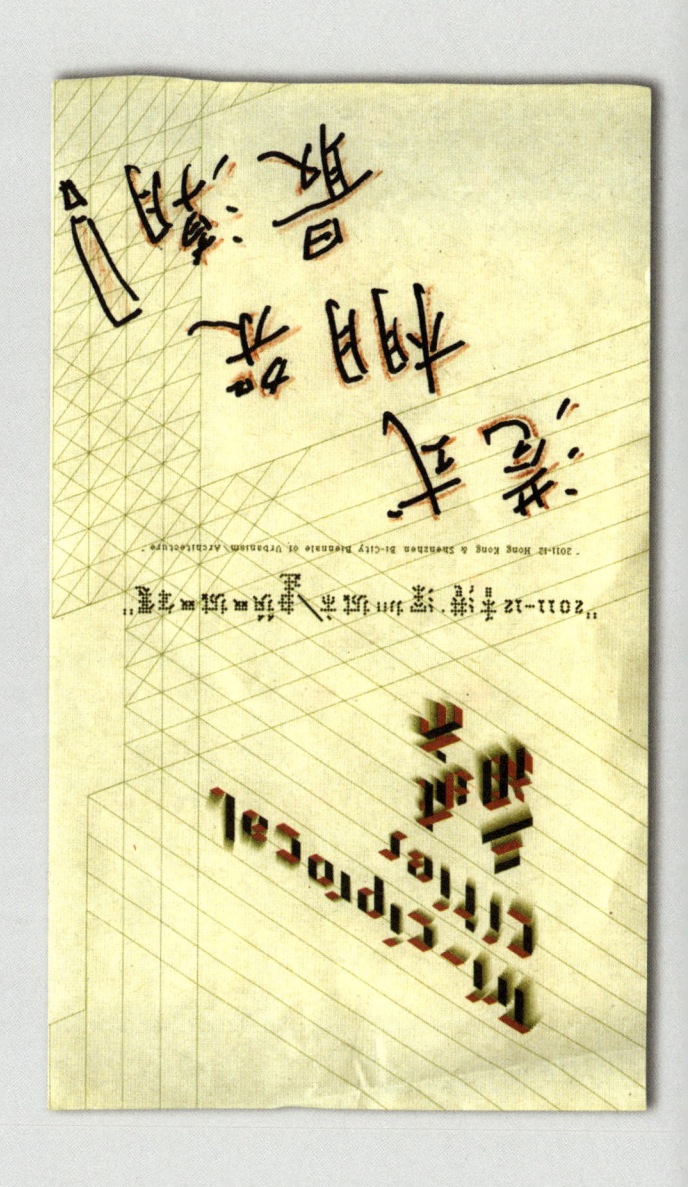

"2011-12 Hong Kong & Shenzhen Bi-city Biennale of Urbanism\Architecture"

三城记
Tri-ciprocal Cities

EXH 010

PAVILION:

Hong Kong Exhibits

PROJECT:

How much does it weigh?

DESCRIPTION:

This installation sought to explore factors that affect Hong Kong's public realm, and inspire viewers to rethink the value of it as we strive to develop sustainable places. Inverting the model allowed the audience to have a look at the Hong Kong of the 1920s. Pulling on various hanging objects, symbols of materialism and commercialism, revealed the city fabric that results from the inevitable conflicts balancing public and private interests.

EXHIBITOR:

Athena Kei Yun CHAU, Reine WONG, Chung Yin PO, Stanley Ka Chun PUN, Howard Chi Ho CHUNG

Reine Wong is a multi-disciplinary designer of installation and video works. Stanley Pun and Athena Chau are architects. Chung and Po have been involved in two of the most influential projects in HK – the West Kowloon Cultural District and Kai Tak Cruise Terminal.

ORIGIN:

Hong Kong

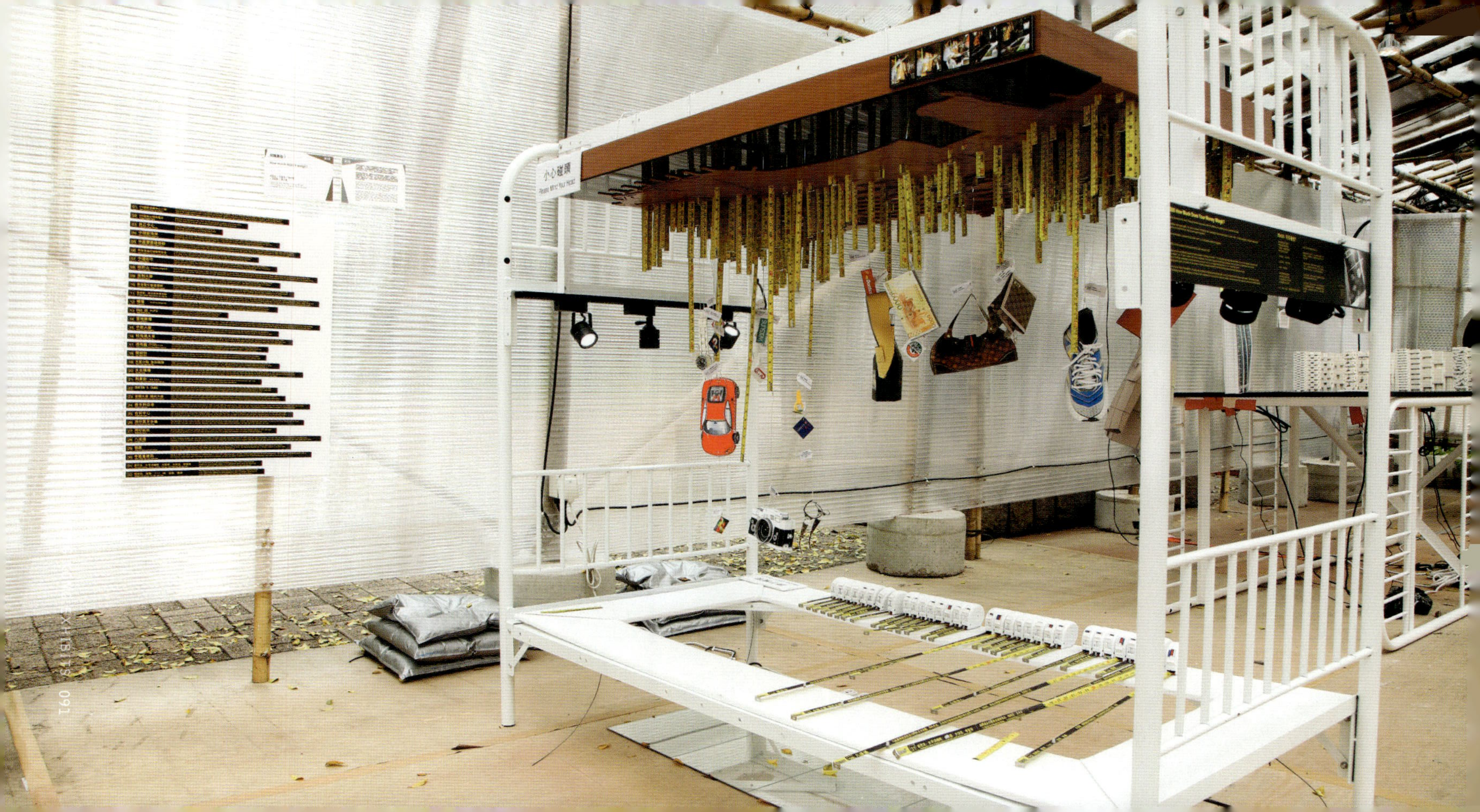
小心碰頭
Please Mind Your Head

HONG KONG EXHIBITS

Dios vio todo lo que había hecho, y era bueno en gran manera.

Teddy Guajardo 10.4.12

EXH 011

PAVILION:

Hong Kong Exhibits

PROJECT:

Density & Openness Revisited: Recoding Building Bulk in Hong Kong

DESCRIPTION:

The exhibit showed an alternative approach to open and public spaces in the context of the city. Instead of extruding building mass, this model incorporates a ratio of open space in the design process, producing varying spaces and densities to generate new forms of public space, semi-public and private exterior and interior spaces.

EXHIBITOR:

Rocker-Lange Architects (Christian J. LANGE and Ingeborg M. ROCKER)

Rocker-Lange Architects is located in Hong Kong and Boston. Founded in 2005 by partners Ingeborg M. Rocker and Christian J. Lange, the office specializes in cultural, residential and urban design.

ORIGIN:

Hong Kong / United States / Germany

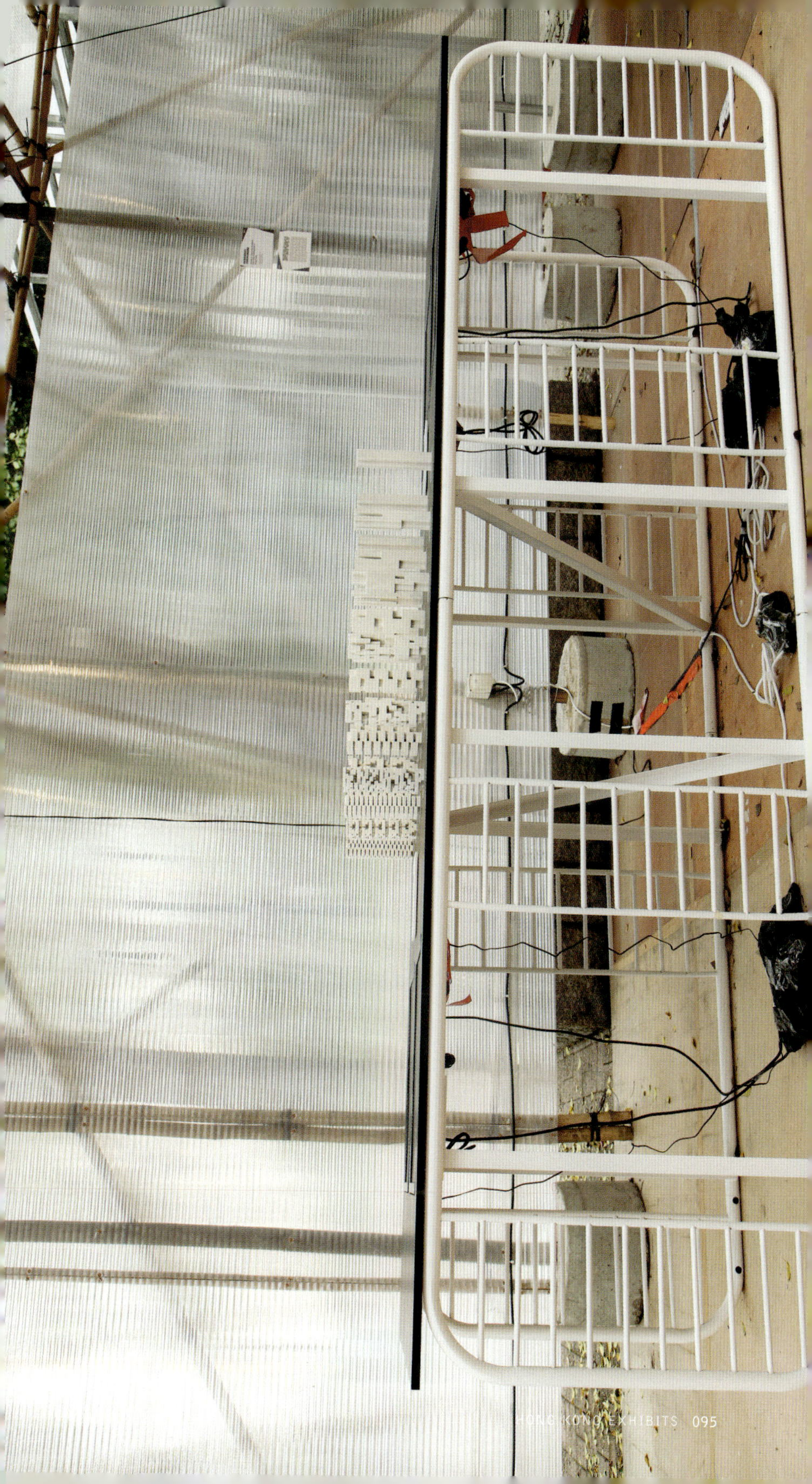

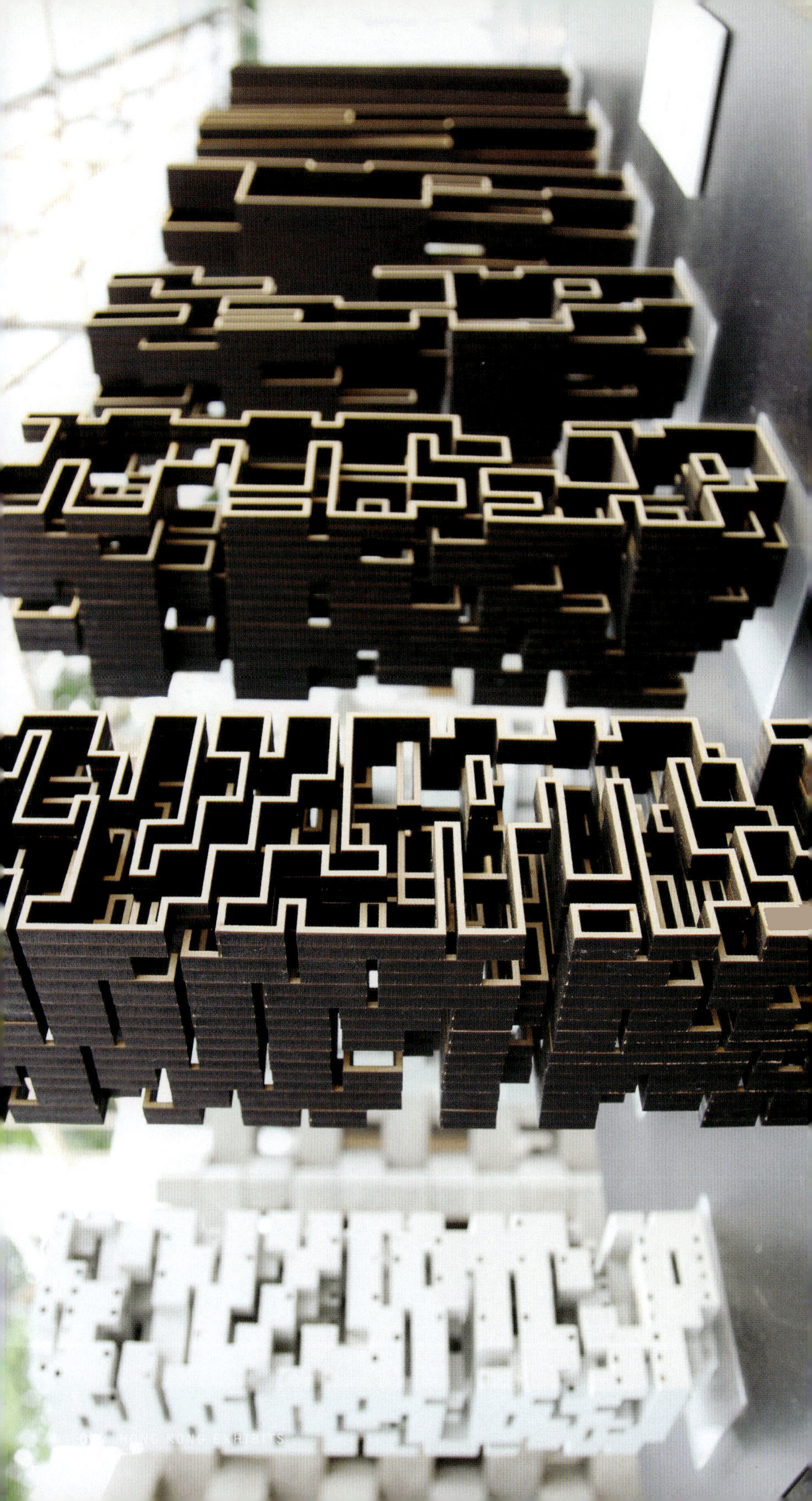

2012.4.11
운전께서
오늘게 하셔서
아침 먹을
치킨에 갔다고
얼마이 남자가
하나 오세요.
사정 합니다.
— 남는 기다하다 —

EXH 012

PAVILION:
Hong Kong Exhibits

PROJECT:
Choi Yuen Ecological Village

DESCRIPTION:
Choi Yuen Ecological Village is in the New Territories of Hong Kong. This low-cost eco-village demonstrates sustainable design concepts including the conservation of fishponds and orchards, allocation of communal land for organic farming and vehicle-free pedestrian system. The project opens up new opportunities for community architecture diverging from the mainstream mode of housing development in Hong Kong.

EXHIBITOR:
Wang Weijen Architecture; Choi Yuen Village Eco-Community Building Studio

Wang Weijen Architecture has won various design awards through its emphasis in cultural and ecological landscape, and completed projects in Hong Kong, Taiwan, and China. Professor Wang is currently head of the Department of Architecture at Hong Kong University.

ORIGIN:
Hong Kong

HONG KONG EXHIBITS 099

100 HONG KONG EXHIBITS

我愛生氣包

我喜歡人們的笑臉

每次不高興時，如果人家

說你的臉2圓一圓，有扭扭，

身心因為聞了朋友一句話，

Third: What I see into it is foremost cultural. It is my belief that the city belongs to all, and not just to those in power, be it political or financial. Old buildings represent collective memory, be it 'official' like religious (temples) or military (statues) buildings. But to me, the greatest examples are the 'popular' historical buildings, the everyday buildings without great significance that represent everyday life. Their survival layers the morphology of the city in an unplanned, organic way. I do not want to sound paternalistic or even supremacist, but it is my view that the respect and critical appreciation of the existing, is a benchmark for the level of development of society.

Sadly, in my short time as a resident of Tokyo I have seen many interesting buildings disappear without any public reaction. So when in HK I was very pleasantly surprised to visit 30 Western Street.

Hope you are well, and hoping to see you soon, wherever.

Q&A 004

DIALOGUE WITH

Kristof Crolla

TO: Kristof Crolla
FROM: Anderson Lee, Gene King

Your installation 'The Dragon Skin Pavilion' inside our Shenzhen Pavilion of the Biennale drew quite some attention by its sheer visual and interactive aspects. We were particularly intrigued by its strong sense of digital fabrications and the intricate construction techniques involved. Each panel is similar yet slightly different in order to create its enclosure and tectonics. You mentioned that the design and fabrication are a combination of a production system from the developed and developing world, something high and low tech all at once.

How would you see your current design practice and current works from your office as a continuous pursuit of this kind of high/low tech combination now you have based your practice in this crossroad of the Pearl River Delta?

TO: Anderson, Gene
FROM: Kristof

Let me know if this is too much or too little text. I have full papers written on these projects, so I don't really know where to stop...

The Dragon Skin Pavilion combined digital design and fabrication techniques with limited required onsite project knowledge or building skill: the prefabricated, numbered shells just needed to be slotted into one another to make the final geometry appear. By using the digital fabrication techniques available in the region, this project was an experiment on how architects could safeguard design control in a context where onsite communication of geometric complexities is often difficult.

In more recent work we have expanded this exploration of strategically applied digital design techniques by integrating unique local craftsmanship and building traditions into the workflow. Our primary research has recently been on the incorporation of typically Cantonese scaffolding techniques. This unique and centuries old custom relies entirely on the use of bamboo for construction, but can be pushed further into the future through combination with contemporary design tools. Bamboo scaffolding is never built according to plans or drawings, but follows a series of structural principals and concepts for its conception. Using a range of knotting techniques, the scaffolding design can respond to unique site conditions and requirements. The intuitive and unpredictable nature of this construction method seems to diametrically oppose the often rigid, top-down nature of computational design – a preconception we tried to change in some built exploratory projects.

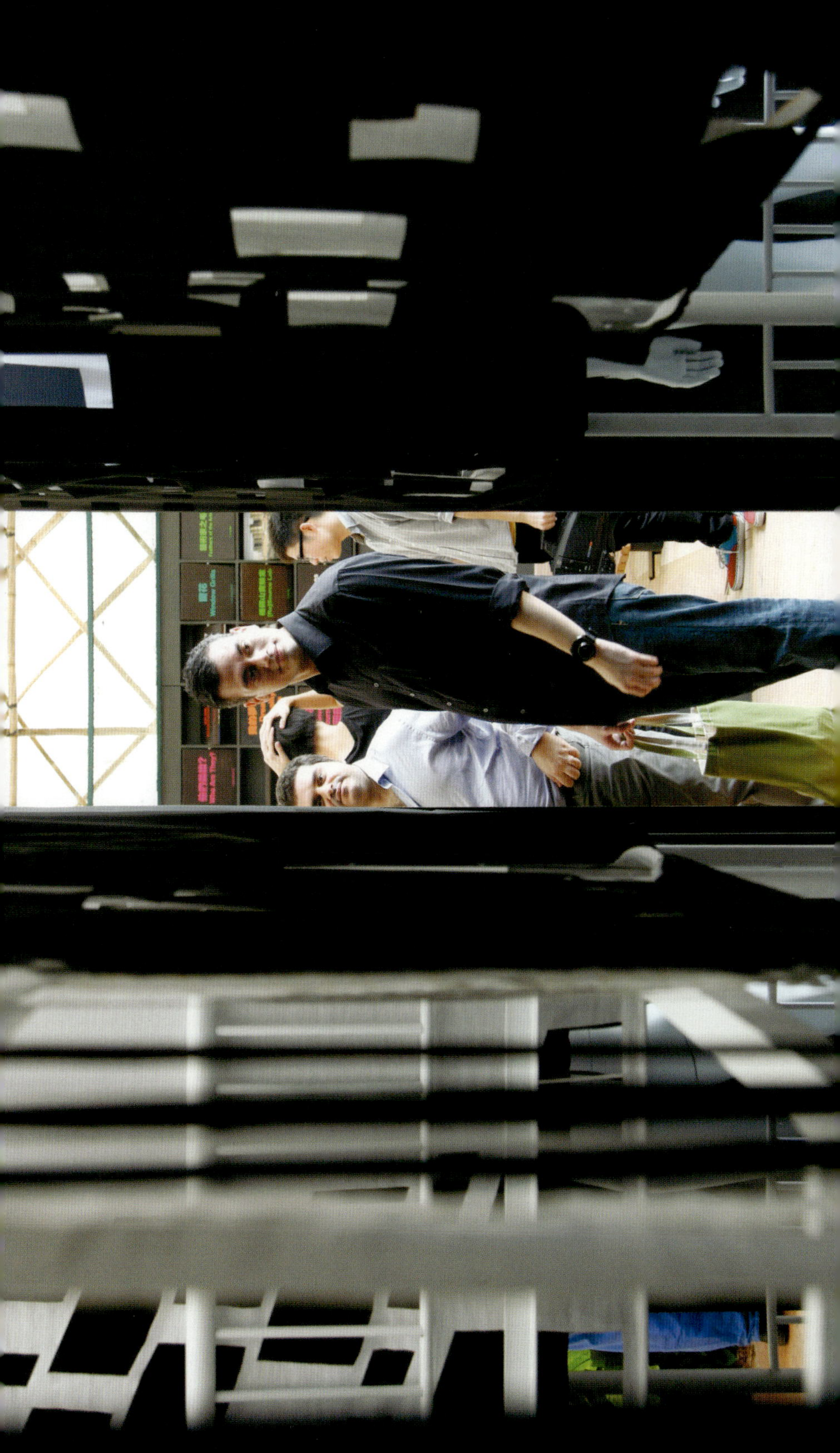

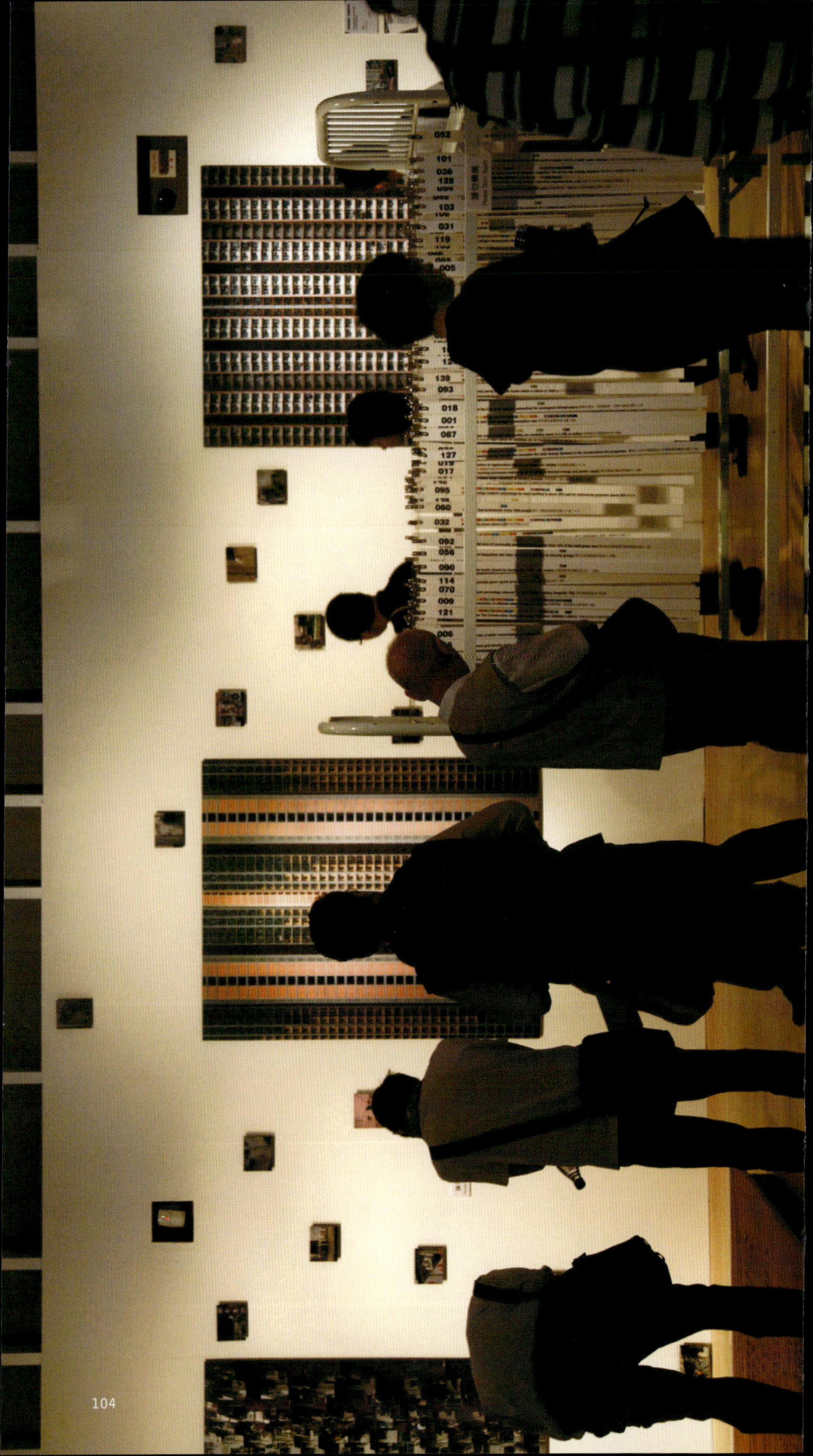

Reciprocal
Cities
雙城

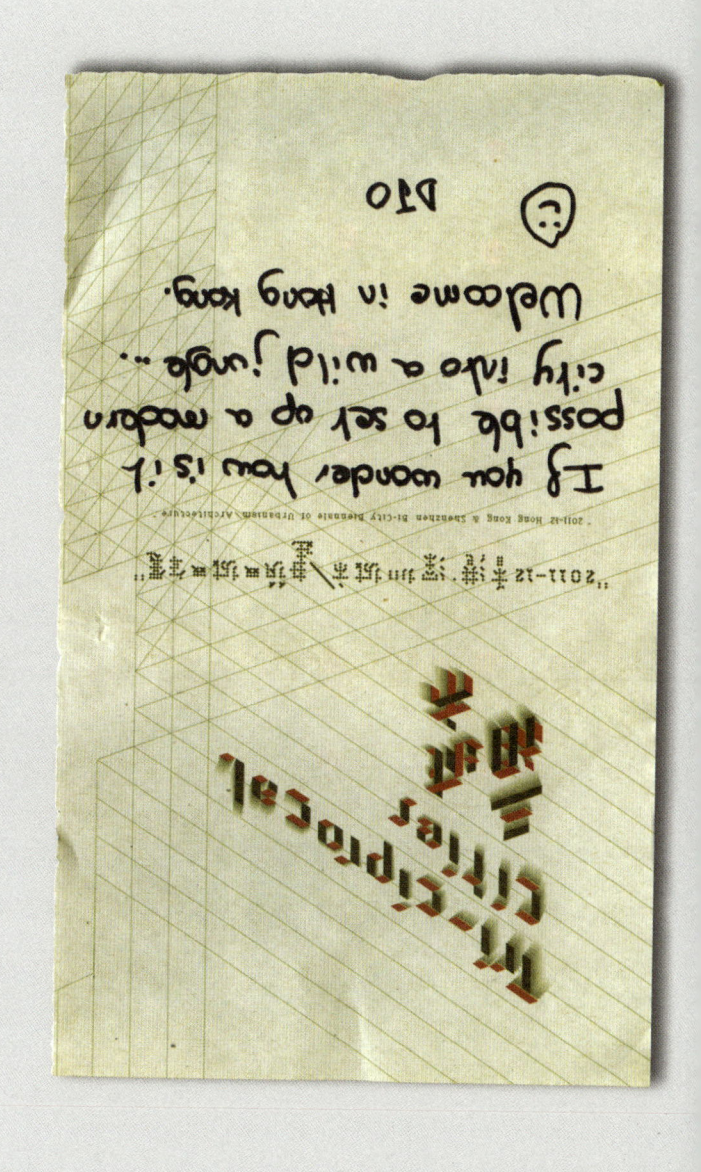

"2011-12 香港．深圳城市\建築雙城雙年展".
· 2011-12 Hong Kong & Shenzhen Bi-city Biennale of Urbanism\Architecture

If you wonder, how is it possible to set up a modern city into a wild jungle... Welcome in Hong kong.

☹ B10

PAVILION 2
Shenzhen and Other Mainland Cities Exhibits

This pavilion included four pieces that moved directly from the Shenzhen venues of the Biennale: 'Coaster Raid – Creative City Exploration,' '10 Million Units: Housing an Affordable City,' 'Qianhai Workshop,' and 'Counterpart Cities: Climate Change and Cooperative Action in Hong Kong and Shenzhen.' By sharing these selected exhibits, Hong Kong and Shenzhen became linked together, strengthening the concept of the Bi-City Biennale as 'one theme, two exhibitions' and emphasizing the continuity of these events. The pavilion also included stories from other parts of the mainland, including established cities like Beijing, Shanghai, and Chengdu as well as growing 'new towns.'

ABOUT THE PAVILION
The bamboo structure housing these exhibits was designed by William Lim. Using bamboo as a medium, Lim has designed many artistic structures for exhibitions and events in the past. This new interpretation took the form of a cocoon, sheltering the development and growth that marks today's China.

SHENZHEN EXHIBITS 107

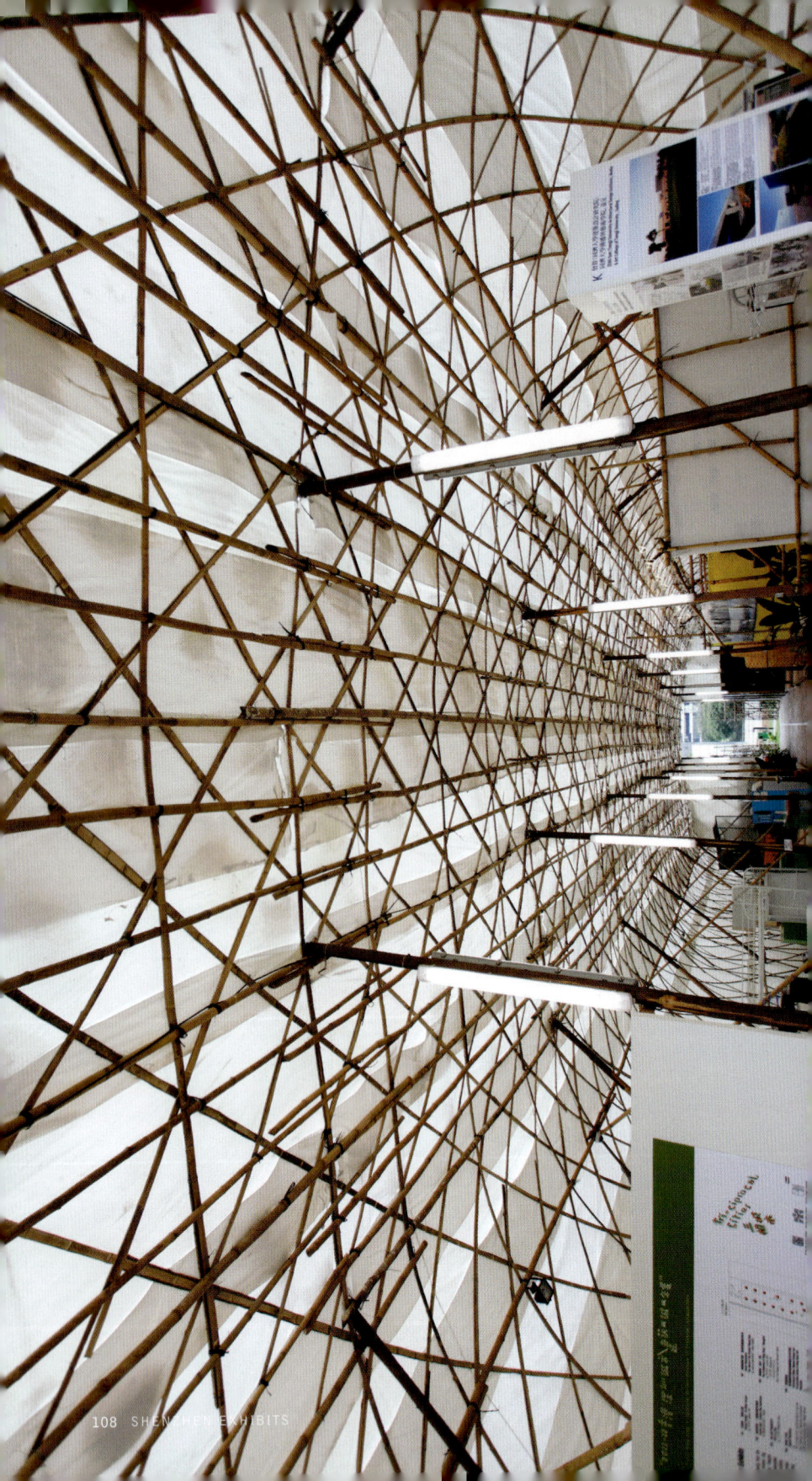

108 SHENZHEN EXHIBITS

我的麼想 My Sharing

这作畫方法问简单，
你知道我的信，
整在实际一代习听
捷径 也杉捉高 有信我
的发挥。

我的麼想 My Sharing

好羡慕 画画 的等师，
希望 有天 我的书 为多 懂；
等生 们 都 喜欢 今

EXH 013

PAVILION:

Shenzhen Exhibits

PROJECT:

Garden Pavilion: An Urban Cocoon

DESCRIPTION:

Urban Cocoon attached itself to a found environment, in this case a Hong Kong-style bamboo scaffolding; it lasted for three months until it had served its purpose, and its impermanence could make it useful in response to global crises and events.

EXHIBITOR:

William LIM

William Lim graduated from Cornell University and has been living in Hong Kong since 1982. A practicing architect, he is also active in artistic pursuits, and has carried out important public art installation works.

ORIGIN:

Hong Kong

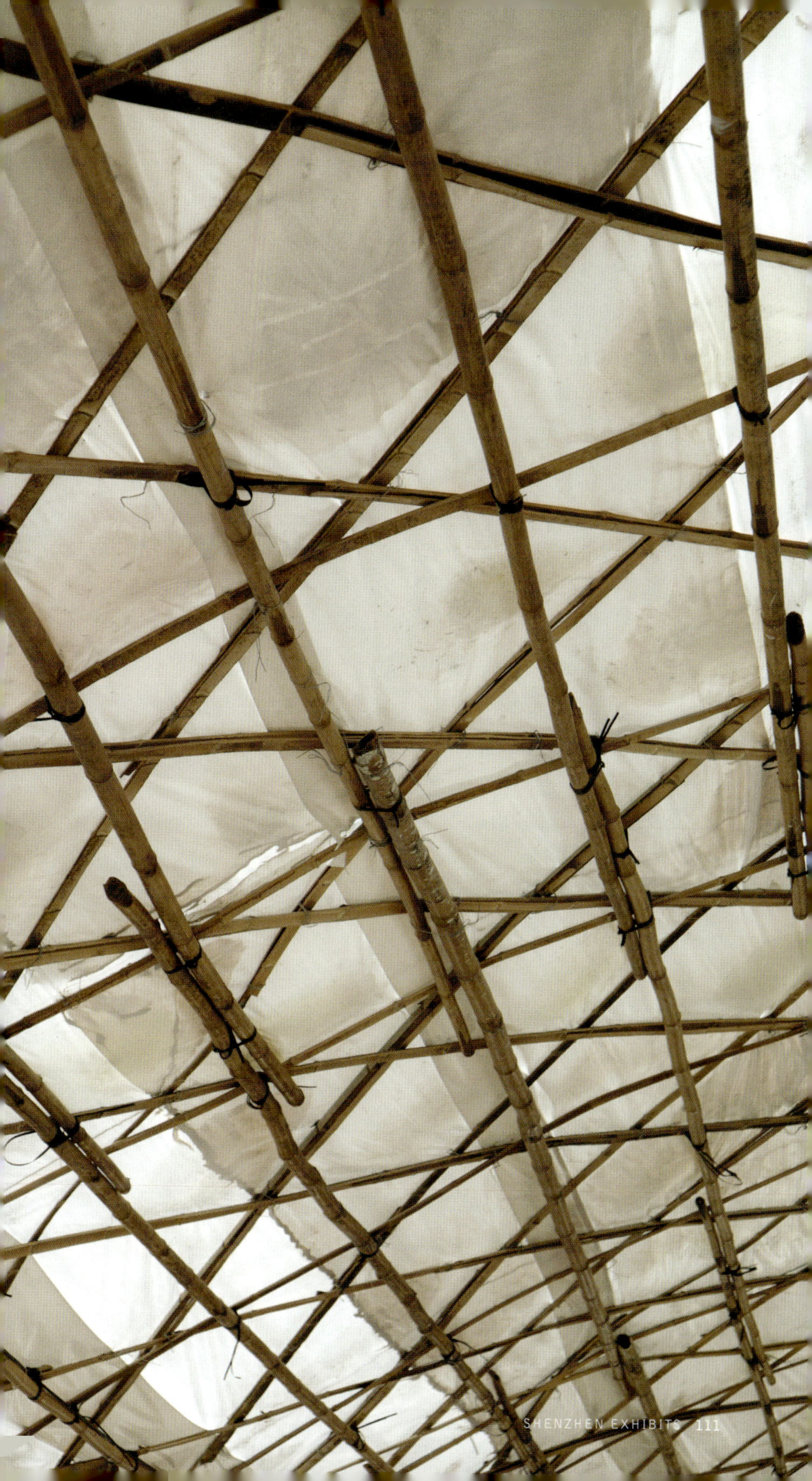

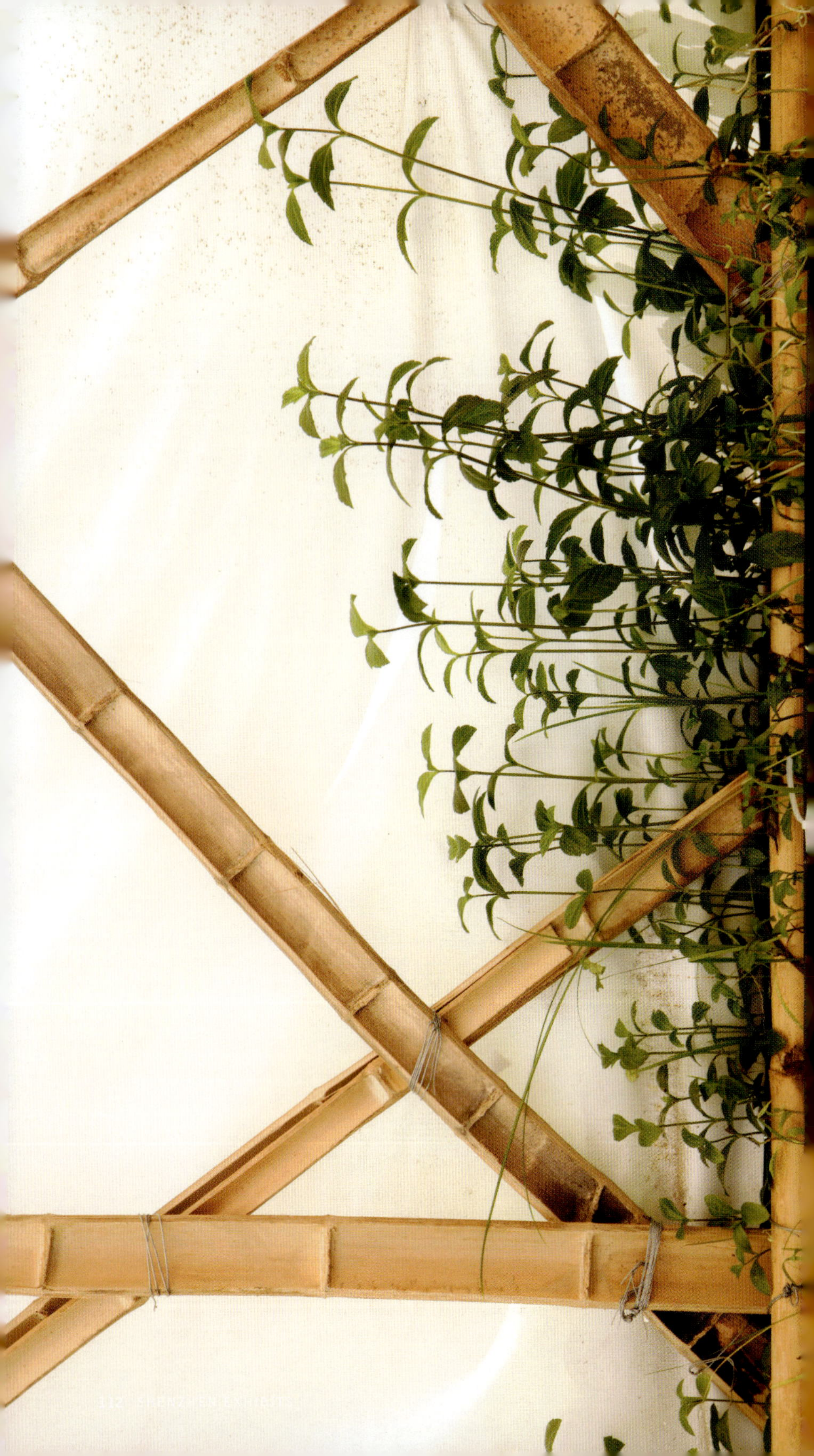

WE ALL ARE NATURE.
CREATION itself; myself

- No matter what you are from.
- No matter Man or Women.
- No matter Richer or Poor
- No matter Human or animal, etc.

We need Nature So Pls do takecare of and Respect eachother. Rem

EXH 014

PAVILION:
Shenzhen Exhibits

PROJECT:
Coaster Raid: Creative City Exploration

DESCRIPTION:
Shenzhen, City of Dreams, after thirty years, a community is blooming in Shenzhen and getting ready to reveal its own identity and values. Coaster Raid scouted this space between people, influenced by time and place. Riptide Creative Collective proposed a platform for local and grass-roots creative expression. Coaster Raid was a new creative event developed by Riptide. Nine raiders – artists, designers and intellectuals – used this event to present their vision.

EXHIBITOR:
Riptide Creative Collective

Riptide's objective is to use creative expression to encourage public participation in the urban environment.

ORIGIN:
Shenzhen

SHENZHEN EXHIBITS 115

梧桐山賞
[Re]Source
生活是舞臺
It's Your Showtime
You Are the Star
你是主角
我的夢想
My Dream
Your Reality
What does
Shenzhen
mean to you
兩面城市
Heads or Tails City?
生活
Living
社區
Community
香沉
Hong Shen
城市
City
扎根
"Radication"
多樣的城市
Divers' City
花樣城市
Fancy City
Fancy Ads
花樣廣告
給弱小的我們
"To our weakness and our fear of the future"
對未來不確定的恐懼
一起吃蛋糕
Come and Share
This Cake
對房屋的
Imagination offers
an enhanced quality
of life
美好想像
都市求生
Urban Survi

无论你走了多远，大家永远不会忘记你！

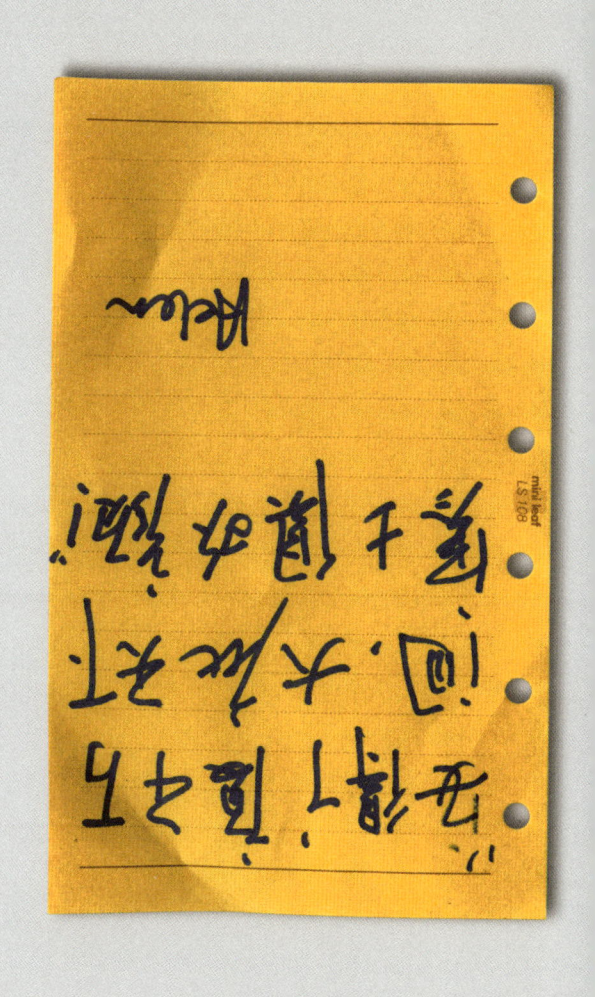

Helen~

EXH 015

PAVILION:

Shenzhen Exhibits

PROJECT:

Fish in a Tree

DESCRIPTION:

Nature has created models that are much more sustainable than our human endeavors. Waste is utilized in a productive way. Therefore, the first principle of smart design should be a reciprocal relationship with nature. This project proposed using biomimicry to create a metaphorical link between humans and fish, forests and oceans.

EXHIBITOR:

Chi Yung WONG

Chi Yung Wong is a media artist whose work is a mixture of technology, popular culture and theatre arts. Wong holds a Bachelor of Fine Arts (Theatre Lighting Design major) with First Class Honors from the Hong Kong Academy for Performing Arts. His versatile stage background has enabled him to participate in over one hundred local and international projects since 1998.

ORIGIN:

Hong Kong

SHENZHEN EXHIBITS 119

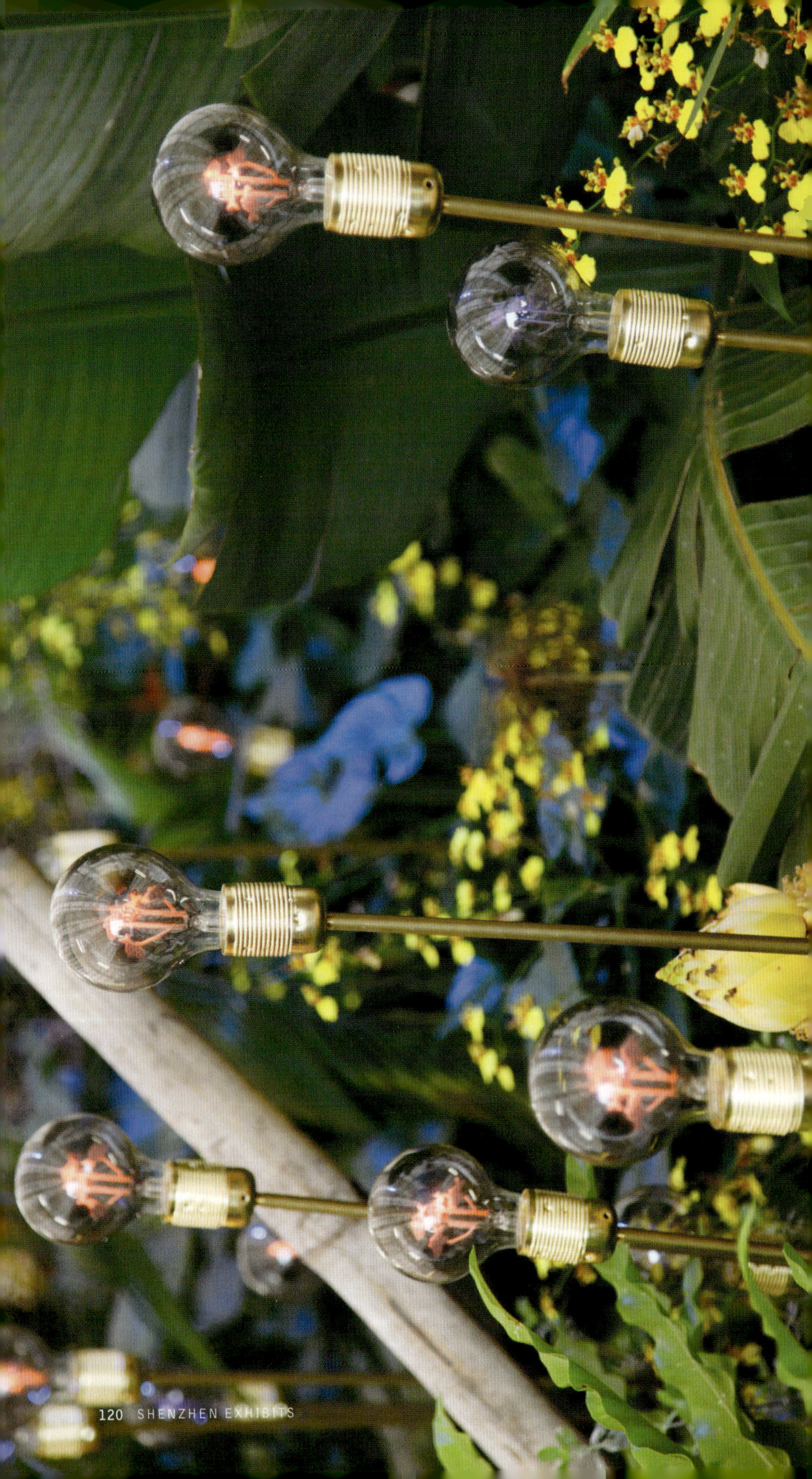

I want to live in
a house with a small garden.

慧眼独(?) PET HEAVEN
EMERSON PERRY

1) 画面小, 有自由.
2) Content is king. (8)
3) 通用好, 不需用图未.
保证每个人看到明确信息.

TO: Kristof
FROM: Anderson, Gene

What kind of prototype or current and/or future production system is happening after the 'Dragon Skin?'

TO: Anderson, Gene
FROM: Kristof

The two recent projects within this research direction that stand out are the 'Golden Moon – 2012 Mid-Autumn Festival Lantern Wonderland,' and the 'Pulse Pavilion.' The first project was a temporary architectural structure for a highly expressive and captivating temporary public event space in Victoria Park. It is the winning entry for the Lantern Wonderland design competition organised by the Hong Kong Tourism Board for the Mid-Autumn Festival. It was on display for six days and was built in eleven days from a curved steel geodesic dome, 2km of bamboo and 475 stretch fabric flames.

The second project is the outcome of an experimental design & build studio held with the 3rd and 4th year students of the University of Saint Joseph in Macau. It is an inhabitable sculpture, a parametrically generated organic lattice structure created from split bamboo rods, interwoven with fabric panels.

Q&A 005

DIALOGUE WITH

Norihiko Dan

TO: Norihiko Dan
FROM: Gene King, Anderson Lee

Your installation at the Biennale takes a zigzag form, like a zigzag passageway, does that carry any meaning?

TO: Gene, Anderson
FROM: Norihiko

It is a white dragon tangling and coiling along with a red bed.

TO: Norihiko
FROM: Gene, Anderson

What is your reflection on Metabolism, Maki's and Kurokawa's era (and you know both of them well)? Do you see a collective concern from that generation for new urban issues? Do you still see that from contemporary Japanese architects?

TO: Gene, Anderson
FROM: Norihiko

Maki was my teacher when I was a student in the masters program at Tokyo University, from 1979 to 1982. I met Kurokawa in the early 1990s when I became a member of Japan Interdesign Forum which he established in 1980s. From my point of view, although their personality and their architecture look so different, there is much in common in their aspect toward cities. Both of them regard cities as 'incomplete' in their growing process.

Metabolism was conceived by young Japanese architects – Kikutake, Kurokawa, Ohtaka and Maki – in 1960s Tokyo, which was still recovering from World War II, and it lead to a criticism toward classic completeness in urbanization of early modernism. The difference between Maki and Kurokawa is that Maki tries to integrate group form with intermediate open space as if it were a growth of villages in such work as Daikanyama Hillside Terrace; on the contrary, Kurokawa tried to encourage the city's growth by

123

124

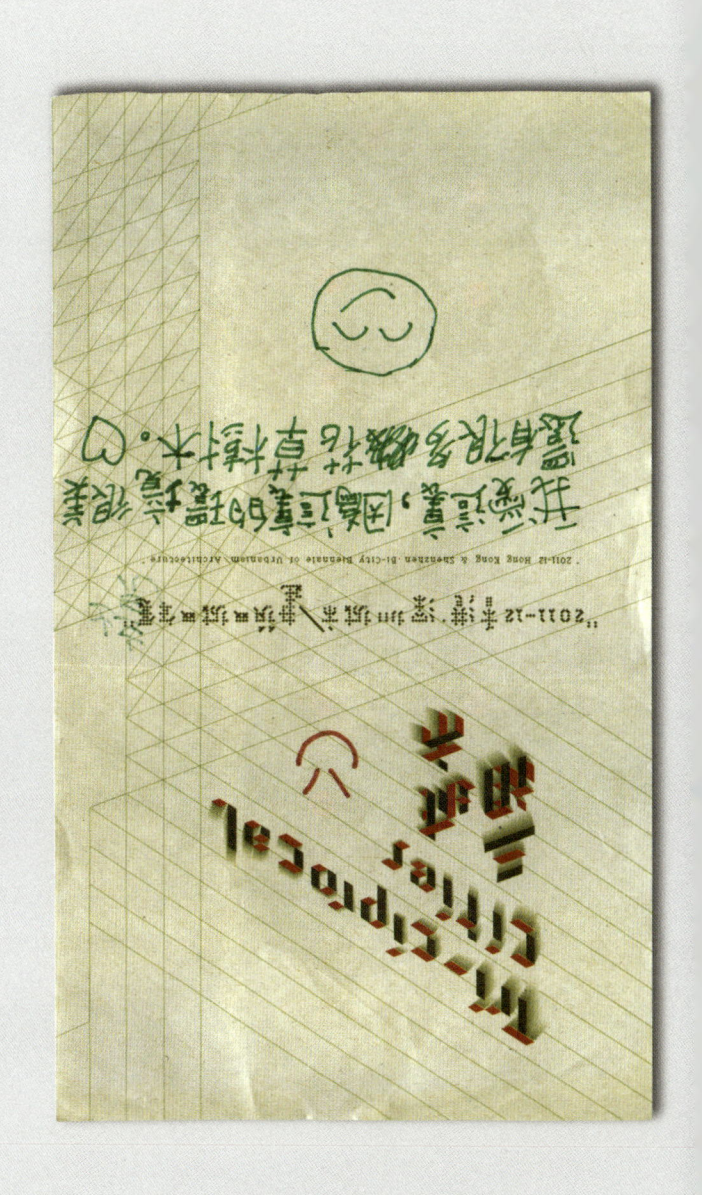

"2011-12 Hong Kong & Shenzhen Bi-city Biennale of Urbanism\ Architecture"
「2011-12 香港·深圳城市\建築雙城雙年展」

我覺得，因為工藝的技藝之珍貴
還是很多家徽技藝存於民工。☺

三項城市
Tricipiocal

EXH 016

PAVILION:

Shenzhen Exhibits

PROJECT:

Qianhai Workshop

DESCRIPTION:

This exhibit aimed to analyze the development direction of Qianhai district in Shenzhen, and also to create an open platform for the public to engage and imagine the future of the city together. Visitors could find out various facts about the development and comment through games, voting, or drawing.

EXHIBITOR:

Urban Planning, Land & Resources Commission of Shenzhen Municipality Urban Design Division; Shenzhen Urbanus Architecture and Design

URBANUS is committed to the Modernist belief that architecture can help create a better life, and hence architects should push the boundaries of their traditional roles and be a progressive force in society. URBANUS has been involved in more than two hundred projects of architectural design and urban planning, spanning various building types and scales and research projects.

ORIGIN:

Shenzhen

前海工作坊
Qianhai Workshop

未来城市形态的复杂性与矛盾性
The Complexity and Contradiction of the Future Urban Form

SHENZHEN EXHIBITS 127

128 SHENZHEN EXHIBITS

Archi-II
Nov 2012.

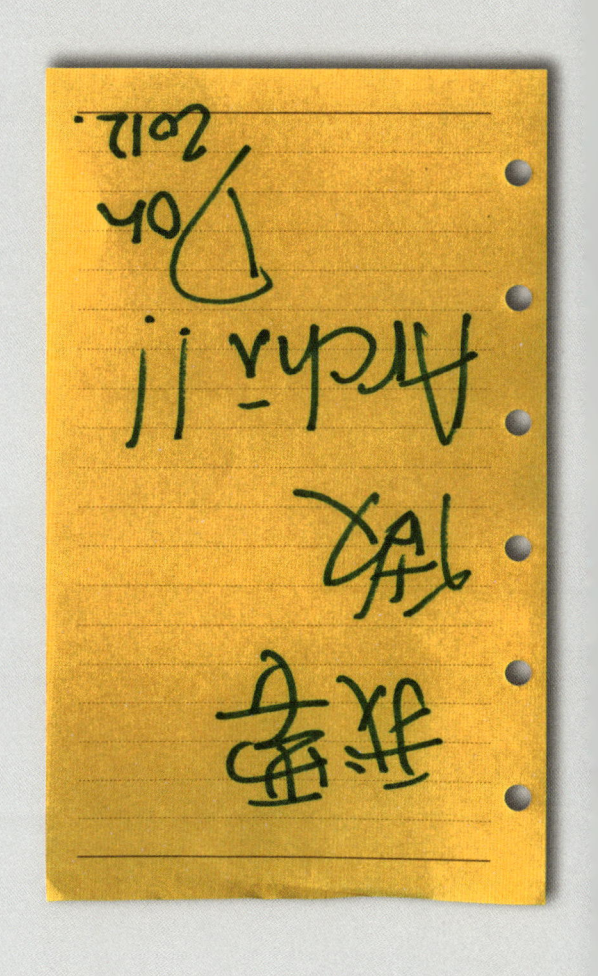

EXH 017

PAVILION:

Shenzhen Exhibits

PROJECT:

10 Million Units: Housing an Affordable City

DESCRIPTION:

Housing an Affordable City brought stakeholders together to examine the challenges and opportunities of providing low- and mid-income housing in the dense environment of the contemporary city. The exhibit presented the winning proposals of Shenzhen's '1 Unit – 100 Families – 10000 Residents Affordable Housing Design Competition.' It also showcased innovative designs and research into the current issues of affordable housing, spanning different stages and scales of intervention ranging from construction details to national policy.

CURATOR:

Juan DU

EXHIBITOR:

Exhibitors include winners of the Affordable Housing Design Competition, Urbanus, Standardarchitecture, Massachusetts Institute of Technology 10K House Design Studio, Hong Kong University Urban Ecologies Design Studio, Urban China Research Center, Bai Xiaoci, Xiepeng Design, Zhuoyue Group, M3house Ltd., UAO Creations

ORGANIZER:

Urban Planning, Land & Resources Commission of Shenzhen Municipality; Shenzhen Center for Design; supported by Zhubo Design

ORIGIN:

Hong Kong / Shenzhen / Beijing / Shanghai / Taiwan / Guangzhou / Xiamen / Xian / United States / Germany

10 MILLION UNITS
广厦千万·居者之城
HOUSING AN AFFORDABLE CITY

SHENZHEN EXHIBITS 131

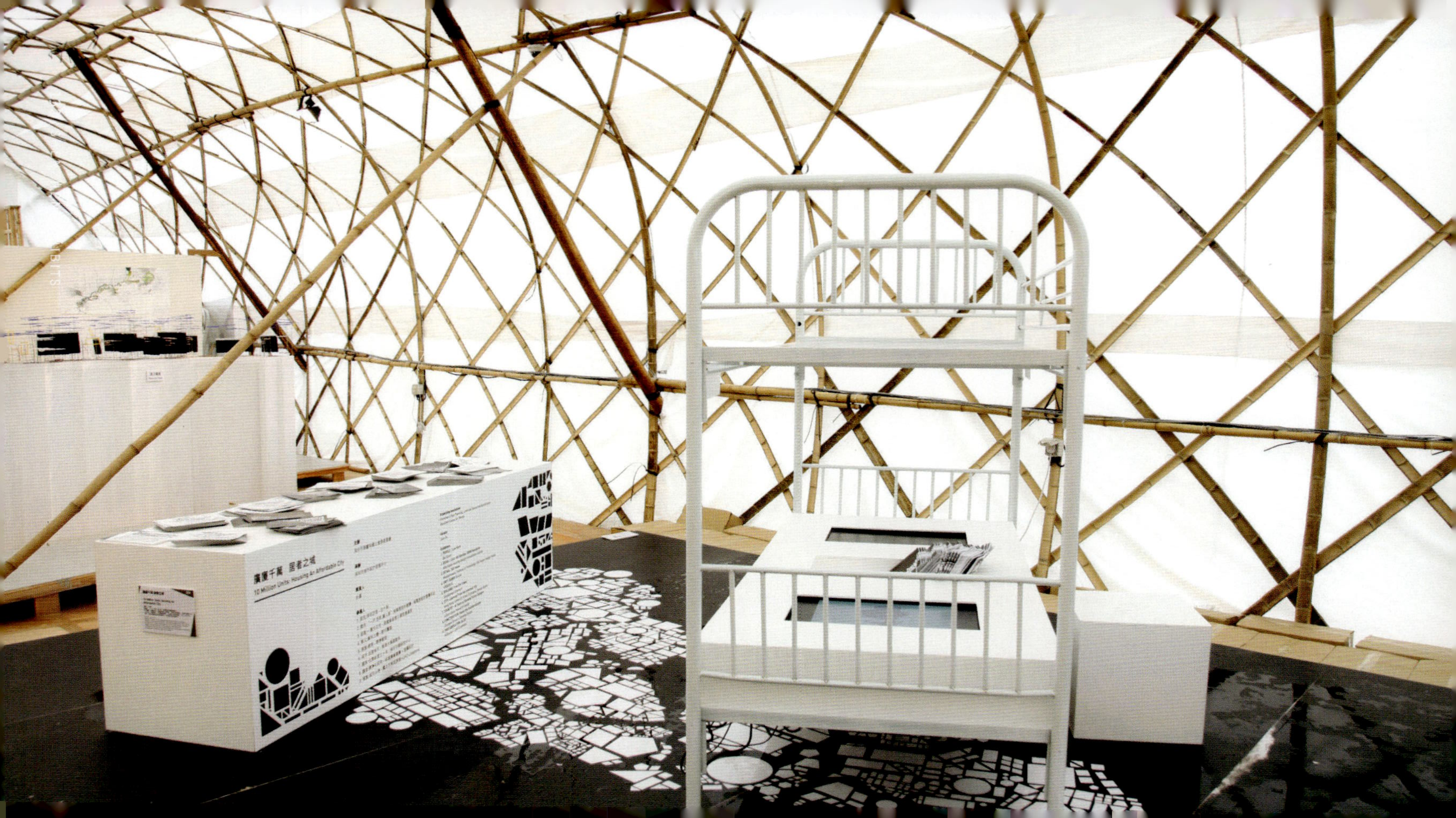
廣廈千萬 居者之城
10 Million Units: Housing An Affordable City

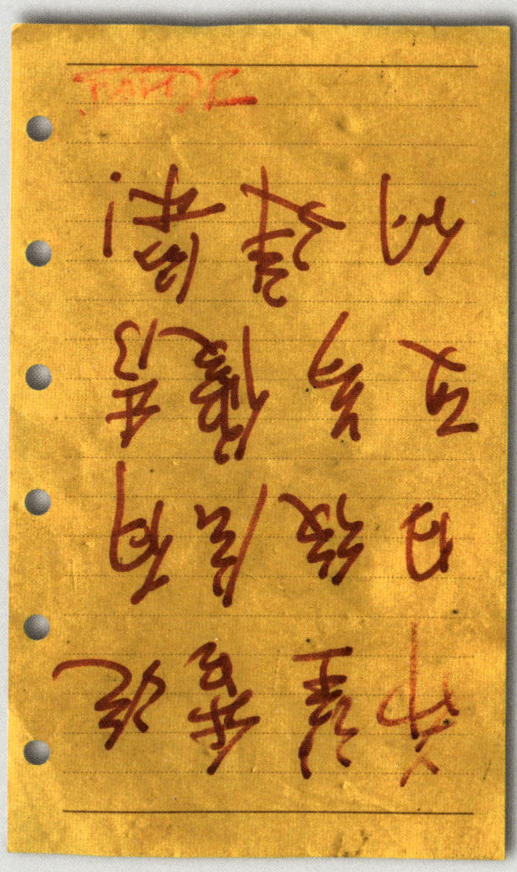

EXH 018

PAVILION:

Shenzhen Exhibits

PROJECT:

Border Metabolism: The Future of The Frontier Closed Area

DESCRIPTION:

What is the future of the Hong Kong's Frontier Closed Area? Park landscape, sustainable buffer, industrial belt, knowledge network or new downtown for a combined Hong Kong/Shenzhen metropolis? In our exhibit we proposed a Mutual Benefit Zone that is adaptable to the future needs of both Hong Kong and Shenzhen. The plan consisted of a series of interlinked interventions across the Closed Area. Activating the existing landscape, these interventions provided new uses and programs to generate a future plan that is able to evolve over time.

EXHIBITOR:

Joshua BOLCHOVER, Peter HASDELL

Joshua Bolchover is an Assistant Professor at the University of Hong Kong. His current research interests focus on the complex urban-rural ecologies of cities in China.

Peter Hasdell is an architect, urbanist, and artist. He is presently Guest Professor at the School of Design, Polytechnic University of Hong Kong and he has his own design office in Hong Kong and China.

ORIGIN:

United Kingdom / Australia

SHENZHEN EXHIBITS 135

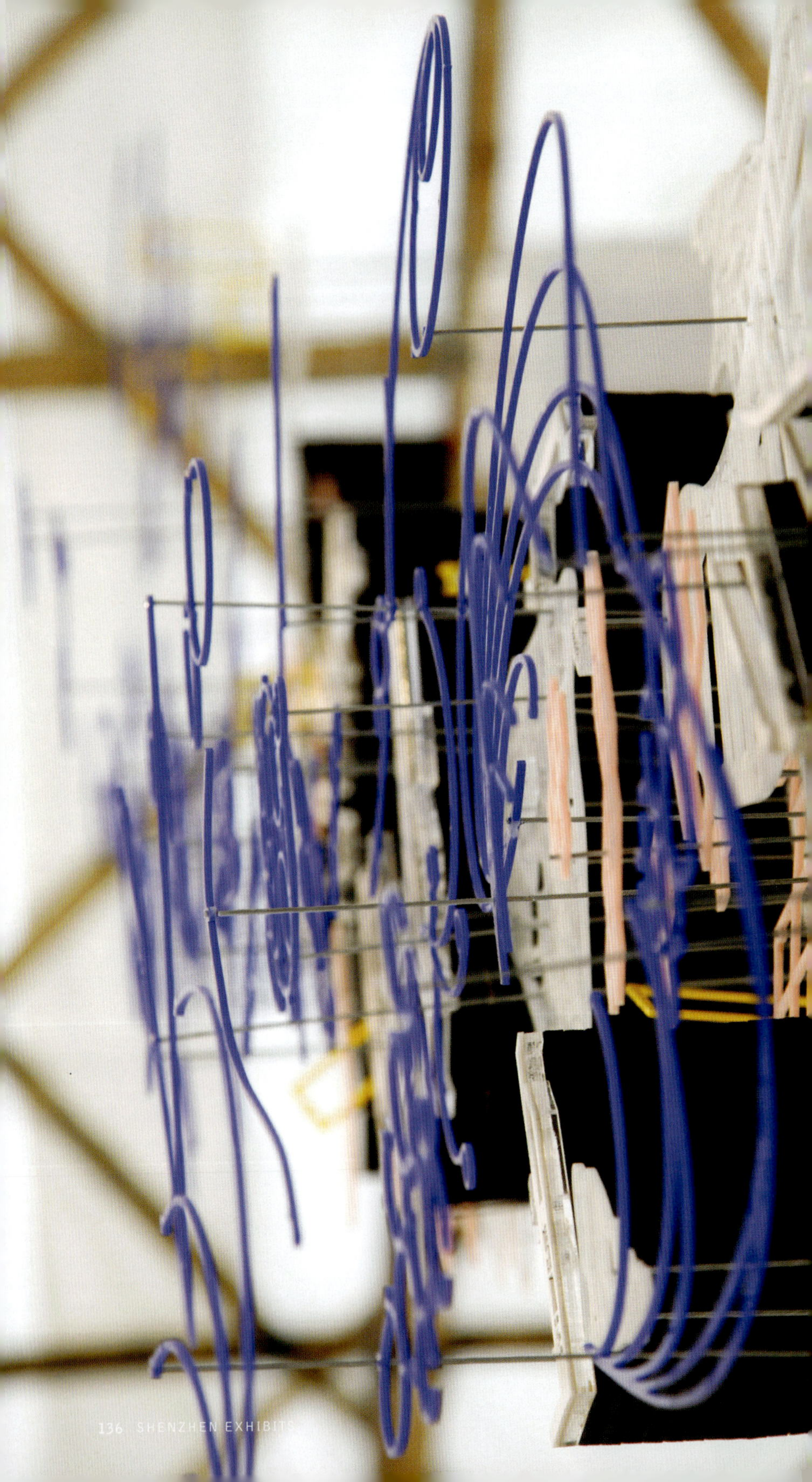

我爱你。

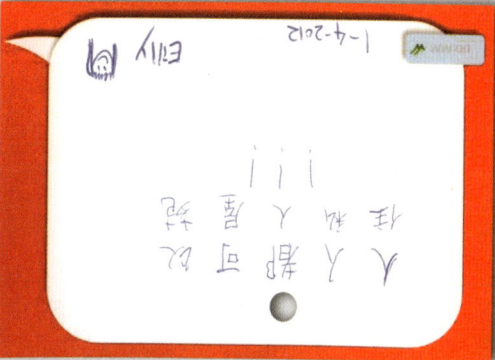

爸爸你

人人都可以
骗我，人骗我
！！！
Elly
1-4-2012

the system, shown in Nakagin Building. Yet both of them recognize a city as growing in diversity and that leads to Metabolism. Kurokawa's Symbiosis was also based on this heterogeneous notion of diversity in reference to Buddhism and biological images.

Since the end of the 1980s, this heterogeneous aspect has been challenged by homogeneous reproduction responding to global commercialization. Architects were also influenced by this gaining power, not only in their field of work, but also on their psychological attitude towards architecture. Architecture seems to have become a globally consumed cosmetic brand with worldwide propaganda. However, the diversity of the city and natural environment would never disappear no matter how global this world will be.

So I strongly believe that architects holding heterogeneous aspects should play a more important role to weave another better, but continuous locus with a cross-bred creativity based on new Metabolism and Symbiosis. I am not so sure if this concern would come out only from contemporary Japanese architecture, but I hope that this will be shared with many other people from all over the world, who would invent and develop a new interpretation of this thought to include the issue of time and cultural diversity.

Q&A 006

DIALOGUE WITH

Tris Kee

TO: Tris Kee
FROM: Anderson Lee, Gene King

The nature of a bi-city biennale, between Hong Kong and Shenzhen, would inevitably bring into question the differences in organization strategy and implementation approach for each side on the 'same' event, and ultimately bring a certain level of the impact and cultural meaning to the city in the end.

Through our own participation, dialogues and interaction with the Shenzhen counterpart during the 2011 biennale, we realized we have much to learn from each other. Since you are involved again, as exhibitor, in this year's 2013 Shenzhen side of the bi-city Biennales, could you shed some light on your observation on their approach to organizing a biennale?

TO: Anderson, Gene
FROM: Tris

Although Shenzhen and Hong Kong are in close geographic proximity, the two Biennales show great differences. Hong Kong often looks at China with envy, as its ample land and resources allow the curators to freely exercise their ideas and artistic direction. In China, large corporations such as private developers, local government or municipal authorities see positive returns from the architectural biennales and are therefore willing to invest in the events. For instance, it has been observed from multiple times in Shenzhen that the Biennale was able to impact its urban setting, either being a catalyst to revitalize a district or more radically, regenerate the economy. Developers have learned to rely on the artistic spark to reactivate districts and bring in profit, economic returns and higher employment.

The availability of space and land has always been an advantage for Shenzhen Biennales, but dealing with a vast site can also pose problems. This year's Shenzhen Biennale 2013 has moved its location from OCT Contemporary Art Terminal (OCAT) to two sites in Shekou – one an abandoned glass factory, and the other the old Shekou Ferry Terminal. Part of the reason for this move was the successful urban transformation of OCAT: the idea is to replicate that success here by transforming abandoned sites in Shekou into a cohesive and vibrant district. The venues were selected with the purpose of generating an adaptive reuse strategy after the Biennale is finished. This Biennale, like previous Shenzhen editions, is mainly funded by private corporations led by developers who saw

return home

relative's or
nd's house

8,000

140

"花开花落人来人往，月圆月缺。"

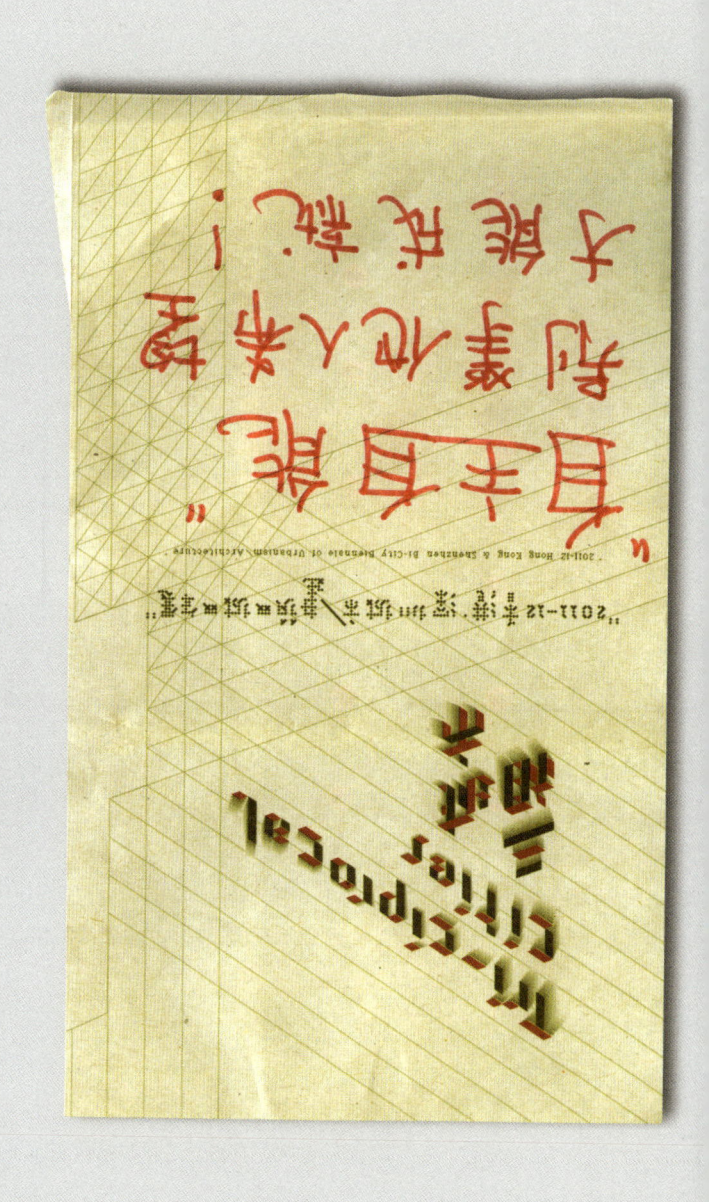

"2011-12 香港・深圳城市\建筑双城双年展"

城市
互働
in-ciprocal
cities

EXH 019

PAVILION:

Shenzhen Exhibits

PROJECT:

The In-Between of Hong Kong / Shanghai

DESCRIPTION:

We found the bunk beds that were provided a powerful parallel with a basic inhabitable unit, starting from the human body. From within each unit people begin to reach out into their surroundings. The In-Between of Hong Kong / Shanghai offered a glimpse into some of these moments of engagement particularly the constant dialogue between old and new in both city's soaring densities.

EXHIBITOR:

Neri & Hu Design and Research Office (Lyndon NERI and Rossana HU)

Founded in 2004 by partners Lyndon Neri and Rossana Hu, Neri & Hu Design and Research Office is a multi-disciplinary practice based in Shanghai that provides architecture, interior, master planning, graphic, and product design service.

ORIGIN:

China

SHENZHEN EXHIBITS 143

144 SHENZHEN EXHIBITS

打倒日本帝国主义！
苦難的中国人民站起来了！

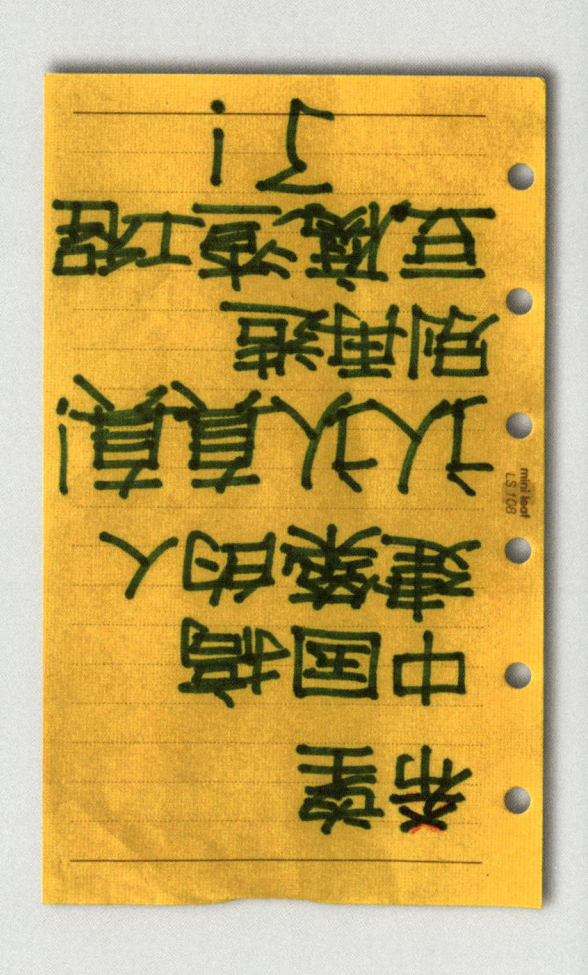

EXH 020

PAVILION:

Shenzhen Exhibits

PROJECT:

Counterpart Cities: Climate Change and Co-operative Action in Hong Kong and Shenzhen

DESCRIPTION:

Hong Kong and Shenzhen are counterpart cities in a single interdependent system. Climate change will ultimately have profound effects on the region and require new infrastructure strategies. Counterpart Cities brought together six design teams from both cities to research and propose collaborative responses to the systemic challenges of climate change in the region.

EXHIBITOR:

Curators: Jonathan D. SOLOMON, Dorothy TANG

Research partner: ARUP; coordinators: Dr. Ricky TSUI, Dr. Iris HWANG; design team leaders: Stefan AL, Guochuan FENG, Doreen LIU, Vincci MAK, Tom VEREBES, Xiongyi ZHU

ORIGIN:

Hong Kong / China

SHENZHEN EXHIBITS 147

148 SHENZHEN EXHIBITS

我的名字叫
我还喜欢画画
就是我的名字

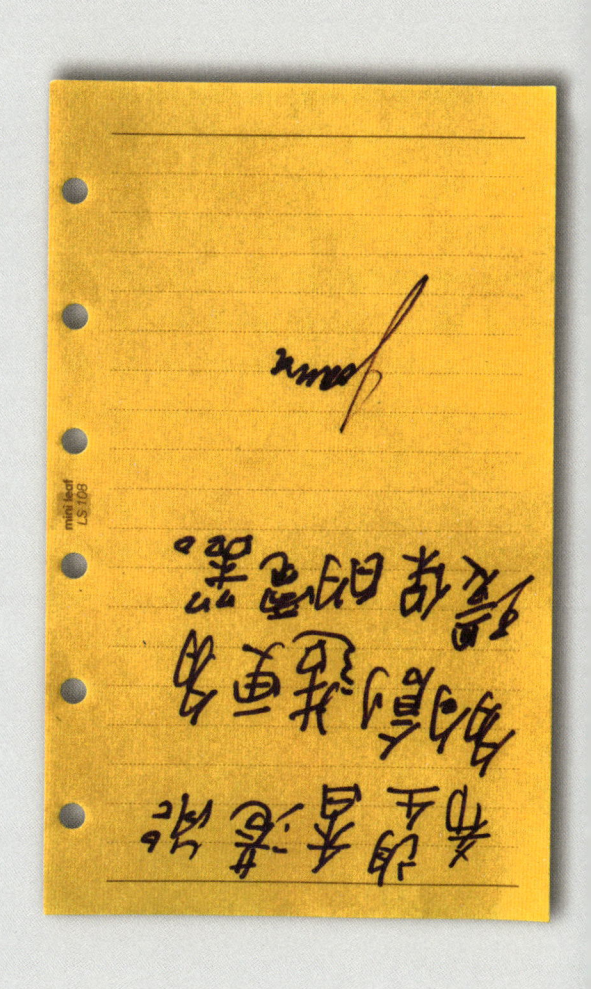

EXH 021

PAVILION:

Shenzhen Exhibits

PROJECT:

Dragon Skin Pavilion

DESCRIPTION:

The Dragon Skin Pavilion was a proposal for an architectural art installation that explored the spatial, tactile, and material possibilities offered today by revolutions in digital fabrication and manufacturing technology. It inspired passersby to reevaluate and reimagine what defines the space we live in today if tomorrow's technologies were combined with industries of the past. The installation was a highly experimental temporary structure, designed from 163 unique pieces of post-formable plywood, a new environmentally friendly material.

EXHIBITOR:

LEAD (Kristof CROLLA and Sebastien DELAGRANGE);
EDGE (Emmi KESKISARJA and Pekka TYNKKYNEN)

Laboratory for Explorative Architecture & Design Ltd. (LEAD) is a Hong Kong / Antwerp based architectural design and research practice founded in 2011 by Kristof Crolla & Sebastien Delagrange. LEAD explores the potential of contemporary design techniques and fabrication technology.

EDGE Laboratory for Architectural and Urban Research serves as a research infrastructure provider for the Tampere University of Technology School of Architecture.

ORIGIN:

Belgium / Hong Kong / Finland

SHENZHEN EXHIBITS 151

DRAGON SKIN PAVILION
DRAGON SKIN PAVILION
DRAGON SKIN PAVILION
DRAGON SKIN PAVILION
MAGIC
逆光
AWSOME!

爸媽的家人遠遠
住在雲林，而上
個月有位新的
可愛的家人誕生

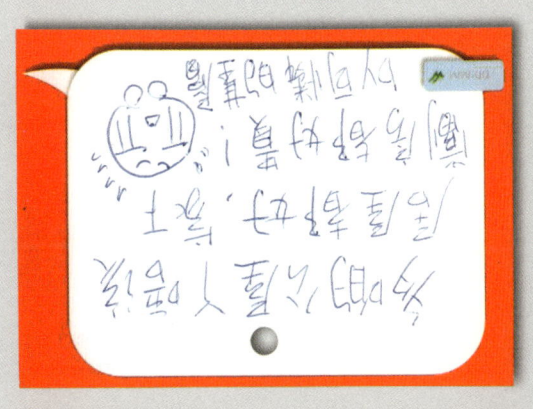

My Dream House

我很有禮貌的話，
自己的玩具分享，還
有把地上的玩具撿
起來放進箱子裡！

the success of the pilot project at OCAT and believe in the potential economic benefit this project will bring.

TO: Tris
FROM: Anderson, Gene

So is it safe to assume that both Hong Kong and Shenzhen are 'young' cities in our 'Triciprocal Cities' theme when it comes to using Biennale as a vehicle to bring impact to a city and its culture?

TO: Anderson, Gene
FROM: Tris

As compared to some of the European Biennale exhibitions that have almost a century of history, the Asian architectural Biennale such as those of Shenzhen and Hong Kong are relatively young, still searching for their own positions in the realm of expositions.

Finding a location for an architectural exhibition is not difficult in China, but interpreting and curating the exhibition remains challenging. Unlike their Chinese counterparts, however, the Hong Kong Biennales have relatively more difficulty in securing venues, resources, and exhibitors. The 2007 venue, the old Central Police Station in Central, was a revolutionary choice: it was the first time that an old existing building had been adaptively reused for this completely different purpose. In addition to seeing the exhibition, most of the visitors were also able to experience unique spaces like the jail cells and police guardrooms. This venue was open only temporarily and is no longer available for public display, as it is currently under development, but the idea of adaptively reusing older buildings seems to be a sound solution for other local exhibitions.

In contrast, the 2009 Hong Kong Biennale chose to look for a tabula rasa, a huge piece of virgin land at West Kowloon. The surprise was that Hong Kong had such a big piece of land available, but the down side was its disconnection with the existing infrastructure network, which affected attendance. That year, the curatorial team seems to have won a good piece of land, but the fundamental question remains: who are the audiences of the Hong Kong Biennale and what messages are the curators delivering? In the past, media has commented that the general public may not be able to appreciate the Biennale's more esoteric content. Therefore, the Hong Kong Biennales of 2009 and 2012 made deliberate attempts to engage the public through community events.

TO: Tris
FROM: Anderson, Gene

It was clear that both curators in the 2007 and 2009 biennale became increasingly aware of the importance of having the public engaged and participated during the span of the event. In our 2011–12 Biennale, we continued to place heavy emphasis on the roles of the community and public participation; clear evidence is that we collected thousands of Post-it notes and comment cards left by the visitors to the biennale, sharing with us their visions of the future of their cities. As curator on Community and Media, would you like to wrap up your thoughts on this particular aspect of the biennale?

TO: Anderson, Gene
FROM: Tris

The 2011–12 Biennale took a step further. Other than the factors of time, people and space, which were the main ingredients for the curatorial theme of the 'triciprocal' city, the community was another critical ingredient in the Biennale. The dichotomy of having intellectual exhibition and community participation has always been a tension of an architectural exhibition. The issues the curators wished to explore were certainly contextual but we hope that the issues might also be reflective and insightful, offering Hong Kong citizens an opportunity to speculate what our impact on our built environment could be.

155

156

I ♡ HK

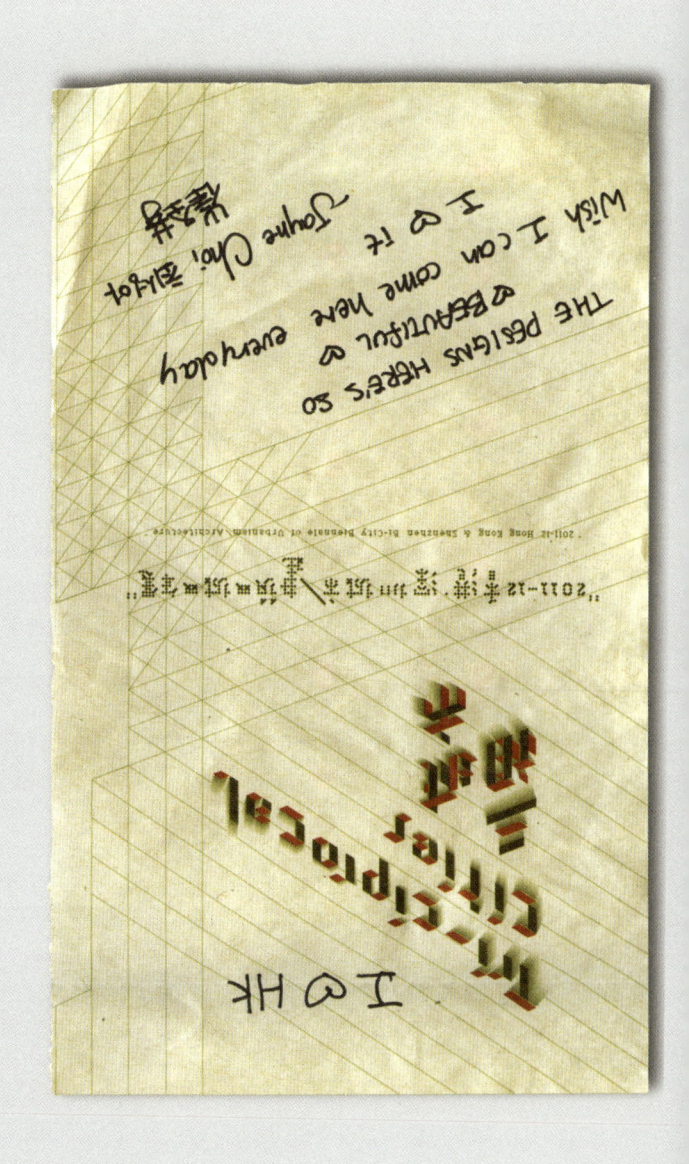

in-ciproca/
互惠

"2011-12 香港·深圳城市\建築雙城雙年展"

2011-12 Hong Kong & Shenzhen Bi-city Biennale of Urbanism\Architecture

THE DESIGNS HERE'S SO
@BEAUTIFUL @
I ♡ it
Joyne Choi, 최진아
최진아

Wish I can come here everyday

EXH 022

PAVILION:

Shenzhen Exhibits

PROJECT:

Stories from Beijing: Memory, Transition, Arraignment, Practice

DESCRIPTION:

Beijing possesses a kind of spiritual quality that adds some intangible element to its architecture. Stories from Beijing was an ensemble of recent projects making connections with its rich historical fabric, both architecturally and culturally.

CURATOR:

WANG Shuzhan, Associate Chief Editor of Archicreation Magazine; ZHANG Yan, Associate Chief Editor of Archicreation Magazine; WANG Xiangdong, Editor of Archicreation Magazine

EXHIBITOR:

CUI Kai, China Architecture Design Master and Chief Architect of China Architecture Design & Research Group; ZHU Xiaodi, President and Chief Architect of Beijing Institute of Architectural Design; LIU Jinbiao, Photographer for Archicreation Magazine; WANG Jinsong, Artist

ORIGIN:

China

SHENZHEN EXHIBITS 159

160 SHENZHEN EXHIBITS

（鄧麗君

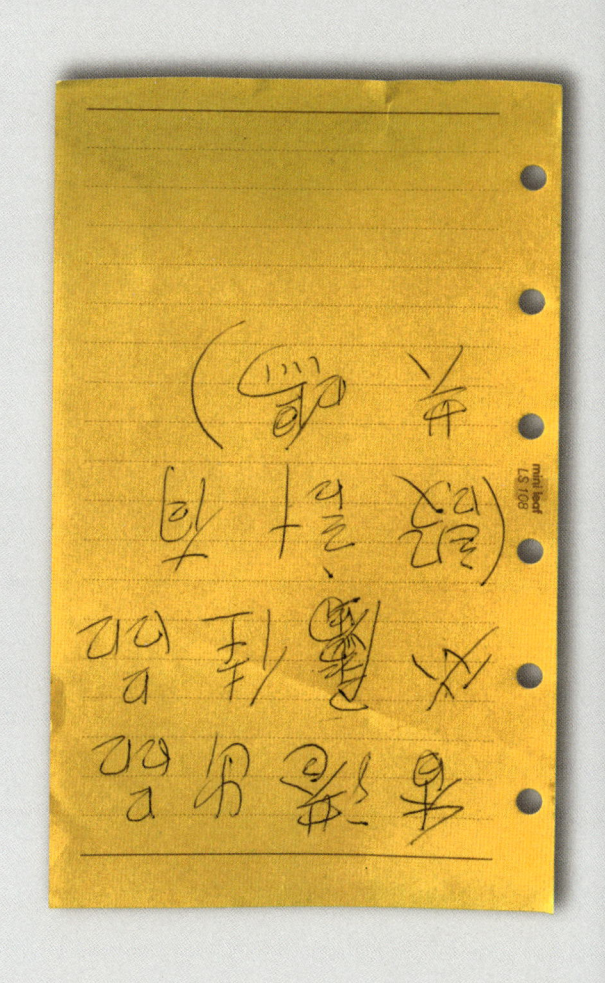

跌倒）

你到數吗
a

你是誰呀
a

EXH 023

PAVILION:
Shenzhen Exhibits

PROJECT:
Department of Design, Sichuan School of Fine Arts Institute New Campus

DESCRIPTION:
The Huxi Campus architectural complex is composed of seven multistory buildings that vary in form on the top of a hill. Drawing from Chongqing's mountain habitat and historical industrial fabrics, the project applied locally accessible cheap materials to create a uniform yet diversified ensemble. Exterior stairs and various layers of rooftops echoed mountain paths. Together they provided an industrial looking space with avant-garde touches.

EXHIBITOR:
Jiakun Architects

Jiakun Architects is headed by Jiakun Liu, whose projects have been selected to appear in many international exhibitions and won various design awards. Mr. Liu also lectures worldwide.

ORIGIN:
China

SHENZHEN EXHIBITS 163

164 SHENZHEN EXHIBITS

2013.11.18

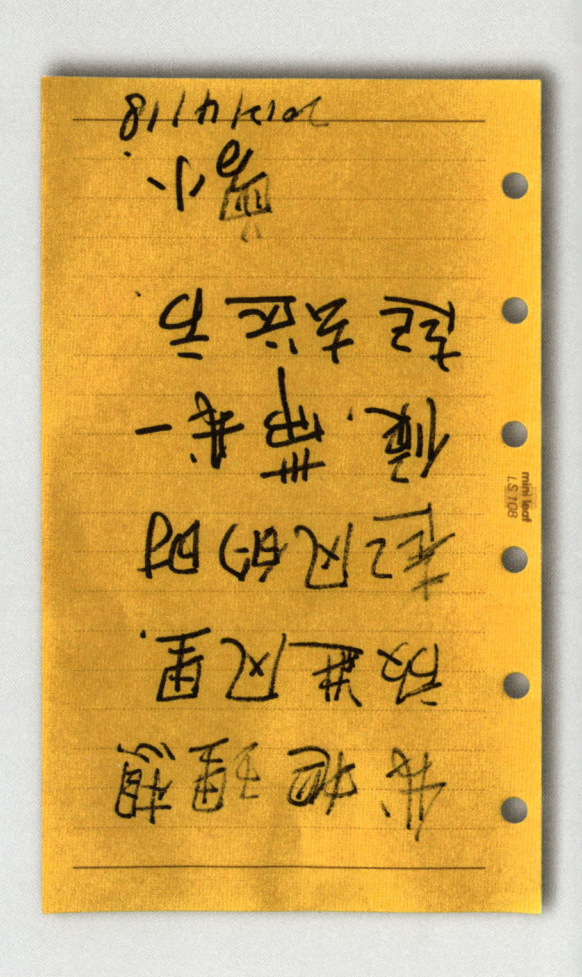

小品

믹 웨딩 구현

進. 曲조~

축가의 메

장면 설명.

부케 받는 사람

EXH 024

PAVILION:

Shenzhen Exhibits

PROJECT:

Edge of Public: Contemporary Architecture in Shanghai's Qingpu and Jiading New Towns

DESCRIPTION:

Countless 'new town' developments in China are an increasingly privatized, both spatially and socially, source of architecture commissions and missed opportunities. The exhibit introduced a group of Shanghai-based architects and examined how they have responded to this phenomenon with works in the public realm.

CURATOR:

LIU Yuyang, LI Xiangning, Harry den HARTOG

EXHIBITOR:

The exhibiting architects represented a diverse and dynamic group of emergent architects, all of whom base their practices, research, and teaching in Shanghai: LIU Yichun, CHEN Yifeng, YU Ting, YUAN Feng, WANG Fangji, WU Jing, ZENG Qun, ZHANG Ming, ZHANG Zi, ZHANG Bin, ZHOU Wei, ZHANG Jiajing, ZHUANG Shen, ZHU Xiaofeng, Harry den HARTOG, LI Xiangning, LIU Yuyang. Installation and Exhibition Design: LI Danfeng and QIU Yuanshen

ORIGIN:

China / The Netherlands / United States

SHENZHEN EXHIBITS 167

168 SHENZHEN EXHIBITS

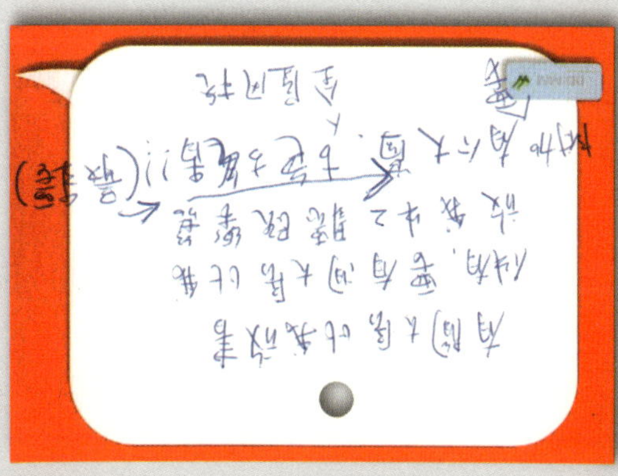

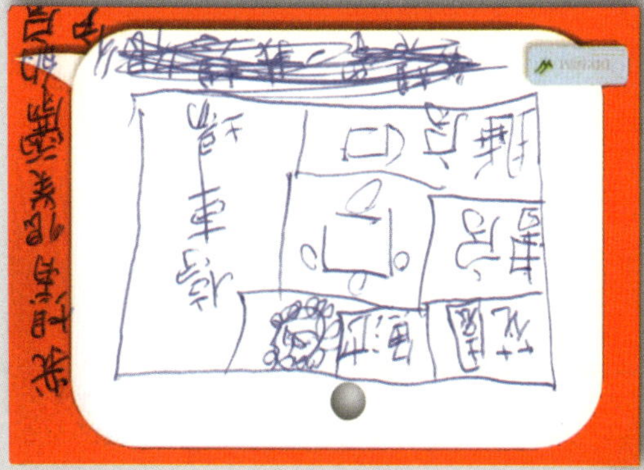

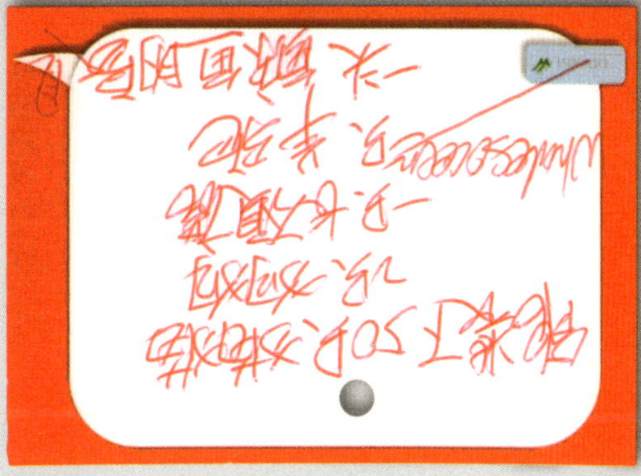

Regardless of site, budget, and curatorial direction, the fundamental value of a Biennale is to offer an open platform for dialogue. By continuing to build upon citizens' interests and participation, a Biennale can become a useful vehicle to formulate visions of progressive thinking. The Biennale essentially becomes the backdrop for creative speculation and it brings forth the critical question of how architects can help to define and share public culture.

Q&A 007

DIALOGUE WITH
Shu-Chang Kung

TO: Shu-Chang Kung
FROM: Gene King, Anderson Lee

Hong Kong Biennale 2011 was over one and a half years ago and we are finally publishing a book. Anderson has a great idea that in addition to documenting the exhibition, we shall also make reflections. So we have prepared the following questions, but please write more and don't get confined by them.

While in the past, people would say 'I am sorry, our city is a little shabby,' we can now find some new confidence from Taipei for its own identity as a livable and interesting city. I guess what has made the difference is the people and the life style they have created. Even though there is neither exciting landmark architecture nor designs of international masters, we can always find this charming and lively atmosphere in the alleys, and I think that's what makes a city captivating. Is this the message you and Mr. Zeng Wei tried to convey in your exhibition 'Urban Network Booting'?

Taipei is perhaps in a 'comfort zone' now. The three factors in our theme – The Time, The Place, The People – seem positively intersecting. Nonetheless, urban renewal is becoming one of the most heated discussions in Taipei these days. Whether a city can keep advancing depends on both its software and hardware, and how these two elements interwork in response to emerging urban issues. Policies in recent few years seem quite out-of-focus in this sense. What do you think?

TO: Gene
FROM: Kung

I am sorry for the late submission, please see below. Please call if there is any questions.

How Adaptive in Urban Network Booting: If a city is to earn its significance in this ceaselessly evolving world, creative thinking must go beyond the mere pursuit of aesthetics. And only by intervening with the nature of what's present can creative thinking lead to a future. Creative thinking has gone through a remarkable change since the 20th century. Today all forms of creativity shall be people-oriented, and bear the social and environmental responsibilities.

Design has become an intermediary in which citizens with integrated social values can participate in building a rich and diverse innovative mechanism. Design provides a platform for social participants with diverse perspectives to discuss the relationship among space, environment and people. All social changes will therefore be based on positive social responsibility. What should be the source of a city's creativity? Could creativity become a social system?

Bottom-up, an organic solution: I think Taipei is a mature middle-aged city in which middle-class and intellectuals are quite homogeneous while individuals have strong self-consciousness. Young men begin to pursue their ideals through self-will and personal competence. These have filled Taipei with abundant unique and diverse life-styles and humanistic attitudes. And that's what makes Taipei unique among all other Southeast Asian cities.

171

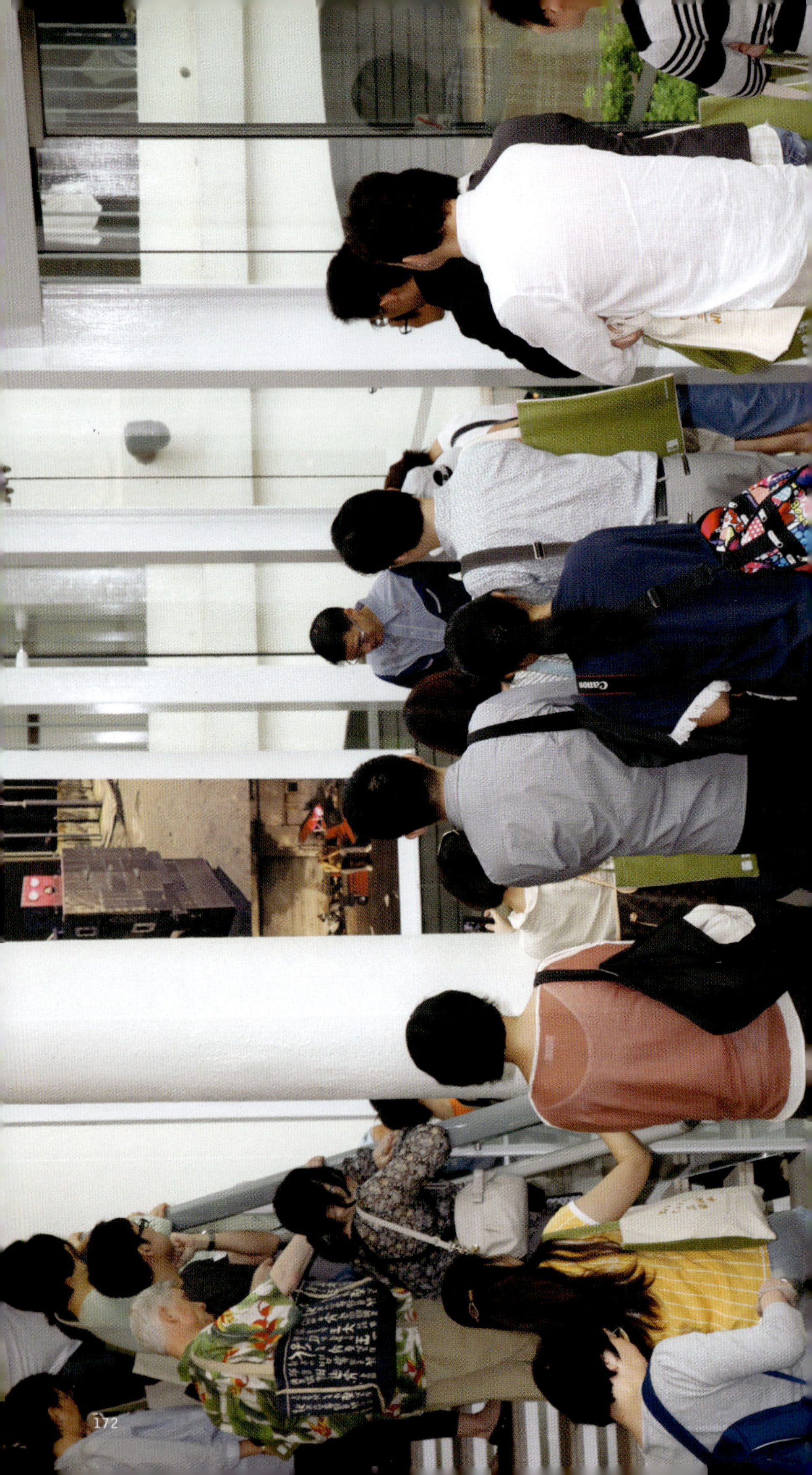

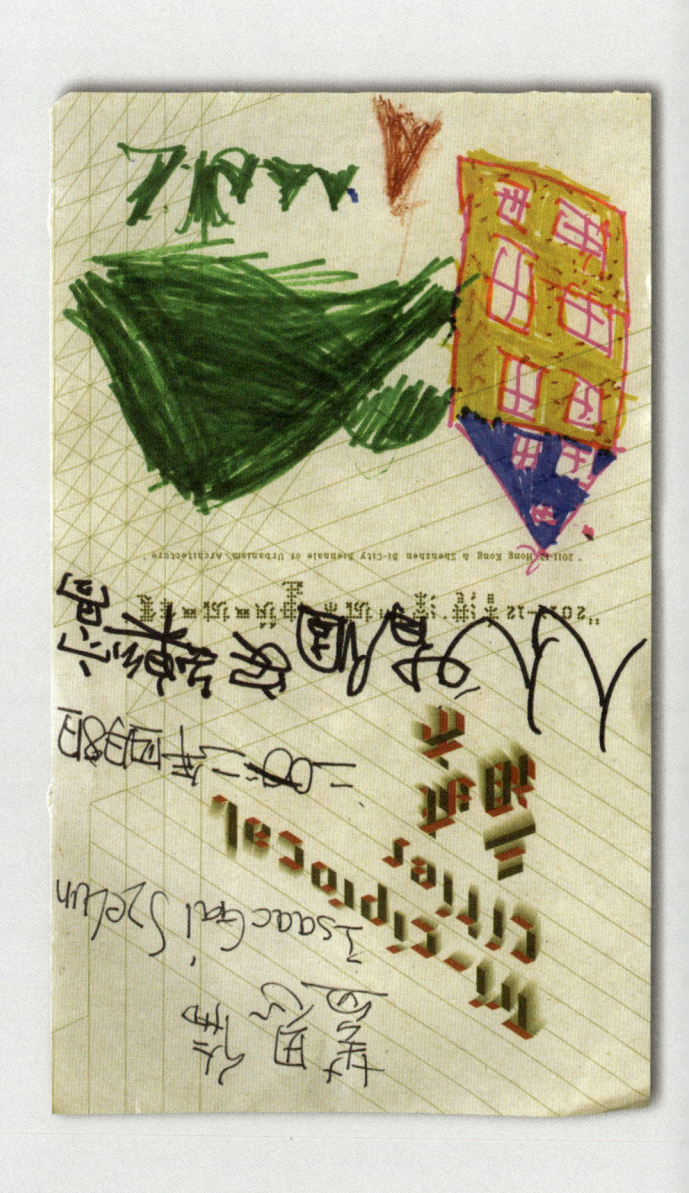

2011-12 Hong Kong & Shenzhen Bi-city Biennale of Urbanism\Architecture

"2011-12 香港。深圳城市\建築雙城雙年展"

二〇一二年二月廿八日

Reciprocal
cities
Isaac Chai Szelun

春到佐敦谷

PAVILION 3
Taipei Exhibits

This exhibit showcased Taipei's recent development in its city, architecture, and also attitude. As a city that has gone through incredible growth since the 1970s, Taipei is developing a new approach that puts equal emphasis on buildings new and old, large and small, tangible and intangible, international and local, with ultimate goal of creating a real place for its people and culture. The exhibit included ambitious projects like the Taipei Arts Center (designed by OMA), Taipei Pop Music Center (by RUR), and the re-use of historical buildings and industrial relics.

ABOUT THE PAVILION

The pavilion was supported by the Taipei City Government. The exhibit was organized by the Graduate School of Architecture at Chiao Tung University, with Shu-Chang Kung as chief curator. The structure, designed by Wei Chang, was linked to the other indoor/outdoor spaces of this exhibition by its innovative use of bamboo, polycarbonate panels, and bunk beds as a response to the Biennale's overall theme and design motif.

TAIPEI EXHIBITS | 175

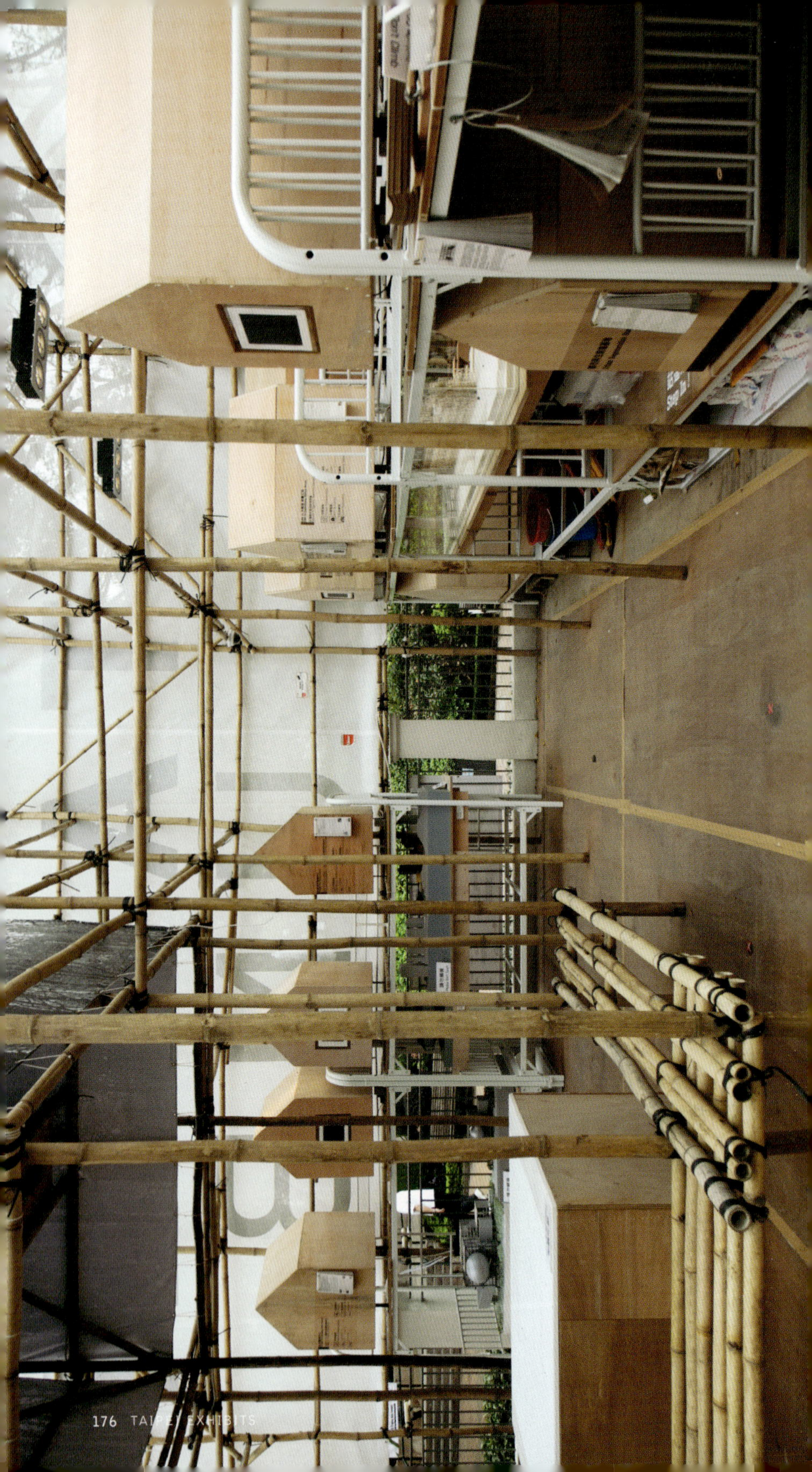

TAIPEI EXHIBITS 179

180 TAIPEI EXHIBITS

I WANT TO
HAVE A
SAKURA 🌸
PARK WHICH
I CAN SIT &
DO NOTHING
JUST RELAX!

EXH 026

PAVILION:

Taipei Exhibits

PROJECT:

Taipei Old Apartment Renovation 2010, 2011

DESCRIPTION:

Lane 204, Songjiang Rd, Lane 9, Chingtien St.; ∞ ; Fuzzy Green Lines: Garden / Apartment; Butterfly Apartment; Xizang Rd, Wanhua District Yungchi Rd., Hsinyi District Section 2, Jianguo South Rd, Daan District; Lane 45, Minsheng West Rd. Furong St, Shihlin District; Songshan District; Birdcage City: Space in Thickness Skin; Xinsheng North Rd, Zhongshan District; No. 316, Tayou Rd, Songshan District: Staircase Passage x Life

Since 2010 the City Regeneration Office has held competitions for old building renovations, in the hope of promoting the redefinition of the urban environment. Regeneration of existing buildings and urban landscapes is encouraged through reviving original uses or inventing new ones. It has been a successful campaign, which provides another dimension for urban renewal.

EXHIBITOR:

ACHL Architects; Jr-Gang CHI (AR-CH Studio); Wan-Lin TSAI; Po-Yu HUANG; Hui-Juan WANG; Guo-Rui LAI; Xian-Hong CHEN; Hsing-O CHIANG; Sheng-Ming WU (Whole+Design Architects & Planners); SCYS ASDD; Chia-Hao TSAI; Pu-Ming TSENG; Hideki HIRAHARA; Bi-Hsin WANG (Grand Hope Architects & Planners)

ORIGIN:

Taipei

TAIPEI EXHIBITS 183

184 TAIPEI EXHIBITS

Home, should be
a place of relaxing.
Instead of sleeping,
HK people still need
to 🌟 strive for
getting on 'ideal home'.
Instead of being
content with our own
"hey space"!

Nic
9 Apr 2017

EXH 027

PAVILION:

Taipei Exhibits

PROJECT:

Taipei Performing Arts Center

DESCRIPTION:

The performance complex is an ambitious project by Taipei City Government. It is composed of three halls for drama performance, one of 1500 and two of 800 seats. The site is located next to the famous Shilin night market, creating special urban characters through the combination of permanent and makeshift facilities.

OMA's innovative proposal providing possibilities of combining halls was selected through international competition in 2009. Construction is scheduled to be completed in 2015.

EXHIBITOR:

Office for Metropolitan Architecture (OMA); Artech Architects

ORIGIN:

The Netherlands / Taipei

TAIPEI EXHIBITS 187

188　TAIPEI EXHIBITS

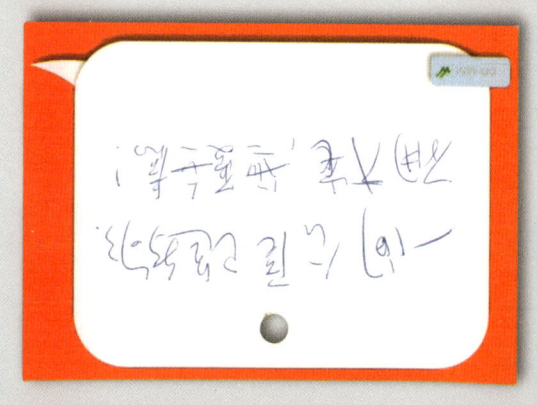

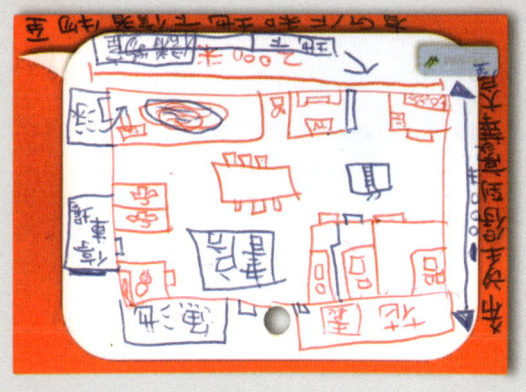

FOR ME HOUSE IS IMPORTANT EVEN ITS SMALL OR BIG. THE IMPORTANT THING IS LOVE & CONTRIBUTION AND HAVE A HEALTHY FAMILY LIFE ASWELL.

一间'n'z'z'z'z
对大家,好温馨!

In the Biennale, we presented the time and spatial dimensions of Taipei's history and life-styles. As a response to the topic 'Architecture Creates Cities, Cities Create Architecture,' we demonstrated a city that is both ordinary and great. Through contemplating the tangible and intangible 'publicity' and 'privacy' of our city, we aspired to eventually reestablish an active dialogue with the cityscape, in order to accomplish the visions of spatial sustainability and development of creativity. This is why we decided the theme of Taipei's exhibition should be 'Urban Network Booting.' Through this exhibition, we would like to put forward the concept and application of 'Social Design,' in which design would become the stem cell for a city's regeneration. The public and the authorities have to confront the severe social development issues, including population, economic, medical, ecologic and residential issues, together. Under the existing public-policy mindset, a city shall adjust and grow constantly through multi-disciplinary communications and creative thinking.

I think, to someone engaged in the field of design, an 'adaptive' mindset is of the utmost importance. Concepts shall adapt to different possibilities. Everything shall be adjustable, and every idea shall be sharable, variable, and combinable. That is going to make our city a better place. To explore and continue the spirit of an Adaptive City, the source of such adaptability should come from the citizens, the mass, and that's also where creativity shall be implemented. The power of design is most revealed when individuals manage to come up with their own unique solutions to tackle their difficulties. The idea of 'Social Design' is a movement that goes beyond visual aesthetics. To meet the rising social issues with limited resources, on one hand we need to establish a solid ground with the vigorous design power of the mass. A city with such collective individualism as the foundation of design strategy would truly belong to its people. On the other hand, we shall also audaciously implant the creative mindset into government's administrations. Through conversations and adaptation, design shall be implemented on both the individual's livelihood and social networks. This is how we shall seek solutions to various kinds of social issues and build the future of Taipei together.

The mass is the initiator of city's changes: If design is to meet the ideals of citizens, its source must come from the mass. When individuals respond to Taipei's natural constraints, social problems and globalizations, they eventually become the fundamental driving forces that allow Taipei to develop and evolve spontaneously. When we try to 'change' and 'resolve' our own difficulties, these micro-changes will alter the development of our cityscape. In the exhibition we emphasized 'How Adaptive.' The major concern was how designs adjust and change the city. By demonstrating such, we were revealing citizen's values on publicity, society, individual livelihood. Through the discussions and initiations in this exhibition, we wished to establish a consensus and shared vision between the citizens and the authorities, and re-examine Taipei's publicity and society. We would also like to ignite civic consciousness and participations among the citizens to intervene the design of a city, and hence eventually bring up a new wave of Taipei's city movement.

Q&A 008

DIALOGUE WITH
Julia Lau

TO: Julia Lau
FROM: Gene King, Anderson Lee

Here I throw out some questions for you to ponder/respond to ... it is part of the format in the publication in which Gene & I ask other curators, exhibitors, symposium speakers in a Q&A dialogue format...

You have always been interested in the potential use and definition of public space in Hong Kong. In our last biennale, we have practically transformed the Kowloon Park, one

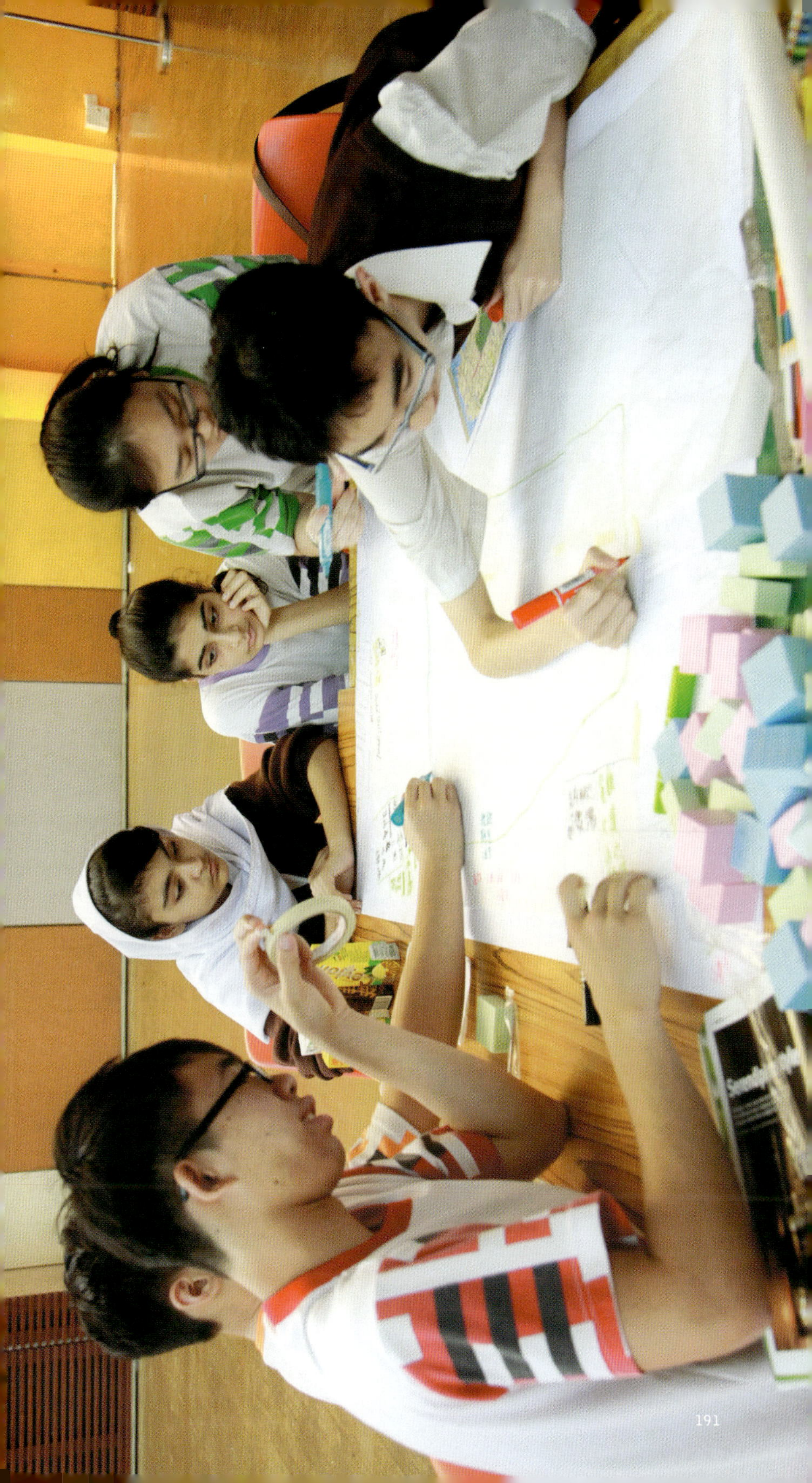

192

"2011–12 香港 · 深圳城市\建筑双城双年展"

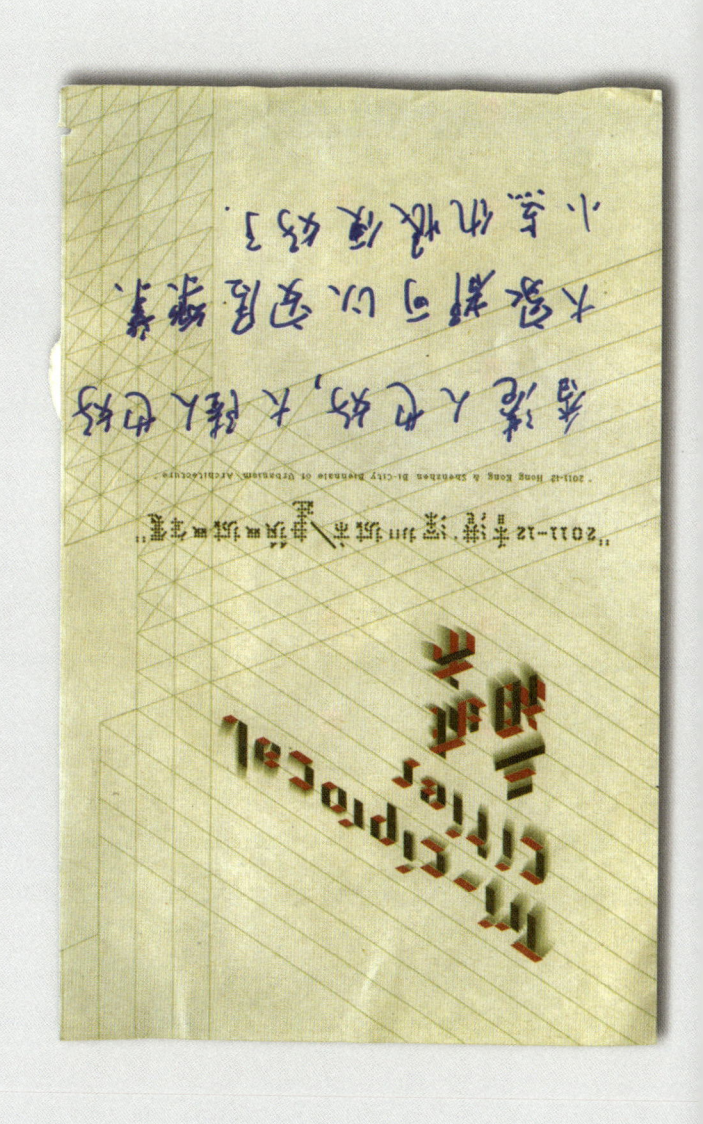

Reciprocal Cities
互补城市

香港人有钱，大陆人有货
大家相互交一下可以互通

小商铺被淘汰了。

EXH 028

PAVILION:
Taipei Exhibits

PROJECT:
Taipei Pop Music Center

DESCRIPTION:
The Center was another ambitious project by Taipei City Government as a base to sustain Taiwan as the leader in Chinese Pop Music. The site was located next to Nankang station, a new transportation hub in the east part of the City. The Project was composed of a main hall, with 3000 seats or 6000 standing capacity, a hall of fame, and several live houses, shops, and restaurants.

Reiser Umemoto of New York won the competition in 2010, and construction is scheduled to complete in 2016.

EXHIBITOR:
RUR Architecture (Reiser + Umemoto); Fei & Cheng Associates

ORIGIN:
United States / Taipei

TAIPEI EXHIBITS

196 TAIPEI EXHIBITS

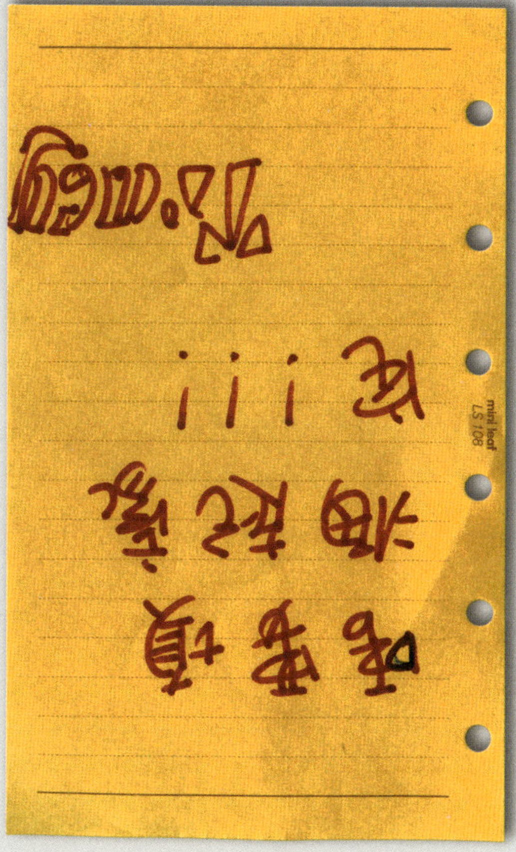
唔要填
海起豪
宅!!!
mini leaf
LS 108

EXH 029

PAVILION:
Taipei Exhibits

PROJECT:
Taipei Creative Districts Map

DESCRIPTION:
'Taipei Creative District' Map was a book published by the Taipei City Cultural Bureau in 2011. It covered 11 urban districts, as well as surveyed 30 shops and studios with cultural creativity, all of which have been naturally developed in urban alleys. These shops emphasize creativity as a part of the life and vitality of a city, and stand as counterpoint to 'policy' projects such as the Taipei Art Center and Pop Music Center.

EXHIBITOR:
Wei-Kung LIU

ORIGIN:
Taipei

「台北創意街區」地圖
"Taipei Creative Districts" Map

都市再生前進基地
Urban Regeneration Station

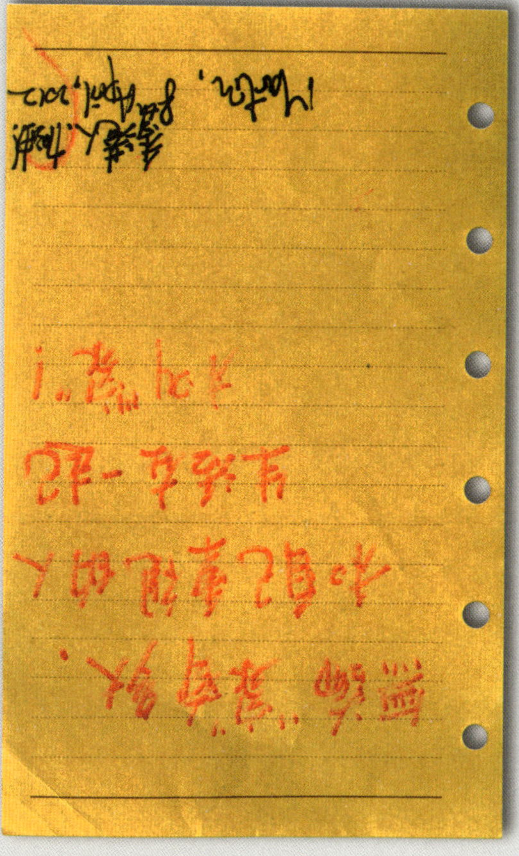
無論"家"有多大，
和自己重視的人
生活在一起
才叫"家"！
香港人
Martin, 8th April, 2012

EXH 030

PAVILION:

Taipei Exhibits

PROJECT:

URS (Urban Regeneration Station)

DESCRIPTION:

The Urban Regeneration Station was established to create a new urban forum and opportunities for public participation along with a sustainable strategy for the future. Seeds needed to be planted in the deadlocked urban development framework, and we collectively called these seeds 'Urban Regeneration Stations,' abbreviated to URS.

URS was a platform, a network and a campaign. It was a quiet urban revolution initiated by the Urban Redevelopment Office of Taipei City Government. Each URS was named by its house number. These spaces are used today for various public events such as workshops, exhibitions, information, and outposts for tourist rest areas.

EXHIBITOR:

Play Ground Exhibition, former Nangang Bottle Cap Factory ('Revived Vanguard,' URS 13) by Artfield (Curator: Hui-Chen WU, Fram KITAGAWA, Shu-Chang KUNG); 'Taipei Extra-Ordinary' Exhibition, The Grand Green (URS 27) by Jay W. CHIU (Chief Curator: Yao-Hua SU); Dadaocheng History House (URS 44) by Institute of Historical Resources Management, Taiwan; Dadaocheng Design Gallery, TKU Architecture Incubator (URS 127) by Dept. of Architcture, Tamkang University; Dadaocheng Academie Urbaine (URS 155) by Urban Redevelopment Office, Taipei City

ORIGIN:

Taipei

TAIPEI EXHIBITS 203

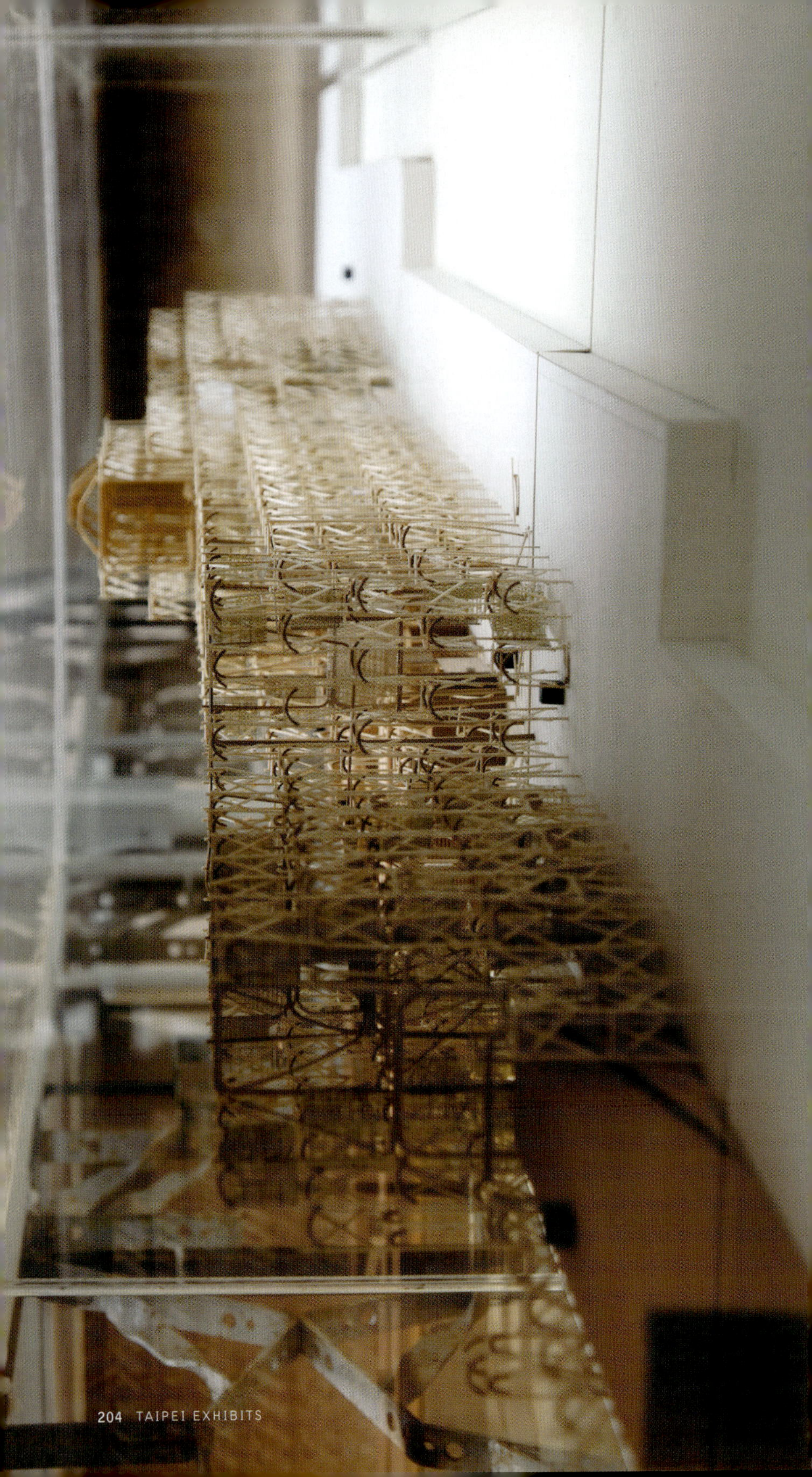

205

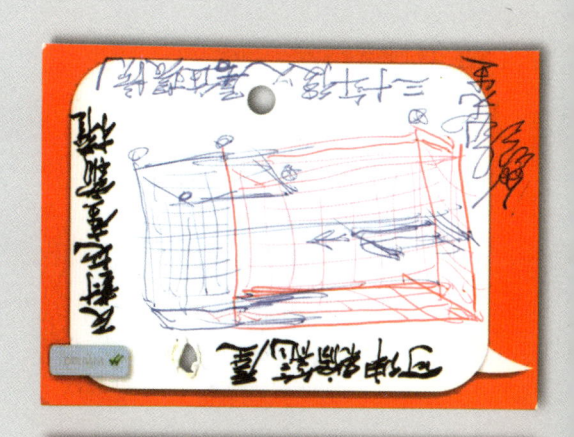

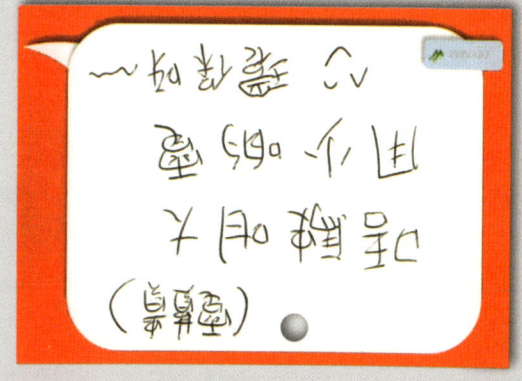

of the most visited outdoor space by tourists, domestic helpers, families with kids, young teenagers, into an outdoor gallery/temporary museum for a duration of 4 months. I know that you have continued to investigate the potential (alternative) usage on these public spaces in Hong Kong. In the past 2.5 years, have you seen that there is a changing trend in how the public perceive this kind of public/outdoor space, or have you been involved in refining their usage?

TO: Anderson
FROM: Julia

When the bunk bed concept first came up, I thought it could be an interesting idea. Though nostalgic, it is precisely those mesmerizing thoughts that leave much room for imagination. The idea was also born out of limited time, limited space, and limited participants. Just like when Hong Kong was going through a period of urbanization, bunk beds were born out of limited space at home; at a larger scale, matchbox apartments on the streets forming the streetscape; and rows of pre-war (slot type) lined buildings making up the city fabric.

Much of these were once zoned as 'Commercial/ Residential' (C/R) mixed use. This gives the architect or the owner a certain freedom to create a mix of different use, different facades enabling different activities fronting the streets, making the streets vibrant. Lot size grew from 2000 sq ft to 4000 sq ft and beyond over the years. Some of these streets with a longer history, were categorized as 'balcony streets.' The faces (facades) of these buildings, although owned by private owners, form the backdrop of the streets, which is a form or type of public space.

Just experience the pedestrianized Mongkok area which is championed by singers and performers in the evenings and holidays, or similarly, the pedestrianized area in Causeway Bay: streets can definitely be successful public space too. As the building facades, or 'backdrop,' are visually captured by the public, they are perceived as part of the public space; hence there is a duty for the owners, architects, and designers to respect the context when designing this backdrop. Individual lot sizes grew bigger and are now often zoned as CDA while C/R zoning is phased out.

We are building bigger, taller and wider ... and sometimes it is easy to get lost in that large context. We should not forget that it is the envelope design of the public space that needs careful treatment and articulation at human scale. Besides the everyday public streets, there are also many other forms of purpose-built public spaces like sports arenas, parks, cinemas, libraries, community gathering places, etc. The same theory applies: we are designing the 'envelope' of the space, not just the facades or the backdrop. Our owners, architects, and designers should use this freedom wisely when designing the 'envelope' of these public spaces, and not forget the touch of human scale for their interaction to enliven the space and enable intimate dialogue of both humans and spaces.

Q&A 009

DIALOGUE WITH

Ulf Meyer

TO: Ulf Meyer
FROM: Anderson Lee, Gene King

In our Biennale you have shown large scale photographs which depict various Chinese cities and their development. It is interesting to realize that while there are physical similarities between each of the 'young' cities, there are certain characteristics or one might say 'an aura' about each city. The idea of 'non place' or 'any-place' has not totally manifested itself in the formation of new Chinese cities.

Since the Biennale you have taken up a teaching position at Tamkang University in

OMA | 庫
OMA | Storage

207

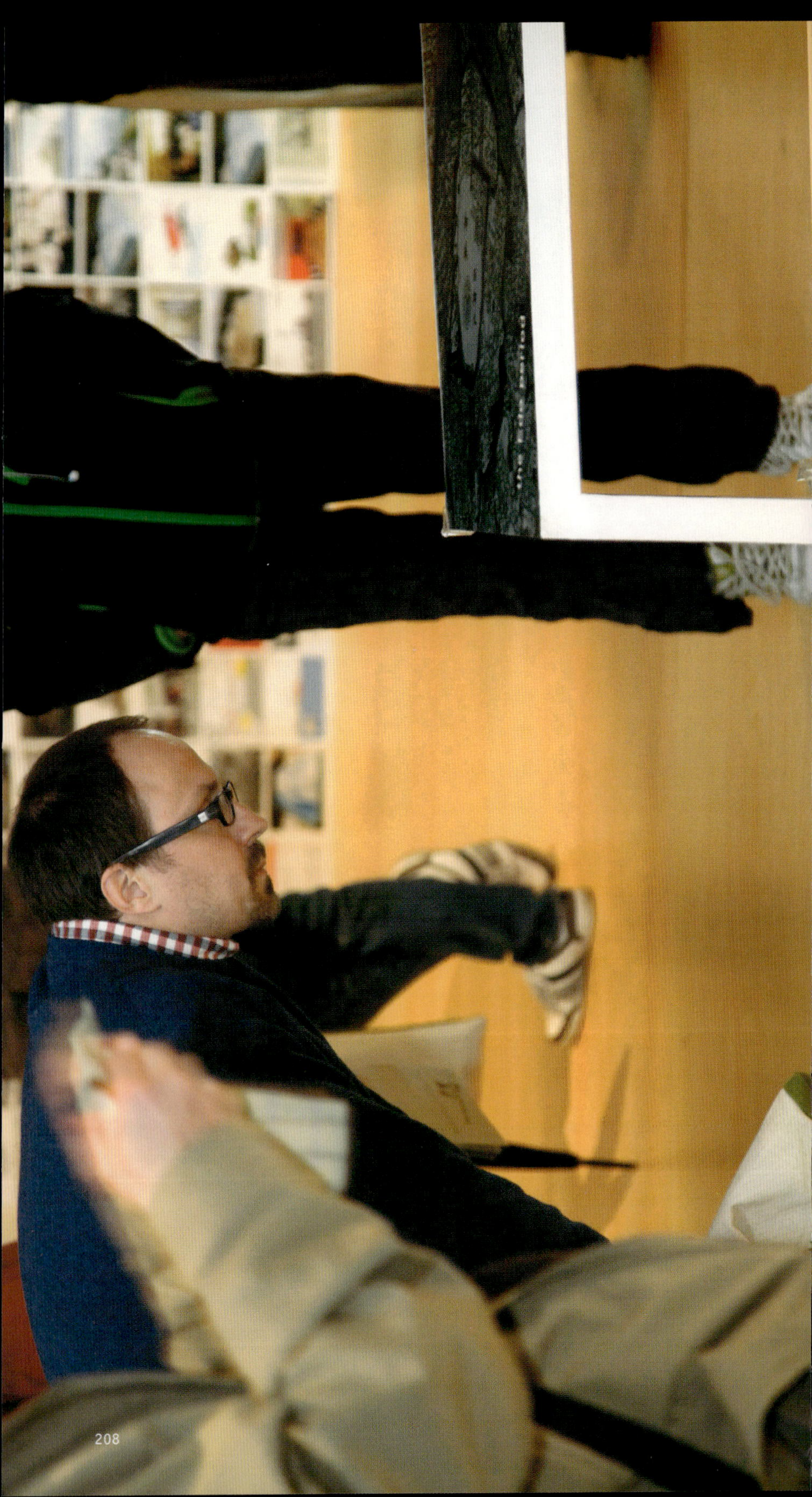

"2011-12 香港·深圳城市\建筑双城双年展"

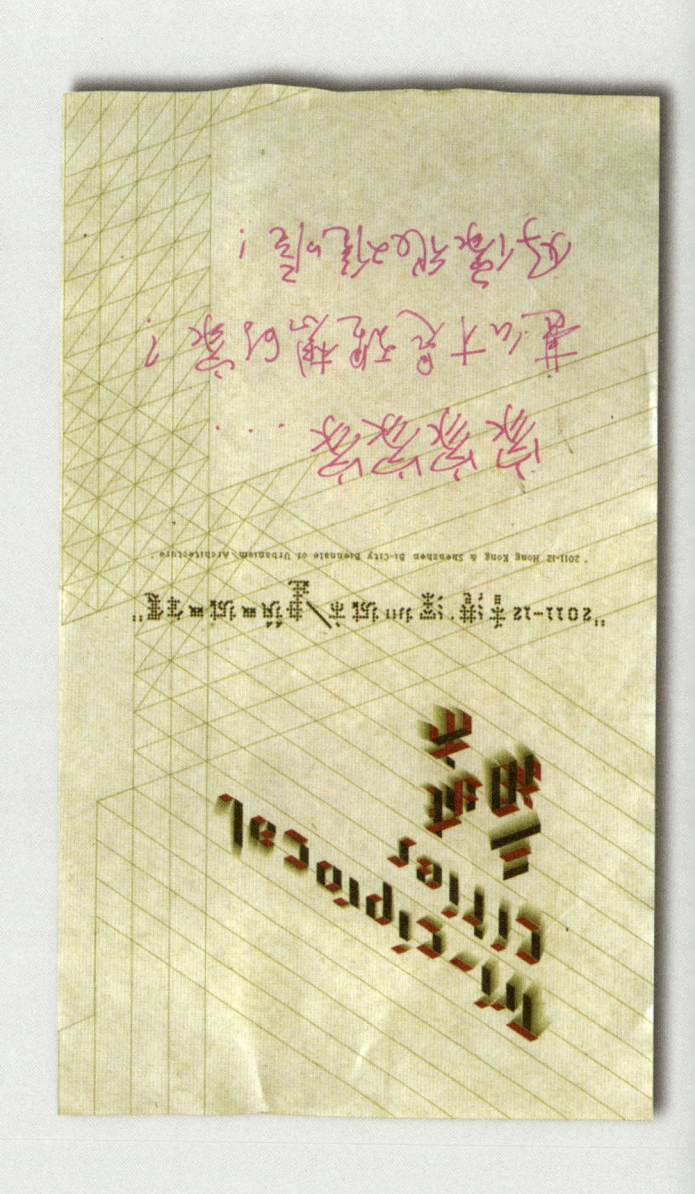

2011-12 Hong Kong & Shenzhen Bi-city Biennale of Urbanism\Architecture

这就是…
难以开启建构的篇章？
或以探究建构的篇章！

PAVILION 4
Asian Urban Portraits Exhibits

This pavilion showcased JUT Foundation for Arts and Architecture's research on Asian urbanism in recent years. The three projects focused on formal and transient aspects of Asia-specific spatial and urban development, particularly the way in which a modern megalopolis may still hold within it a resilient village structure, challenging the definition of urbanism and architecture.

JUT Foundation for Arts and Architecture was founded in 2007 by its parent company JUT Construction with two goals: to rediscover the role of architecture in our cities, and to empower the artistic and creative industries to influence urbanism. Our individual contributions can be magnified through a collective effort.

Since 2007 JUT Foundation has staged a series of exhibitions around the theme of 'The Museum of Tomorrow,' which have won various local and international awards.

ABOUT THE PAVILION
The pavilion itself was a variation on the traditional bamboo shed, with two layers of bamboo frames holding up polycarbonate panels, allowing a dialogue between skin and frame.

ASIA EXHIBITS 211

212 ASIA EXHIBITS

我的圖示　My Sharing

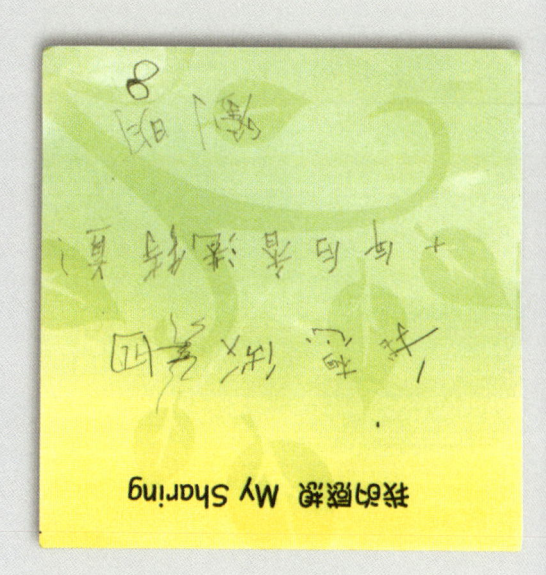

我不知道為一隻蝙蝠在等我

我的圖示　My Sharing

謝謝你告訴我有那麼多影片

EXH 031

PAVILION:

Asian Urban Portraits Exhibits

PROJECT:

Illegal Architecture

DESCRIPTION:

Wang Shu and Hsieh Ying-Chun derived ideas from illegal additions on rooftops and back alleys in Taipei for 'Square also Round' and 'Walden, back alley' installations on Taipei old neighborhoods dating back to the 70s along with exhibits of their past works to provide a poetic perspective on architecture, dwelling, and power.

CURATOR:

ROAN Ching-Yueh, Associate Professor and Director, Department of Art and Design, Yuan Ze University

EXHIBITOR:

WANG Shu, Professor, Director of Architecture Department, Dean of Architecture School, China Academy of Art in Hongzhou, 2012 Pritzker Prize winner

HSIEH Ying-Chun, Architect, 2011 Curry Stone design prize winner

ORGANIZER:

JUT Foundation for Arts & Architecture

ORIGIN:

Taipei

ASIA EXHIBITS 215

216 ASIA EXHIBITS

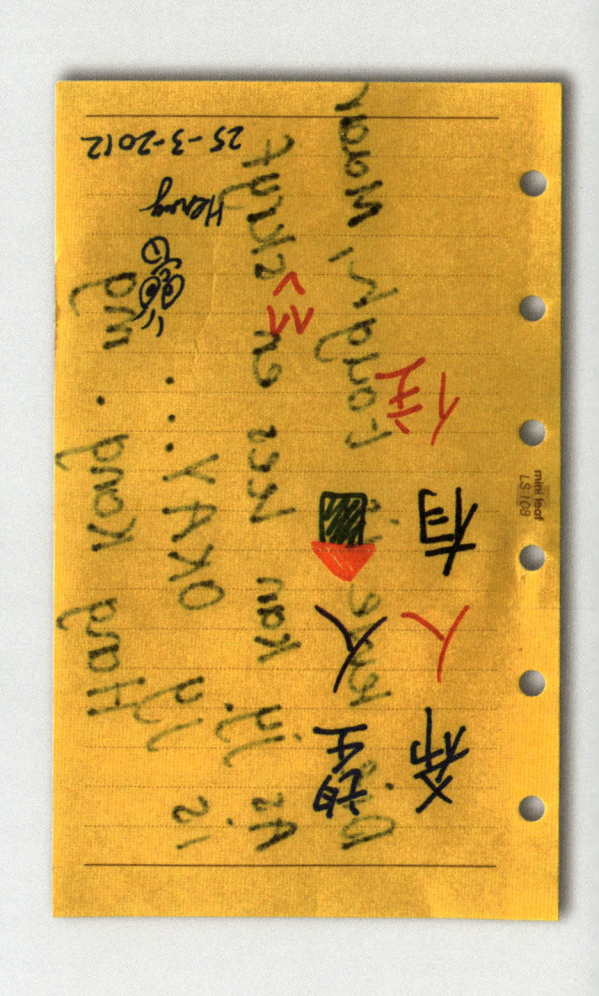

25-3-2012
Hang
Sunshine
Nooi, Vlody,
安 人 有
爱 你 ❤️ 每 day
Hi, you can not even try forget, me!!
OKAY...
Hard xard .
Din

EXH 032

PAVILION:

Asian Urban Portraits Exhibits

PROJECT:

Ruins Academy

DESCRIPTION:

Ruins Academy was an experimental platform to pursue knowledge about Third Generation Cities, a category proposed by Marco Casagrande. Located in an old four-story apartment in western Taipei, the Academy invited participants to engage in workshops on urban, environmental and cultural issues to generate an organic symbiosis of the manmade environment and nature.

EXHIBITOR:

Marco CASAGRANDE

Marco Casagrande, a Finnish architect, founder of C-Lab, since 2000 has been teaching with cross-disciplinary approach including architecture design, urban planning, and environmental art, a methodology also reflected in his works.

ORGANIZER:

JUT Foundation for Arts & Architecture

ORIGIN:

Taipei / Finland

ASIA EXHIBITS 219

ASIA EXHIBITS 219

220 ASIA EXHIBITS

220 ASIA EXHIBITS

1. 搭飞机12.
2. 好好休息一下 HK!
3. 可以休息到一个人走走啦.

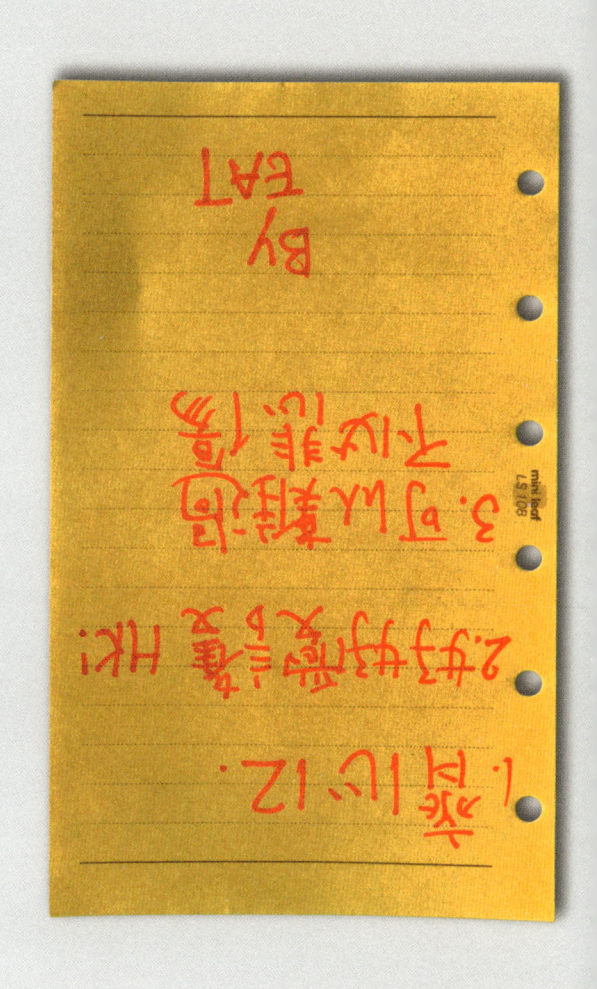

BY
EAT

EXH 033

PAVILION:
Asian Urban Portraits Exhibits

PROJECT:
The Vertical Village

DESCRIPTION:
The Vertical Village exhibited the outcome of research conducted by Dutch avant-garde architectural team MVRDV and their think tank The Why Factory, including their investigations and proposed solutions in various Asian cities experiencing drastic changes in populations and economies. The exhibition emphasized the freedom of individuals and the diversity of neighborhoods during the development of a city, reestablishing the meanings of urban architecture and reconnecting individuals to society.

EXHIBITOR:
MVRDV / The Why Factory

MVRDV was founded in 1993 in Rotterdam by three architects: Winy Maas, Jacob van Rijs and Nathalie de Vries. The Why Factory is a think tank founded by MVRDV and the Graduate School of Architecture at Delft University of Technology. It conducts research globally to explore the challenges cities might face in the future, and proposes possible paths of development to solve these problems.

ORGANIZER:
JUT Foundation for Arts & Architecture

ORIGIN:
Taipei / The Netherlands

ASIA EXHIBITS 223

224 ASIA EXHIBITS

Maison avec plein de
rire et d'espoir.

苗木一本。
用意をととのへて
春を待つ私は

똘똘 마시멜로 크림같이,
폭신폭신 사서 안고싶은
녹일이 없이 이쁜이!
이토도 읽날을 본 기억은
시고서도 않는다시기.
2012.05.04.
17:12
마시멜로
눈

Taiwan, and you are submerging yourself in the cultural and social aspects of a particular Asian city, do you come to any new realization on your juxtaposition of presenting an overall image of cities versus actually living and working in one? Have you and Hans-Georg Esch continued to photograph more of these anonymous cities? And does it change your perspectives in dealing with cities as your subject?

TO: Anderson, Gene
FROM: Ulf

Unfortunately I have to disagree with your observation: I think HG Esch's work shows the total lack of characteristics and the self-similarity within and between cities and illustrates the notion of a non-place. Where do you find 'aura' in his pictures?

You are right about the fact that I now live in an Asian city (Taipei), but since I have traveled to this and many other East-Asian cities before and have also lived and worked in one before (Tokyo), this experience so far does not change my perception or interpretation as illustrated in my book 'Cities of the Pacific Century.' While I was not involved in photographing any of the cities in HG Esch's project, I know that he continues to work on this subject, having just installed a giant rotunda in front of the Rockefeller Center in New York showing Shanghai-Pudong on a giant panorama screen – quite the provocation I think. It was a huge popular success!

Q&A 010

DIALOGUE WITH

Jesse Reiser / Nanako Umemoto

TO: Jesse Reiser, Nanako Umemoto
FROM: Gene King

I thought you are coming to Taipei again in October, has your schedule been changed? The reason I write is that we are finally going to publish the book on HK Biennale, even though it is almost a year and a half since it was closed. Anderson has a good idea, which is that since it is so long ago, we might we well have a dialogue and reflection about the topic again I think it will make a much more readable book. The following are our questions, you can elaborate, change, or improvise, and talk about whatever you find relevan and interesting.

The film you made for the exhibit, 'Manhattan Memorial,' had 6 un-built project in Manhattan. What was your intention? Were you trying to infer that their ideas are still valid and valuable to us now? What do you draw from them? You also included some clips from the time these projects were conceived. Are they to reinforce why these projects were so innovative and unique?

Between projects never built and demolished, you think they inflicted the same kind of impact on current conditions of the city?

TO: Gene, Anderson
FROM: Jesse, Nanako

Better late than never! We had planned to be in Taipei in october for the groundbreaking in Kaohsiung. The event was postponed to November 9th but we are now scheduled only to be in Kaohsiung for one night. We could schedule an interview on skype if you are interested. Or if you want to come down for the groundbreaking....

TO: Jesse, Nanako
FROM: Gene

Are you still coming to Taiwan as scheduled? Please drop me a few lines on the Biennale questions, we hope to finish it up this Friday, so that the book may have a slight chance to

227

6 Indexes

Spatial Transformation

Arts & Culture

Social Participation

Events

Industry Cluster Revitalization

Awakening Habitat

The Basel Cityscape Rhythm

太陽能
Tri-ciprocal
Cities
三相城市
Ian Ho
2012年4月8日
tree house
2011-12 Hong Kong & Shenzhen Bi-City Biennale of Urbanism\Architecture

PAVILION 5
World Exhibits

The indoor space of the Hong Kong Heritage Discovery Centre (HDC) displayed stories from cities all over the world, including New York, Tokyo, Paris, Singapore, and Amsterdam, including the work of some of the world's leading architectural practices, artists, and academics. Each team put forth a unique theory about the interrelationship of time, place, and people in a city, and many attempted to address both local and global conditions.

ABOUT THE PAVILION
Despite its global view, this pavilion remained firmly anchored to its local context because of its location here at the HDC within Kowloon Park. Bunk beds were given to each exhibitor as the basic unit of display. The beds recalled this building's history as a barracks while also invoking the collective memories of Hong Kong people, many of whom grew up in crowded apartments with bunk beds just like these. The curators coined the term 'weight of reality' to reflect the constraints of this exhibition venue: at a mere 200 square meters for 14 exhibitors, the space itself illustrates yet another interpretation of the word 'density.'

WORLD EXHIBITS 231

WATER PROVING GROUND

Cities Unknown
HG Esch

232 WORLD EXHIBITS

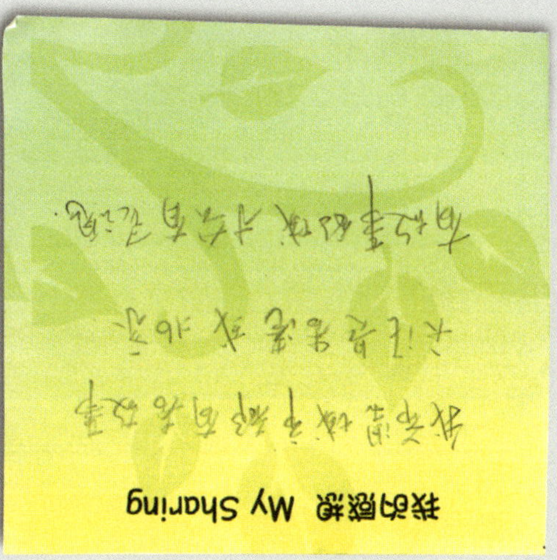
我的感想 My Sharing
我希望城市都有名故事
不论是香港或北京
有故事的城 才会有灵魂.

我的感想 My Sharing
懷念上學
在校園裡的生活

EXH 034

PAVILION:

World Exhibits

PROJECT:

Cities Unknown: Boomtowns in China

DESCRIPTION:

This photographic exhibition presented several large metropolises in the Chinese hinterland. It showed their vitality as much as their ugliness and self-similarity in a clear and straightforward manner.

EXHIBITOR:

Hans-Georg ESCH, Ulf MEYER

Hans-Georg Esch, born in Neuwied, Germany, in 1964, completed training as a photographer. He has been working as a freelance architectural photographer for architecture firms since 1989.

Ulf Meyer was born in Berlin in 1970. After studying architecture in Berlin and Chicago, he became a writer, educator, critic and curator for architecture and urban design.

ORIGIN:

Germany

WORLD EXHIBITS 235

請勿觸摸
Please Don't Touch

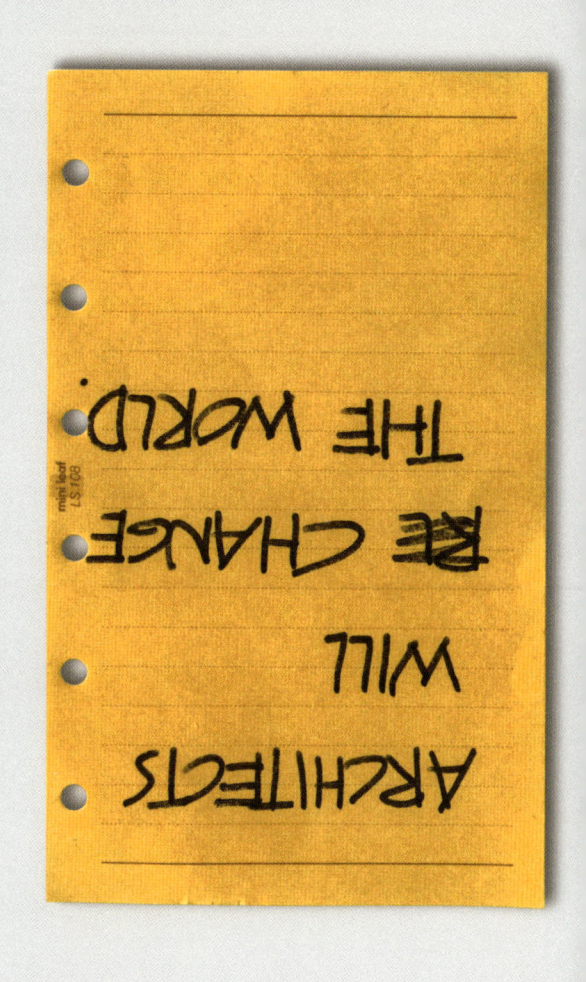

ARCHITECTS WILL CHANGE THE WORLD.

EXH 035

PAVILION:

World Exhibits

PROJECT:

Manhattan Memorious (film)

DESCRIPTION:

This 20-minute long quasi-documentary was comprised of fictional eye-witness accounts of a phantasmagorical Manhattan where the visionary meets the everyday, the absurd and the sublime. The storyline incorporated a series of visionary projects for Manhattan, based on existing documents, drawings, and models that were digitally reconstructed and edited with cinematic format, to provide a reality that Manhattan could have been.

EXHIBITOR:

RUR Architecture (Jesse REISER and Nanako UMEMOTO);
Grahame SHANE

RUR Architecture PC is an internationally recognized multidisciplinary design firm, which has built projects at a wide range of scales. The work of Reiser and Umemoto has been published and exhibited widely, and both partners have taught at various schools in the United States and Asia.

Grahame Shane has taught at numerous universities and has published extensively.

Digital reconstruction: Jun-Hao Ho and Pei-Shen Hsu, both teaching at National Chiao Tung University, Taiwan, along with their digital studio.

ORIGIN:

United States

請勿攀爬
Please Don't Climb

WORLD EXHIBITS 239

240 WORLD EXHIBITS

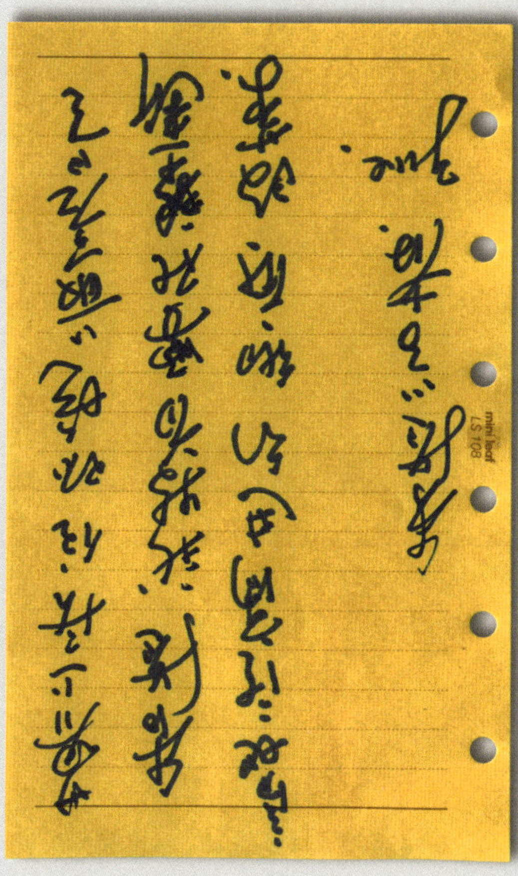

EXH 036

PAVILION:

World Exhibits

PROJECT:

Story From Amsterdam: Great Form Has No Shape (film & installation)

DESCRIPTION:

Starting from its small organically grown medieval centre, the plan of the city of Amsterdam has been the result of a series of planned extensions in the fashion of concentric rings instead of layers on top of each other. This allows co-existence of various areas, each reflecting the political, economic and cultural conditions of the period of their planning and execution for us to experience and study the unity between the urban and architectural typologies of the various periods.

EXHIBITOR:

Felix CLAUS

Felix Claus founded Claus en Kaan Architecten together with Kees Kaan in 1987. The office has establishments in Amsterdam/Rotterdam, Paris and Tokyo, and it has been the subject of several monographs. Claus en Kaan Architecten works on urban design, public buildings, housing, the refurbishment of historical buildings and interior design.

ORIGIN:

The Netherlands

WORLD EXHIBITS 243

244 WORLD EXHIBITS

245

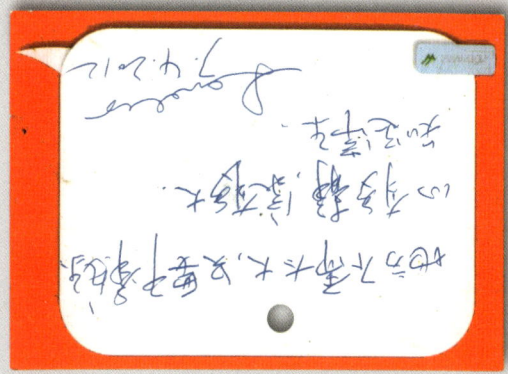

be published before the next Biennale opens. Thanks.

TO: Gene
FROM: Jesse

Sorry to be late with the interview. I was in Europe last week lecturing.
We will indeed be in Taiwan this Saturday for the groundbreaking. We're flying directly to Kaohsiung Friday from Hong Kong and return to HK Saturday afternoon. Will be meeting up with Weijen for dinner. Then we go to Wuhan for a lecture following day.
I am leaving tomorrow morning so will not be ready by end of week. How about recording an interview with you on skype? We return next Wednesday so could do it Thursday evening.

TO: Jesse
FROM: Gene

Sorry to catch you when you are about to be on the road. However, next week may be too late. This needs not be very long, maybe just scribble something down on the plane if you don't carry your computer with you (I don't), and fax it to me when you are in Kaoshiung. Give me a ring (use Michael's phone) when you are in Kaoshiung? Good trip.

TO: Gene
FROM: Jesse

I try to put something together on the plane. Speak saturday.

TO: Jesse
FROM: Gene

Great. Talk to you.

TO: Gene
FROM: Jesse

My answers such as they are.

1) Despite interpretations on some blog posts that the film is an ironic reading of those projects or a parody of the folly of engaging in utopian speculation, we see them as affirmative responses to the metropolis. The medium of film allows us to do something which was not in the minds of the original authors which is to portray the projects not merely as reconstructions of historical artifacts or 'what ifs' but as simultaneous anachronistic universes, in and out of time so to speak. As strong urban ideas they indeed live as traces in projects actually realized and with the potential to inform the future metropolis as well.

2) The clips set up expectations that since the audience is watching authentic contexts the historical facts must be objective as well, but the audience soon realizes that the account is suspect. A paranoid tale in the form a a decades long conspiracy neatly ties together what are otherwise disparate visions. Ultimately the hope is that the audience comes to realize that even the authentic original author narratives are contingent; that paradoxically there is a greater cultural persistence to the designs than to the narratives applied to them.

3) That's an interesting question. In the abstract the difference between projects built but no longer with us and projects unbuilt are two sides of the same coin. They both summon equal pathos. But it seems to me that by and large the demolished projects in New York, what comes to mind is the old Penn Station, had enormous though largely anti progressive effects in the form of the historical preservation movement and how it became institutionalized and codified. There is no doubt that since the 60s the progressive projects

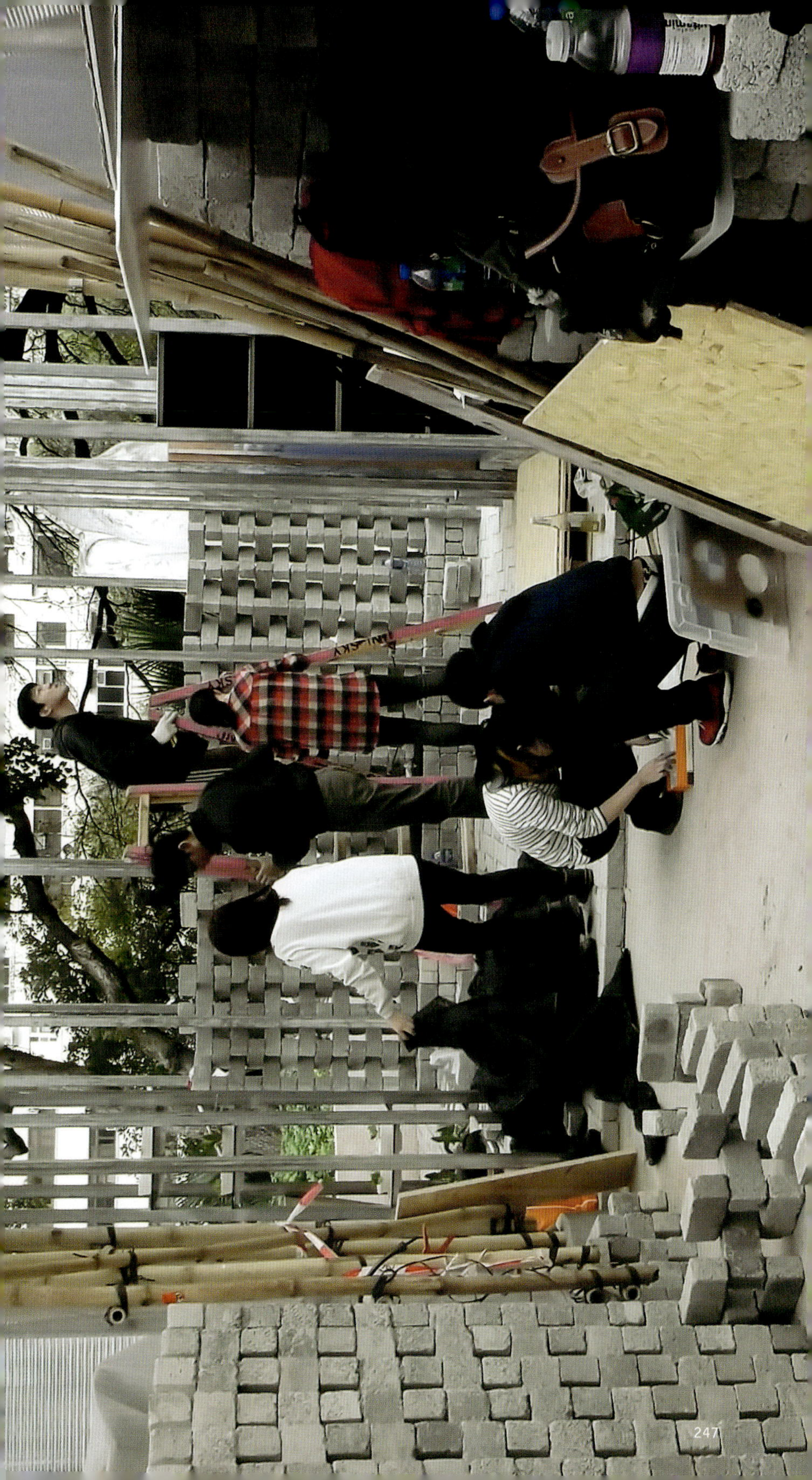

NEW CHOY YUEN VILLAGE 采磡新村

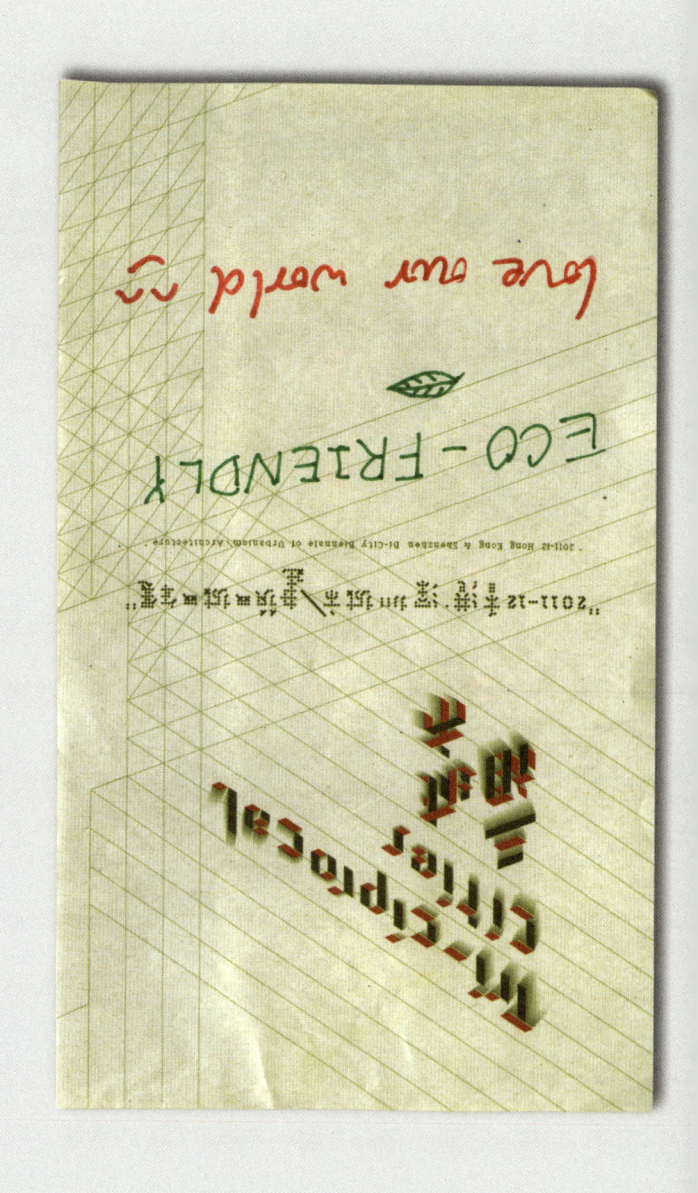

"2011-12年度 深圳 / 香港 城市\建築雙城雙年展"
2011-12 Hong Kong & Shenzhen Bi-city Biennale of Urbanism\Architecture

ECO-FRIENDLY

love our world

互惠
城市
Reciprocal Cities

EXH 037

PAVILION:

World Exhibits

PROJECT:

Combinatory Urbanism

DESCRIPTION:

Combinatory Urbanism, as book as well as this exhibit content, engaged the hybrid space between architecture and urban planning. Against this backdrop, this exhibit surveyed twelve urban projects from the past ten years.

EXHIBITOR:

Morphosis

Founded in 1972, Morphosis is an interdisciplinary practice involved in rigorous design and research that yields innovative, iconic buildings and urban environments. Founder Thom Mayne received Pritzker Prize in 2005.

ORIGIN:

United States

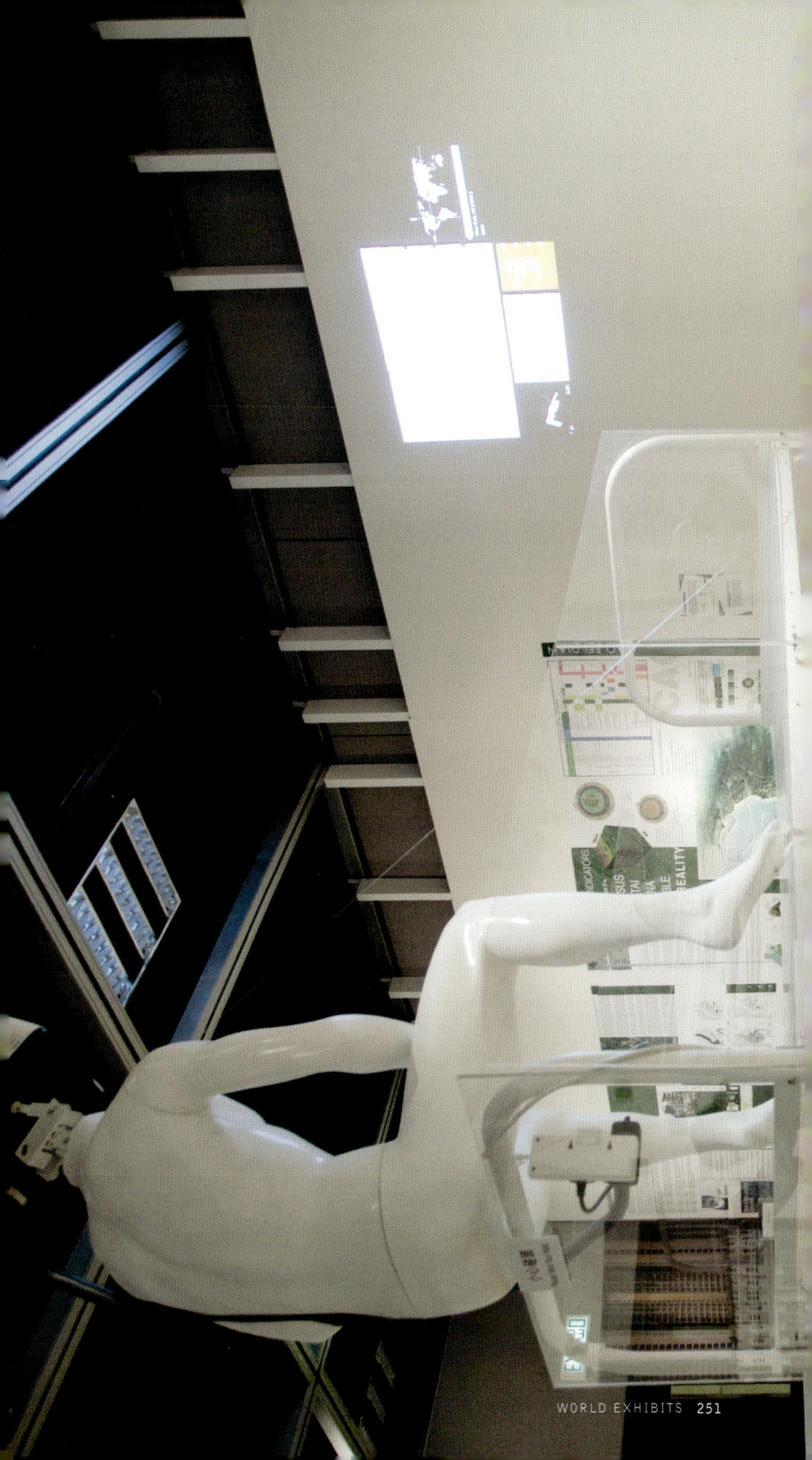

WORLD EXHIBITS 251

252 WORLD EXHIBITS

そ
ンユ草售町
ン多工く満
門售大満！

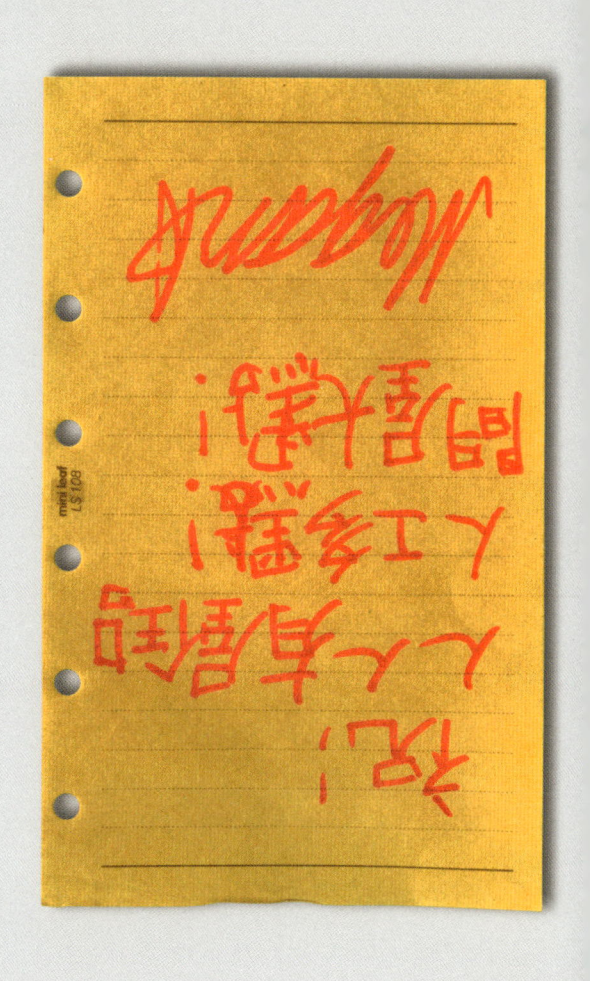

Happiness

EXH 038

PAVILION:

World Exhibits

PROJECT:

Speculative Surfaces for the Chinese Eco-city: Designing an Alternative Form of Development for the Tianjin and Caofedian Ecocities through Landscape and Ecology as Urbanism

DESCRIPTION:

This exhibit examined the phenomenon of the Chinese eco-city through the vehicle of speculative design projects for two seminal case studies, the Tianjin and Caofedian (Tangshan) eco-cities, featured in a film showing the importance of preserving cultural and vernacular landscapes and their potential to be a transformative agent of change.

EXHIBITOR:

Shannon BASSETT, Alex CAMPRUBI, Cesar CABANAS

Shannon Bassett is Assistant Professor of Architecture and Urbanism at the University of South Florida School of Architecture and Community Design in Tampa. Alex Camprubi has been practicing and researching architecture, landscape architecture, urban planning and urban design in Mexico and China for nineteen years. He is currently a lecturer in Beijing. César Cabanas is an architect and cultural curator from Madrid. He is currently practicing in Beijing.

ORIGIN:

United States / Mexico / Spain / China

WORLD EXHIBITS 255

256 | WORLD EXHIBITS

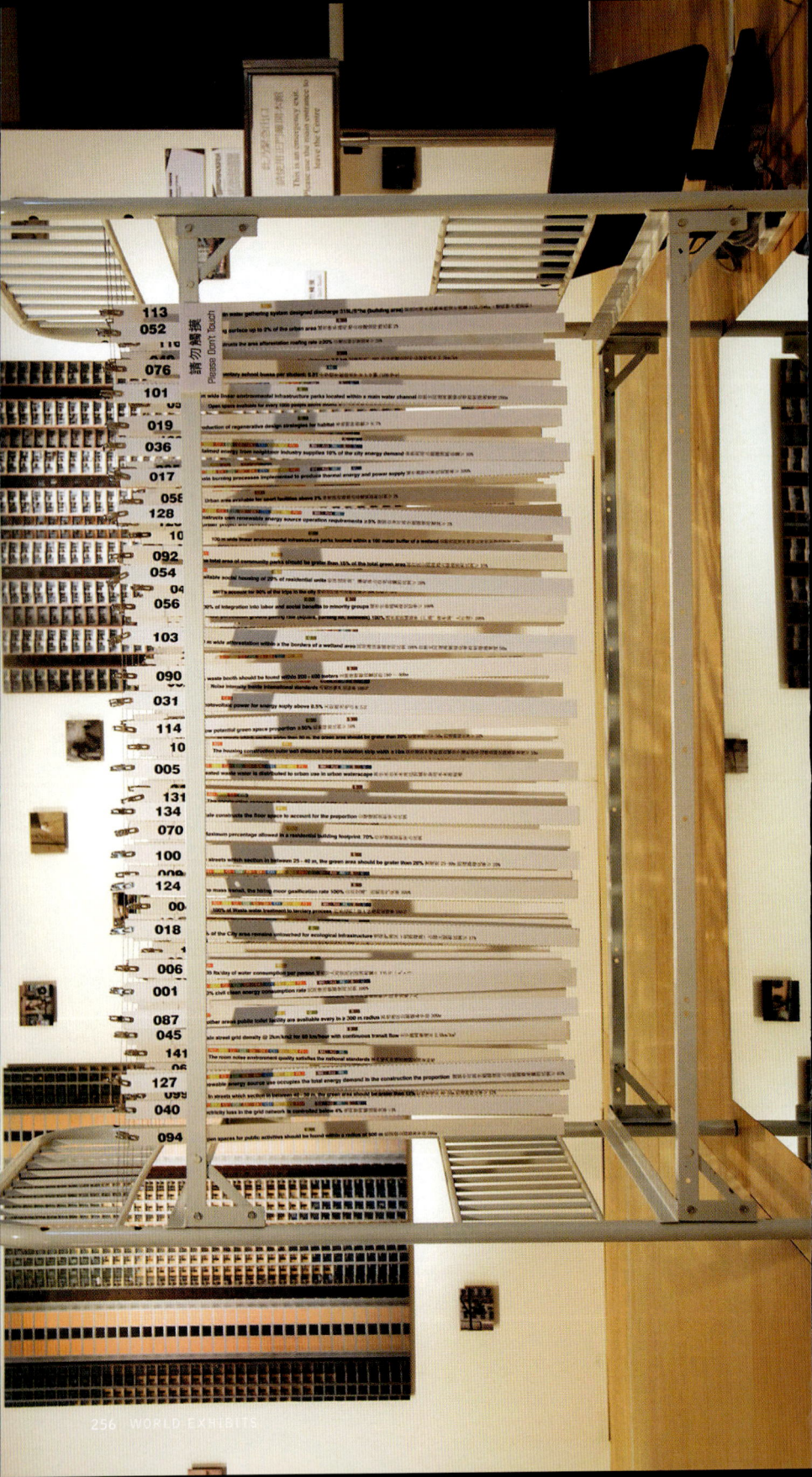

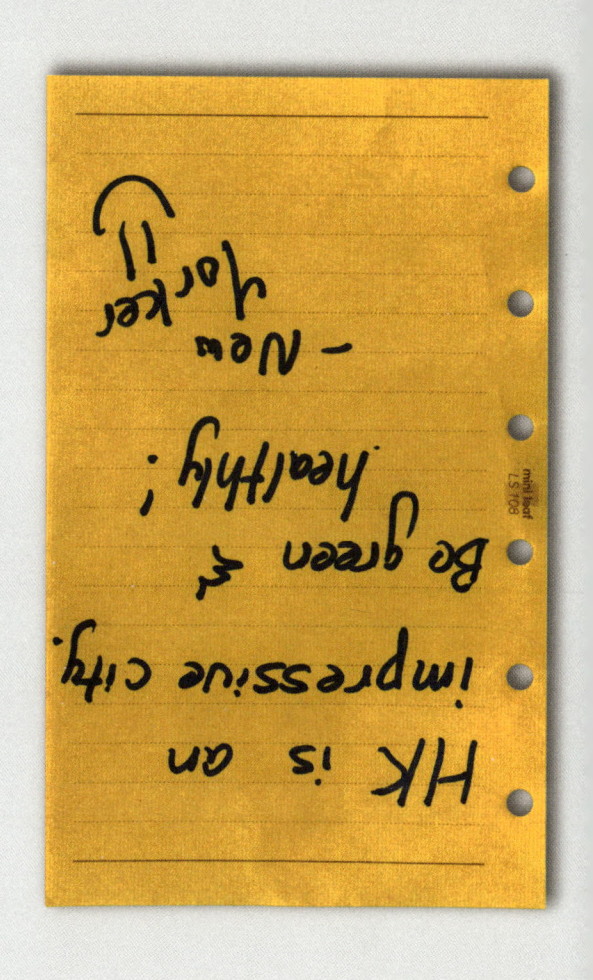

HK is an impressive city;
Be green & healthy;
— New Yorker !!

EXH 039

PAVILION:

World Exhibits

PROJECT:

Architecture of Density / Lost Laundry

DESCRIPTION:

Michael Wolf's images from Architecture of Density were combined in collage form with images from his series Lost Laundry, which showed Hong Kong 'at its intimate best and anonymous worst' (from Alison Bing on the Architecture of Density).

EXHIBITOR:

Michael WOLF

Michael Wolf studied at UC Berkeley and at the Folkwang School in Essen, Germany with Otto Steinert. Wolf's photographic work in Asia focuses on various aspects of life in cities, some using the google street view platform, which have all been published as books.

ORIGIN:

Germany

WORLD EXHIBITS 259

260 WORLD EXHIBITS

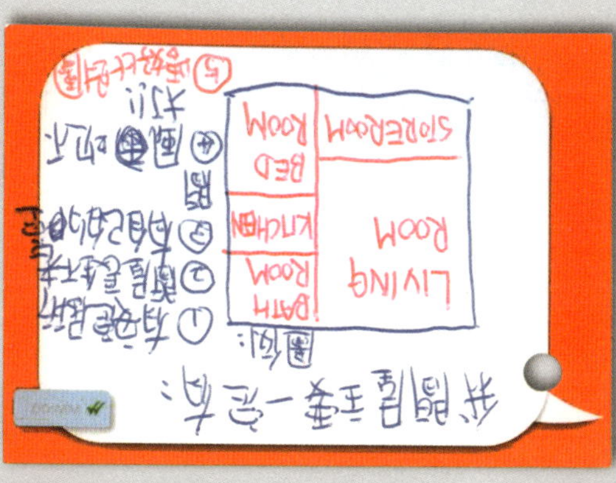

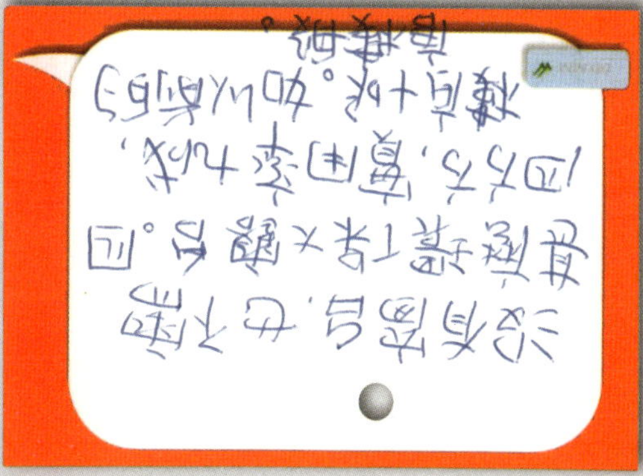

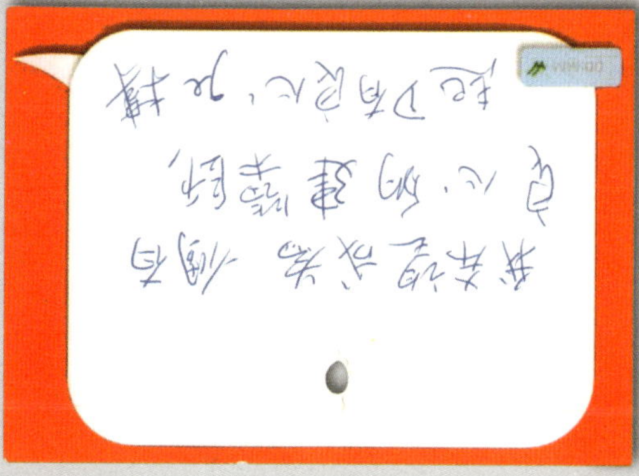

portrayed in the film would have to contend and ultimately lose to that competing vision: a future made by looking backward rather than forward.

Q&A 011

DIALOGUE WITH
Terence Riley

TO: Terence Riley
FROM: Gene King

For your theme for the 2011 Shenzhen Biennale 'Architecture creates cities, cities create architecture, without ends,' I think it is a great description of the state of Shenzhen. The City started from a very baroque sense of planning, simplistic in a modern sense, and millions of buildings emerged along with economic explosion. However, there is a city emerging, or at least aspires to emerge as an unique city. Is that your intention? and if close, what do you see the state of Shenzhen?

TO: Gene
FROM: Terry

Sorry I took so long… To develop a critical point of view with regards to the city of Shenzhen, you have to consider its context. During the high years of Post-Modernism, it was a common argument to compare Brasilia negatively with London, Paris or any other number of traditional cities. Recent visitors to Brasilia are often shocked to find that it is a lush, green city with many pedestrian friendly neighborhoods and with a monumental core that is much more intimate than, say, the Mall in Washington DC.

In this sense we have to compare Shenzhen to other rapidly growing mega-cities. I think that it is too early to tell, but I would argue that Shenzhen is handling its growth better than many, especially those that have basically given up on urban planning and left the future of the city to private developers.

I don't expect Shenzhen to become the City Beautiful overnight, if ever. However, it does have legibility and coherence, which is a goal worth pursuing and sustaining.

TO: Terry
FROM: Gene

Our theme for the Hong Kong Biennale 'Tri-ciprocal city: the time, the place, the people' is a response to your reciprocal relationship between architecture and city, which also indicates the comparison among Hong Kong and Shenzhen. In addition to actual existence of architecture and city, I think Hong Kong enjoys and also suffers from the privilege of over 170 years of heavy pressure for development (most buildings of the past were demolished), but the city also acquires a unique character due to its people, how they react to reality and work out solutions, etc. Do you think people and time, two very intangible aspects, can be grasped for our understanding as well as imagination for the City?

TO: Gene
FROM: Terry

I think that it is inevitable to compare Hong Kong and Shenzhen. While they share the same ecology, they have vastly different circumstances that everyone should recognize. The concept of 'urban time' is important. Despite Hong Kong's tendency to continually erase the architecture of the past, immutable urban traces remain and influence the next generation of building. This is beginning to happen in Shenzhen, particularly in the old CBD.

The culture of Hong Kong has inherited this urban landscape and the people of Hong Kong have inherited the mechanisms that created it and recreate it. The urban fabric

Caged House
1 Bed
床位一千三百元月租
HKD$1300/month

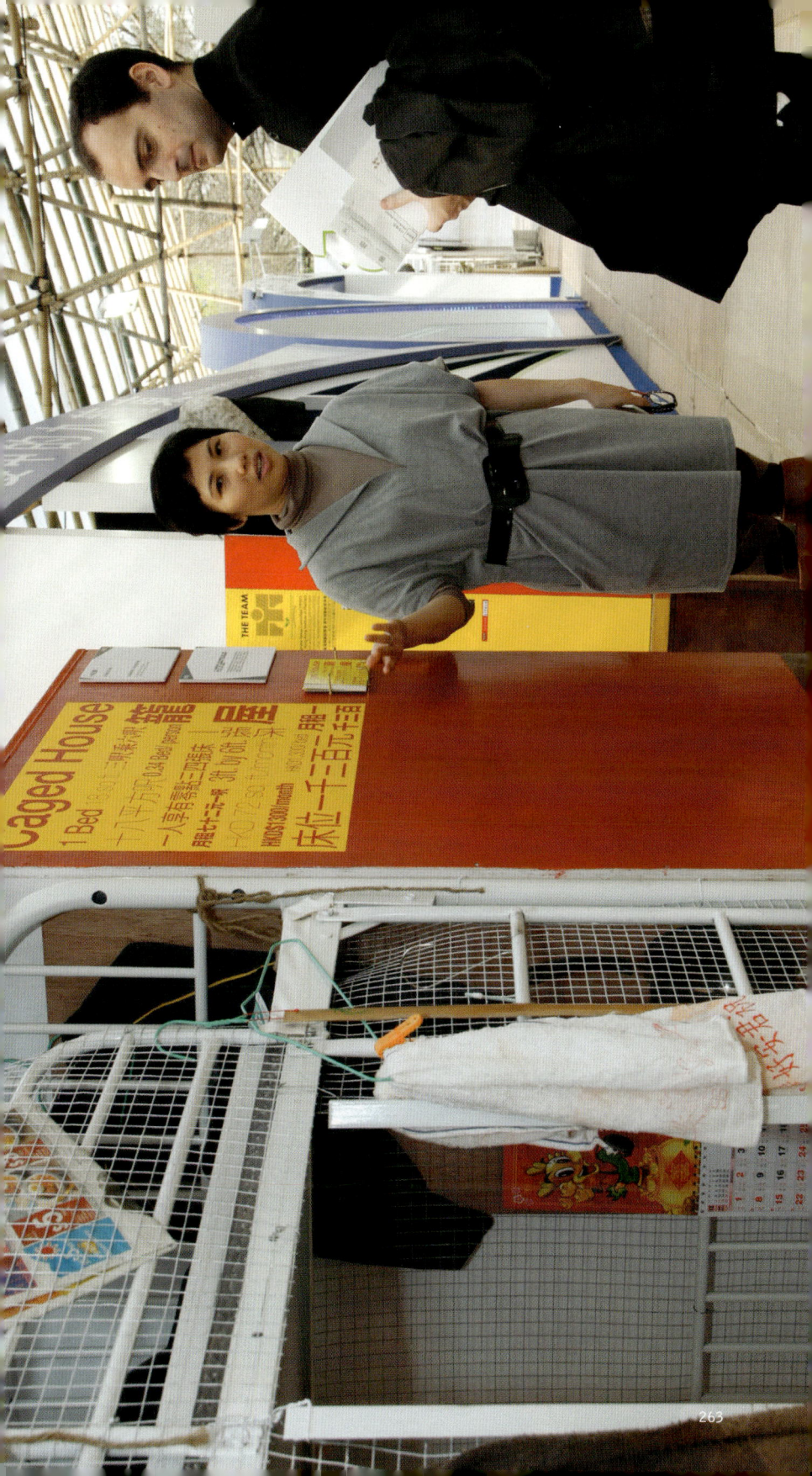

THE TEAM

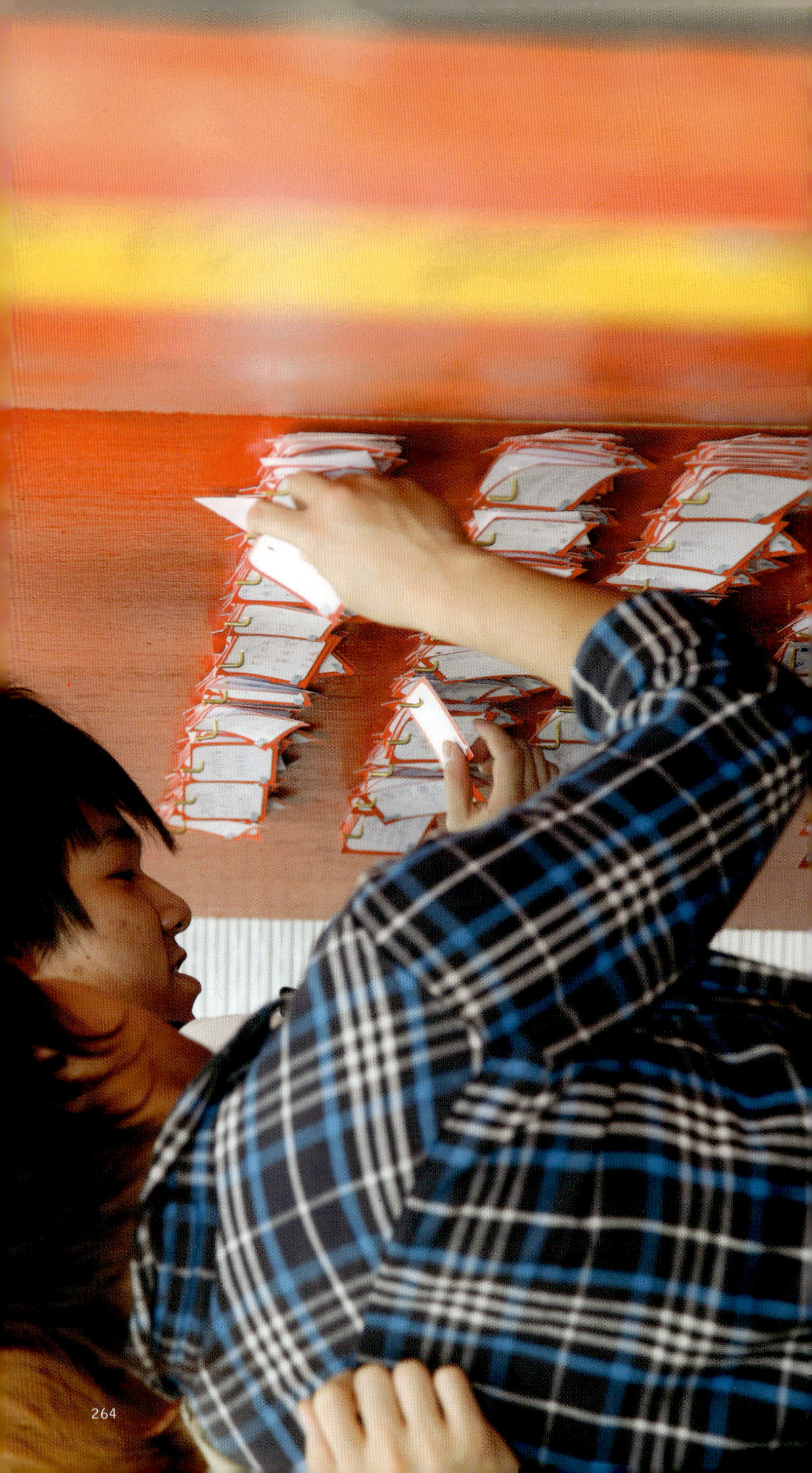

"2011–12 香港·深圳城市\\建筑双城双年展"

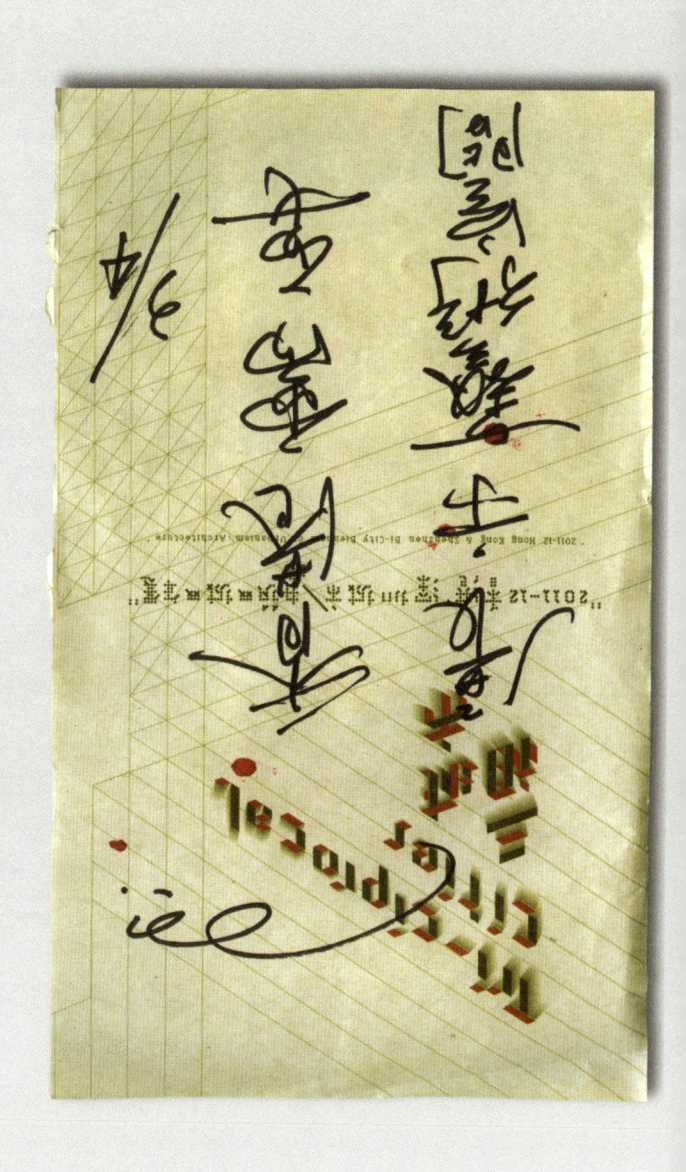

2011-12 Hong Kong & Shenzhen Bi-city Biennale of Urbanism\\Architecture

EXH 040

PAVILION:

World Exhibits

PROJECT:

Dazibao d'architectures Paris-HK

DESCRIPTION:

Atelier Seraji presented a variety of projects in Europe, Southeast Asia and China, which open debate on many other issues pertinent to living in cities. The installation was a table around which we as architects and educators were able to discuss the not-so-bright future of our planet and propose solutions as agile thinkers and doers.

EXHIBITOR:

Atelier Seraji Architectes & Associés

Based in Paris, Atelier Seraji Architectes & Associés is a true atelier: a laboratory for both practice and research. Each project is studied and conceived in strict relationship with a critical analysis of all its conditions: its site and programme, as well as its socio-economic context and cultural specificities. Nasrine Seraji has been Dean/Director of École Nationale Supérieure d'architecture Paris-Malaquais since 2006.

ORIGIN:

France

WORLD EXHIBITS 267

268 WORLD EXHIBITS

WISH...
HK GOV'T
will REALLY
CARE MORE
abt. PROVIDING
AFFORDABLE
HOUSING in HK!

Tbx.
yy-kb.

EXH 041

PAVILION:

World Exhibits

PROJECT:

Water Proving Ground

DESCRIPTION:

This project proposed a new form of landscape in response to changes due to global warming. For the area of New York City's Harbor, this project proposed a vibrant amphibious landscape. Unlike traditional defensive approaches, LTL's proposal increases the coastline to create a wholly new terrain with a variety of possibilities for future urban life.

EXHIBITOR:

Lewis.Tsurumaki.Lewis Architects (LTL)

Lewis.Tsurumaki.Lewis (LTL Architects) is a design-intensive architecture firm founded in 1997 by Paul Lewis, Marc Tsurumaki, and David J. Lewis, located in New York City. The firm has been the recipient of numerous awards. The principals are co-authors of two books, and have been teaching at Princeton, Columbia, and Parsons The New School for Design.

ORIGIN:

United States

WATER PROVING GROUND

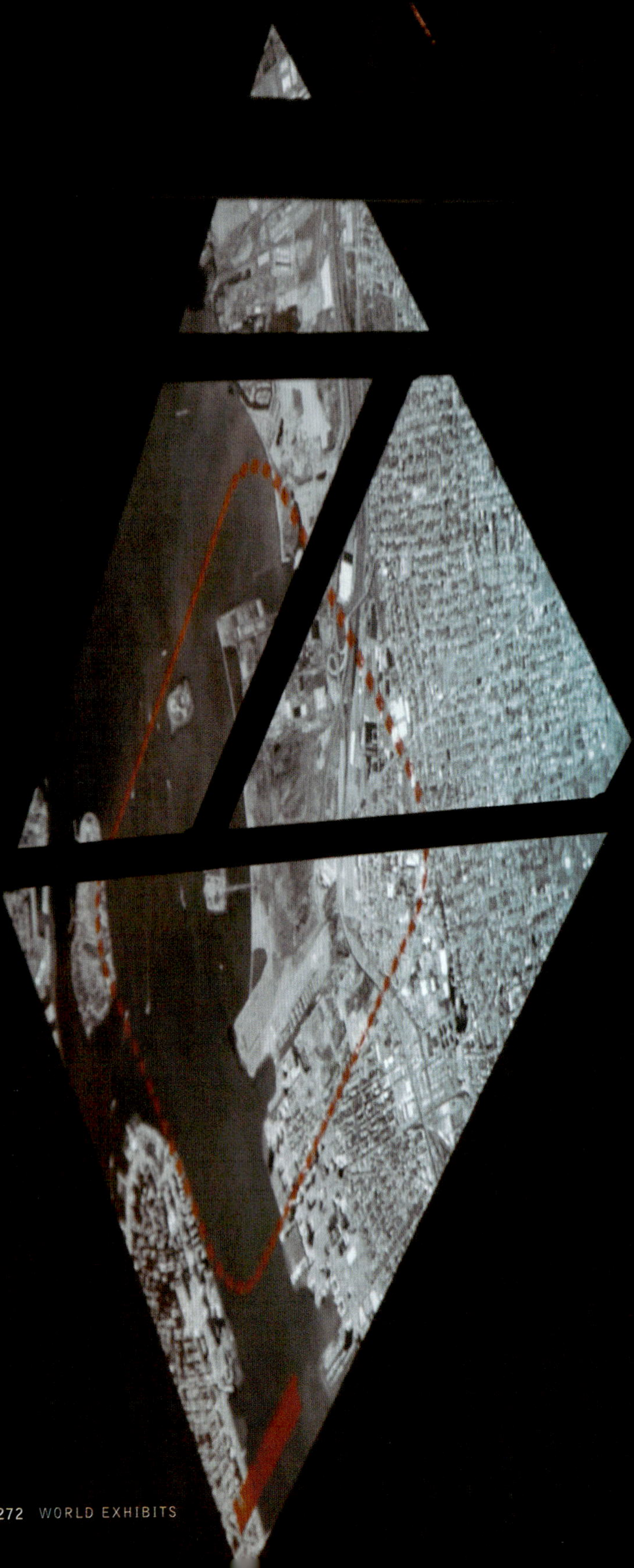

為替相場は国力を反映する！

EXH 042

PAVILION:

World Exhibits

PROJECT:

New Urban Ground: A Sea-Level Rise Sleepover

DESCRIPTION:

As part of The Museum of Modern Art's 2010 exhibition Rising Currents: Projects for New York's Waterfront, the team proposed a new ecological infrastructure for Lower Manhattan. New Urban Ground consisted of two basic components that form an interconnected system — porous green streets and a graduated edge — in response to the prediction that there will be a six-foot rise in sea level by the year 2100.

EXHIBITOR:

Architecture Research Office (ARO); dlandstudio

Architecture Research Office is the recipient of the 2010 Academy Award in Architecture from the American Academy of Arts and Letters and the 2011 Smithsonian, Cooper-Hewitt National Design Award for Architecture.

dlandstudio is a leading New York City landscape architecture practice with projects across the United States and abroad.

ORIGIN:

United States

WORLD EXHIBITS 275

276 WORLD EXHIBITS

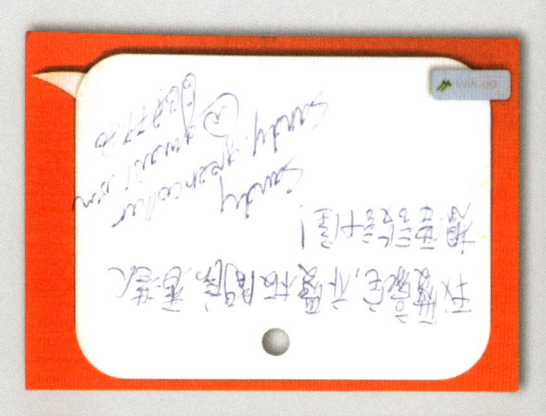

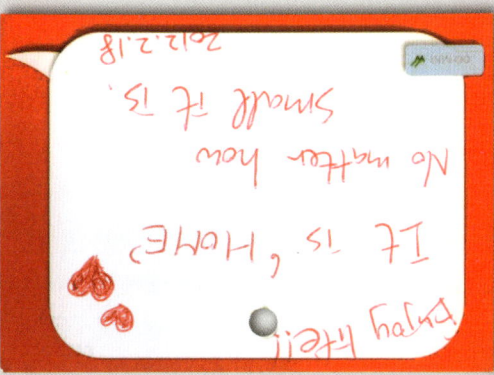

家裡是, 不管味道如何, 還是
最香的!
Smelly Homecoming Sadly
家が一番

It is 'HoMe'
No matter how
Smell it is.
2012.2.18
Enjoy it!!!

2nd floor: kids room
2nd floor: father & mother's room
window
window
Ground floor: big living room
enjoy it!!

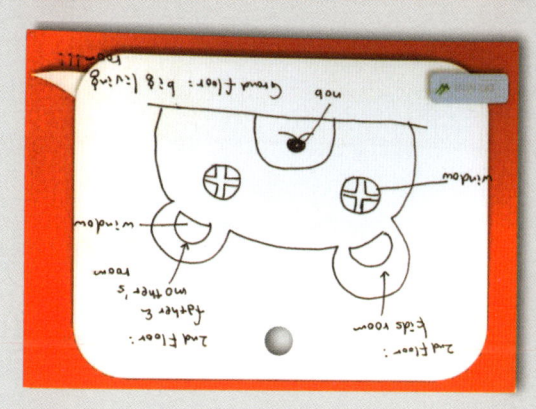

would not be the same without them, just as it is hard to imagine Paris outside of the French culture that created it.

> TO: Terry
> FROM: Gene

I would like to use this chance also to question your interest in coming to Taipei again. I am involved in organizing two competitions for two fine arts museum, one in Taipei suburb and another one in Tainan. Time slots are in February and June. If yes, let me know which slot would work better for you. It would be great to have you here again.

Q&A 012

DIALOGUE WITH
Nasrine Seraji

> TO: Nasrine Seraji
> FROM: Anderson Lee, Gene King

Your installation at the Biennale seemed to have your projects in a crypt, or as sediments of layers defined by the bunk bed dimensions given to you. Is it a message you want to convey to the public how you, as an architect, view your own past projects and that your new works are built upon from your past experiences from the projects? In other words, could the piece be treated as a 'vault' from which you current work is based upon?

> TO: Anderson, Gene
> FROM: Nasrine

Though I like the idea of a crypt and a sort of sanctuary of our projects, our installation at the biennale was an entirely different idea. The bunk bed or at least the pieces that would make one, was a given. It was like a site.

We took the brief and the site very seriously, though we felt that we could change the bunk bed into an entirely different object. We transformed the bunk bed into an infrastructure, a table, an open platform and not a vault. A vault is by definition closed and private. Our installation was open and public.

Perhaps OMA's installation was more like a translucid vault holding all those blue foam models as a serious endeavour to every project of theirs. Or even better, Steven Holl's black room was more like a 'precious vault.' We did with our installation exactly what we do with every project in the office; that is to say that we look very carefully at the brief and the site, the materials and the constraints, the economy of the project in relationship to the socio-political and architectural message it has to give to the public and to its users. Of course your idea of relying on our past experiences is important but not as a crutch. Often architects use past experience as a way of being comfortable in the context of their architectural production. Being able to question the givens of a project and generating a new debate through architecture is our most important goal in every project. Our golden, transparent layered and compressed bunk bed was therefore not a vault nor a container of space but a deep surface, which had as its base the foundation of the city: its infrastructure. Like many of our projects, its main idea was engagement and preoccupation with architecture, the city and geography.

So I guess we could say that the biennale was a big machine allowing some of us to rethink what we do as architects.

> TO: Nasrine
> FROM: Anderson

It seems like a big part of your effort was to create new housing typologies or public architecture among the stringent conditions resulted from code, finance, and most of all,

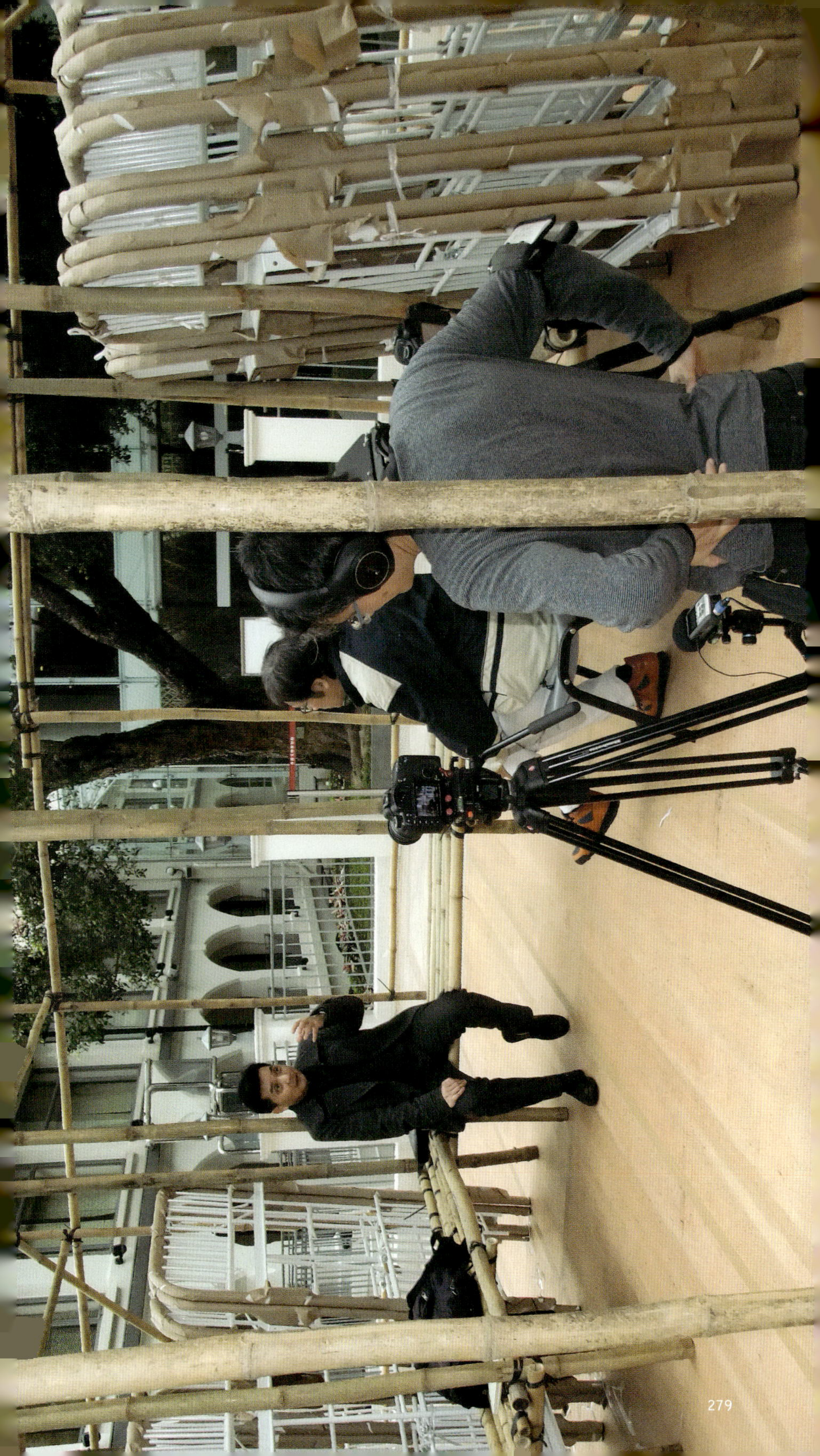

280

In-reciprocal Cities
互城

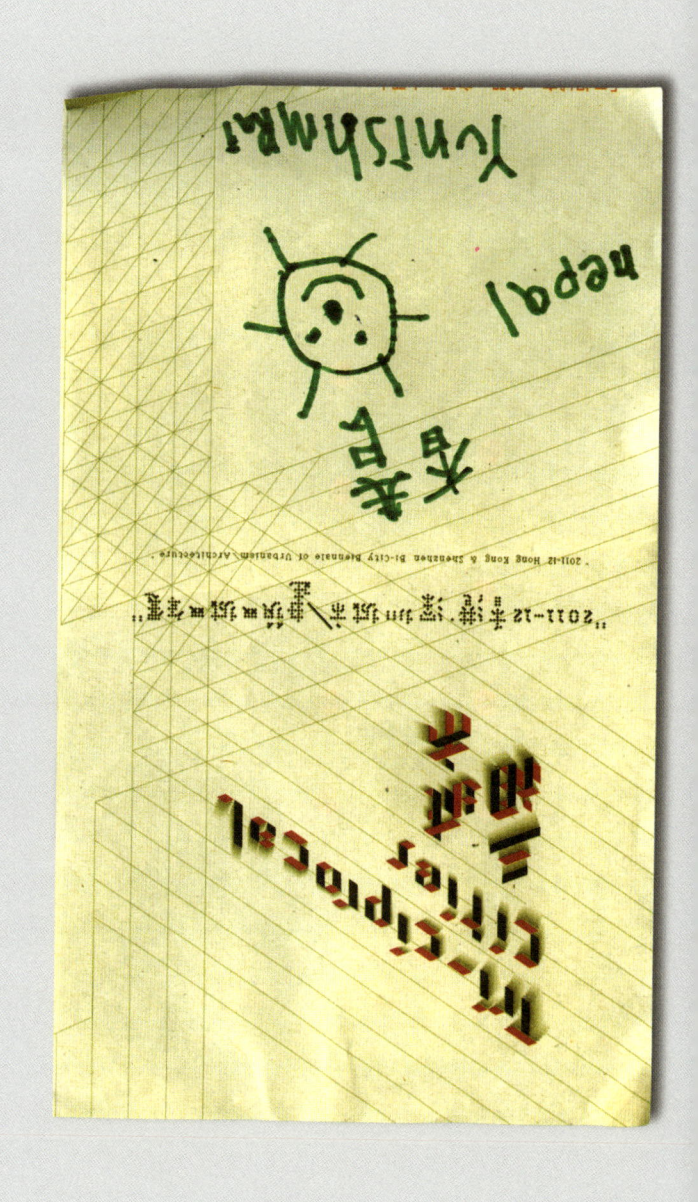

"2011-12年香港·深圳城市\建筑双城双年展"
2011-12 Hong Kong & Shenzhen Bi-city Biennale of Urbanism\Architecture

希望

nepal
Kntshmr

EXH 043

PAVILION:

World Exhibits

PROJECT:

Time in Space: Hong Kong's ICC and Shenzhen's Ping An IFC

DESCRIPTION:

This exhibit studied the spatial relationships formed by the XRL rail line linking of the Pearl River Delta's tallest towers, ICC in Hong Kong, and Ping An IFC in Shenzhen, both designed by KPF. The exhibit studied the spaces these connections make as well as the growth and nature of the two cities.

EXHIBITOR:

Kohn Pedersen Fox Associates (KPF)

KPF is one of the world's pre-eminent architecture firms, providing architecture, interior, programming and master planning services for clients in both the public and private sectors. Within six global offices, the firm's 500-plus staff members come from forty-three different countries, and a diverse portfolio featuring wide range of building types around the world.

ORIGIN:

United States

WORLD EXHIBITS 283

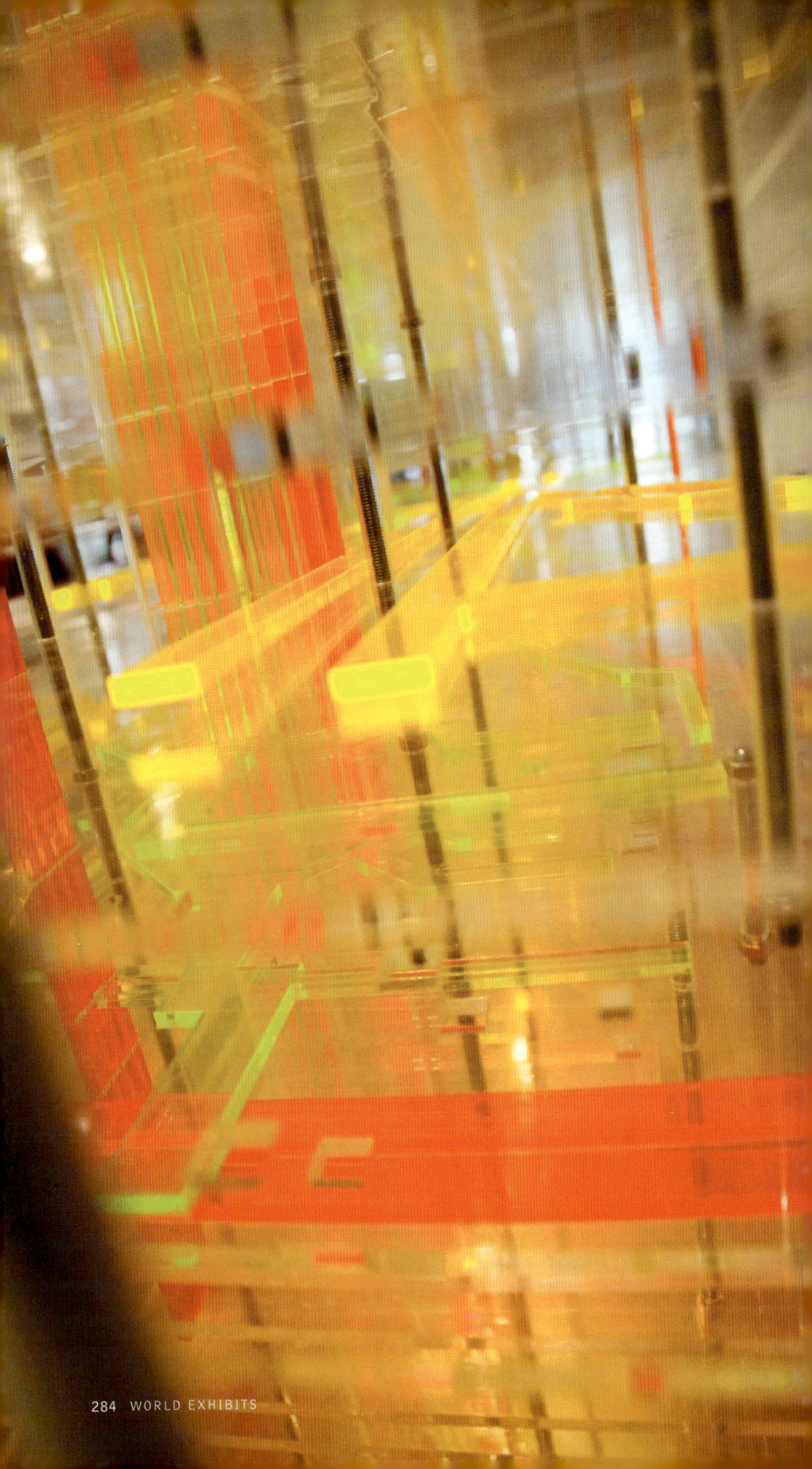

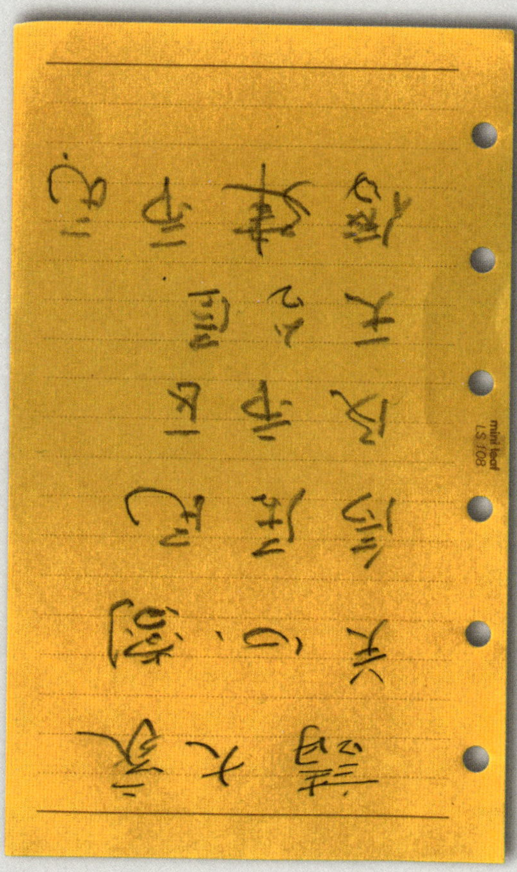
mini leaf
LS 108

EXH 044

PAVILION:

World Exhibits

PROJECT:

Steven Holl Architects: Fusion of Landscape and Architecture

DESCRIPTION:

The exhibition presented four projects of Steven Holl Architects, including Cité de L'Océan et du Surf, Lake Whitney Water Treatment Plant, the Nelson-Atkins Museum of Art Bloch Building, and Herning Museum of Contemporary Arts.

EXHIBITOR:

Steven Holl Architects

Steven Holl Architects is internationally honored with architecture's most prestigious awards, publications and exhibitions for excellence in design. It has realized architectural works nationally and overseas, with extensive experience in the arts (including museum, gallery, and exhibition design), campus and educational facilities, and residential work. Other projects include retail design, office design, public utilities, and master planning.

ORIGIN:

United States

WORLD EXHIBITS 287

288 WORLD EXHIBITS

苹果 米面 茶
鸡蛋 鸡蛋 牙膏
木瓜 固齿
胡萝卜
葡萄
……
蒜蓉豆豉 鲮鱼
切片!!

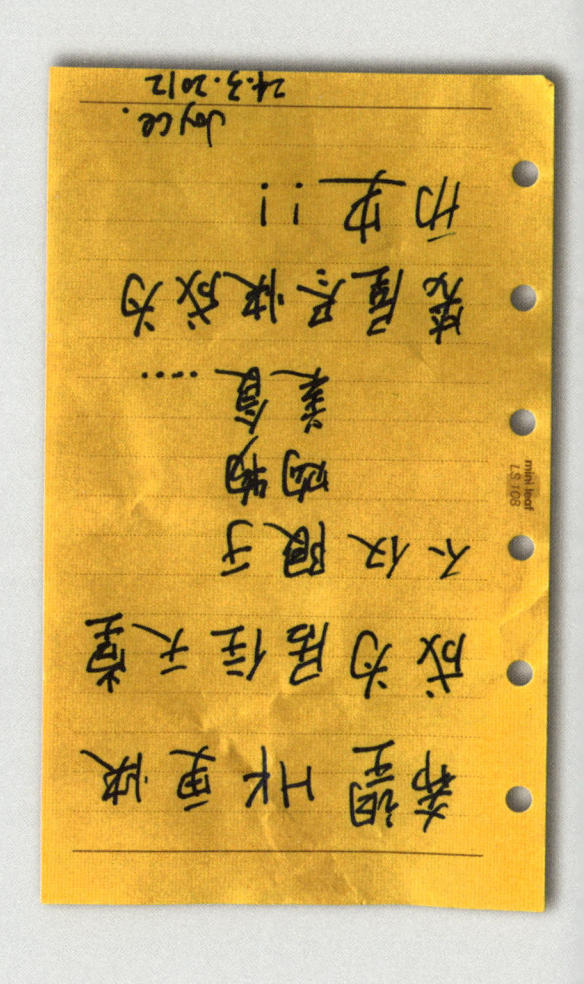

Joyce.
24.3.2012.

EXH 045

PAVILION:

World Exhibits

PROJECT:

Fibercity / Tokyo 2050 version 2.0

DESCRIPTION:

This project focused on Japan's shrinking cities and problems caused by depopulation, especially how to keep infrastructures and public services operating with a lack of available personnel. This exhibition showed two alternative approaches that include one for Tokyo metropolis and another for provincial city of Nagaoka.

EXHIBITOR:

Ohno laboratory, Graduate School of Frontier Sciences,
The University of Tokyo

Hidetoshi OHNO is an architect and professor at the University of Tokyo. He has published widely and has received numerous awards.

ORIGIN:

Japan

291

292 WORLD EXHIBITS

BED CONCEPT
= JAPANESE
TATAMI AS
MEASURE OF
ROOM SIZE!

将来有朝来我妈爸到这里玩
我不会带她去看一个房屋
花色之特色，设计—开打工
等你啊

lovely house ♥

↑ 김민영

the political nature of it. It also seems an urge to break away from the real estate shoe-box syndrome that is prevalent in every city in the world? How does it reflect to your most current practice to-date (2013) now that the installation is almost 2 years old?

TO: Anderson
FROM: Nasrine

As I was saying, the biennale experience did not have a direct effect on how we worked before or after it. But it gave us the impetus to think about our past work at the same time that we were conceiving of the bunk bed. 'It was a sort of lying in bed and thinking actively.' On the other hand every project (especially the ones that we like, as was the case with the bunk bed) are always a reference, a sort of teaser in our minds. We have had two very difficult years of almost no work, no invitations to big glorious competitions, and no exhibitions (that allow us to think about our work) and all because of the current economic turmoil in the world. But then when you travel around the world you see a lot of missed opportunities, trillions of cubic meters of matter constructed everywhere in the world, especially in the fast growing young economies of the world.

I have just come back from Tehran, a city with a beautiful mountain as high as 5000 meters in the northern part of it. It is beginning to look like parts of Kuala Lumpur, parts of China, parts of Lebanon, parts of the favelas in Rio. It has lost its soul, its uniqueness, its rugged dry extreme climate. It is one of the most polluted, ugly, cities in the world, highways on top of highways, saturated almost before completion of the works. High rise shoeboxes popping up like mushrooms just like in China except here they are not empty but are increasing the value of land and therefore excluding a layer of the population that has always lived in the city. Is this the future of cities? I ask myself.

Q&A 013

DIALOGUE WITH

Weijen Wang

TO: Weijen Wang
FROM: Gene King, Anderson Lee

Your installation at the Biennale certainly hit our intention of having an 'after-life' in dealing with the time aspect of Tri-ciprocal Cities. The idea of reinstalling this piece of 'pavilion' somewhat permanently at Choi Yuen Tsuen fascinated both Gene and me a great deal. After almost two years since the biennale, can you shed some light on the current status of this community-driven project and what is the current status of the 'pavilion'?

TO: Gene, Anderson
FROM: Weijen

the pavilion had been shipped back to the choiyuen village by the villagers after the end of the biennale, and now the construction of the village is finally taking place. I saw the material packed nicely – it sat there in a village corner for two years during the preparation of the village construction and it's time for my team to pick it up on the issue of pavilion and public spaces during or after their grand opening.

TO: Weijen
FROM: Anderson

That certainly sounds promising. We are glad to learn that Choiyuentsuen is finally moving forward after so many delays and headaches. During the past two years have there been any design changes and/or any stories you would like to share with us about your working relationship with the village people?

There has been certainly a heightened sense of protecting the environment and local

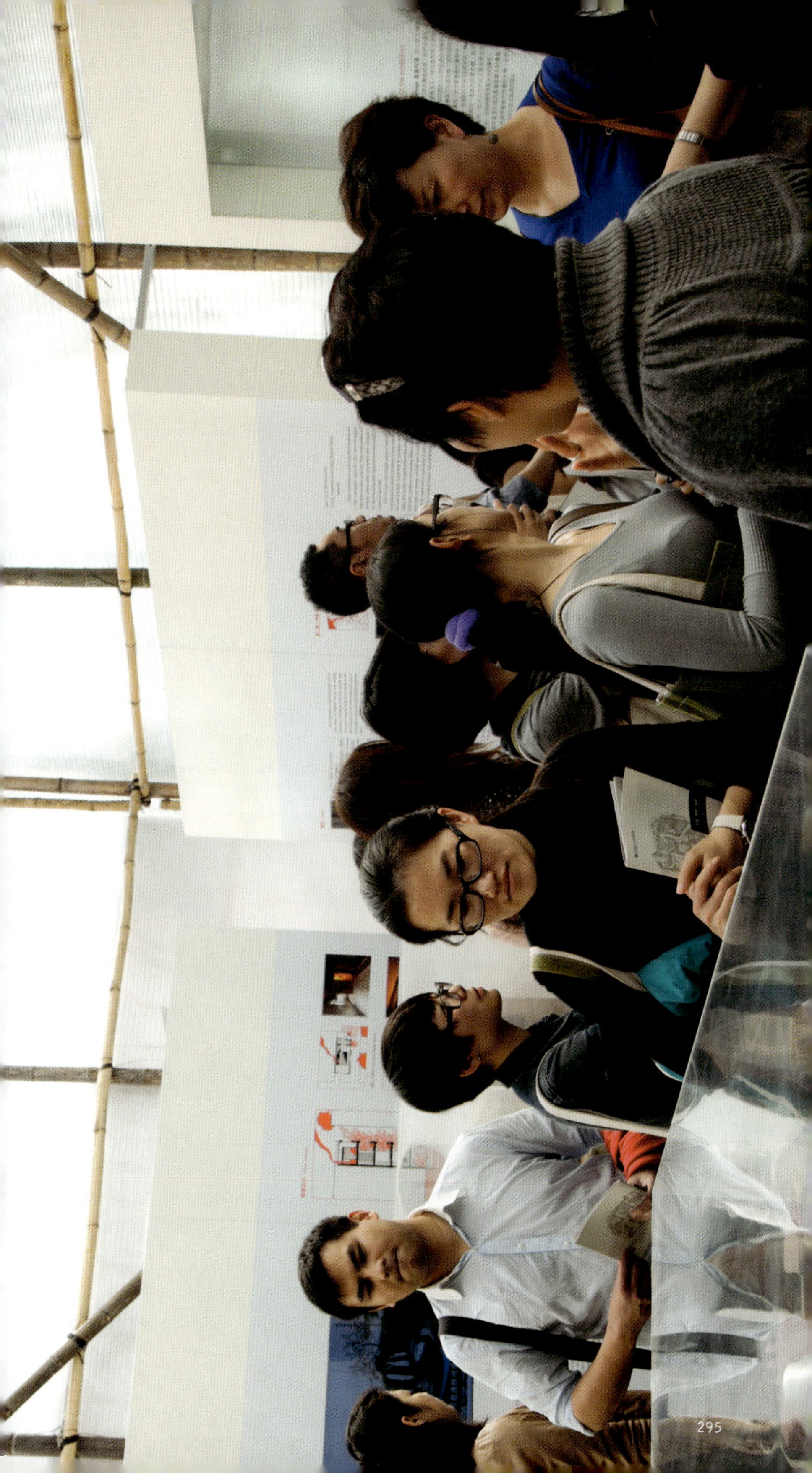

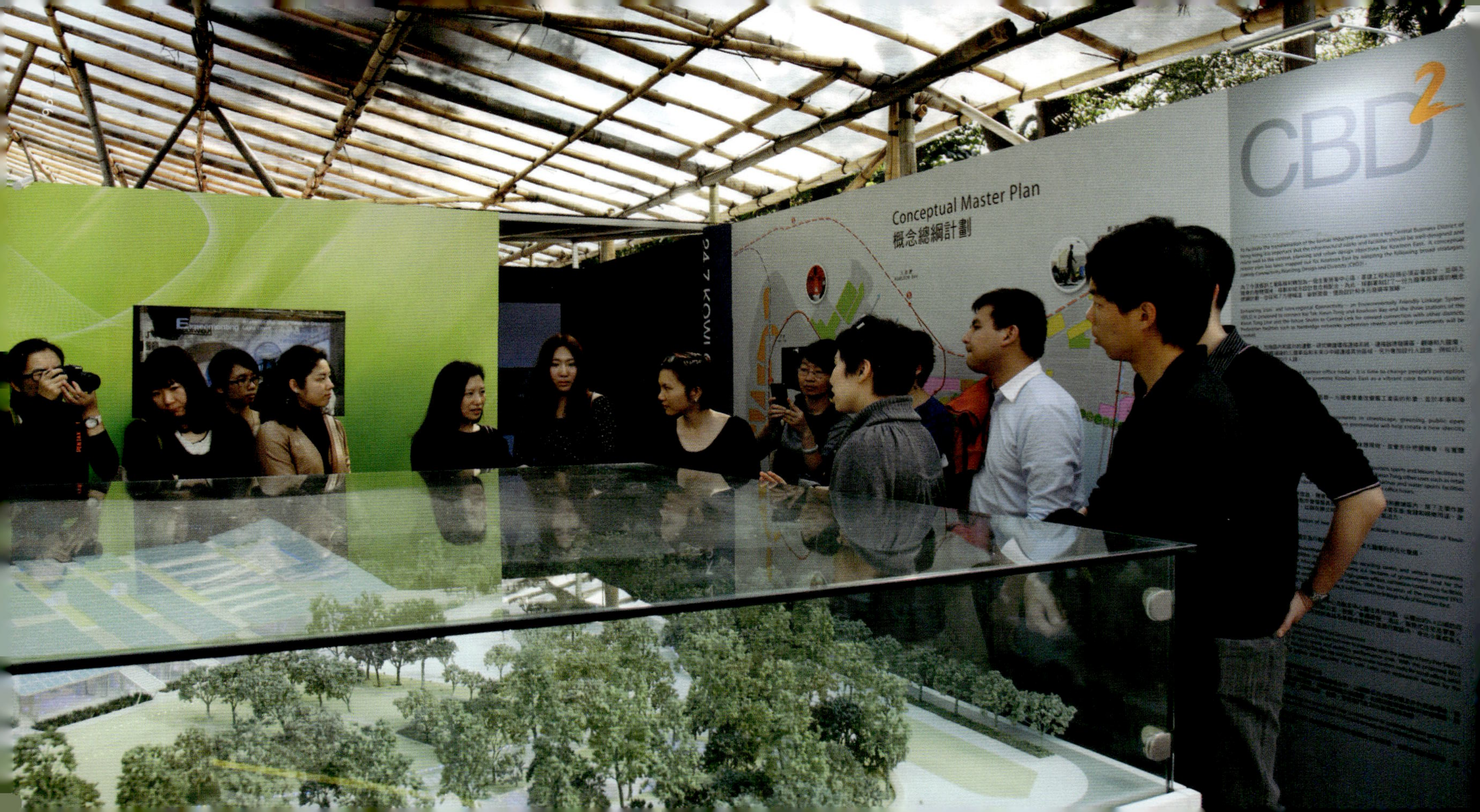
CBD2
Conceptual Master Plan
概念總綱計劃

하지 못하는 일이란 없다고 생각합니다.

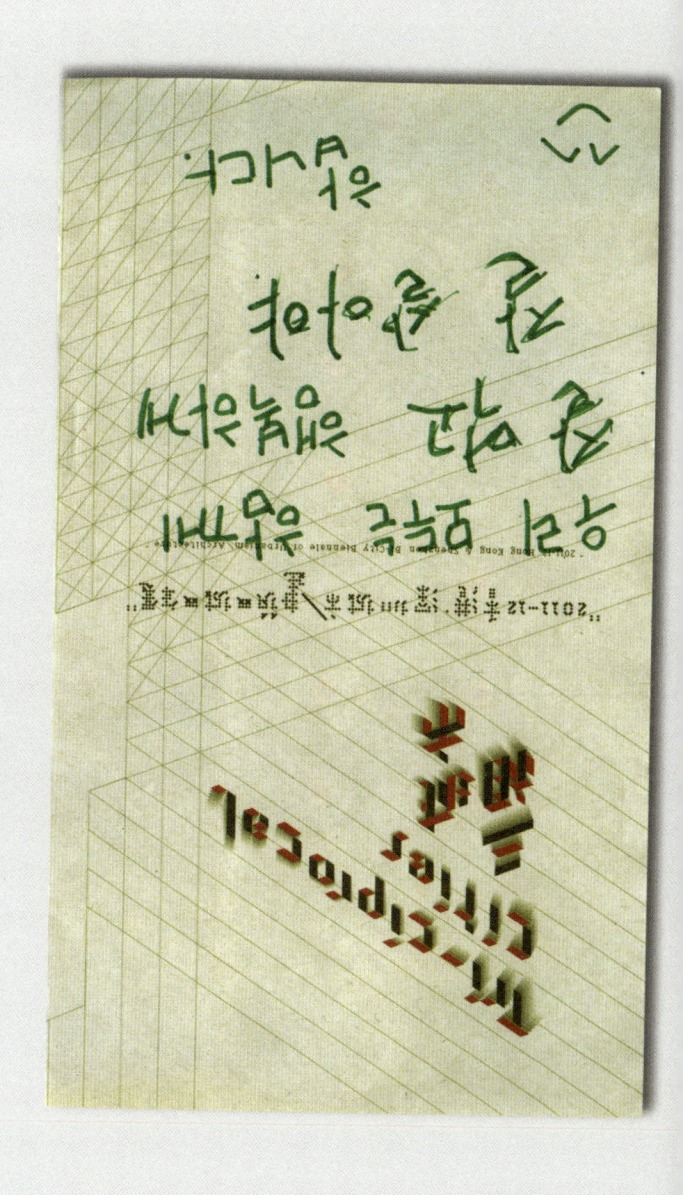

"2011-12 홍콩·심천 도시/건축 비엔날레"
2011–12 Hong Kong & Shenzhen Bienale of Urban\Architecture

In-
reciprocal
cities

EXH 046

PAVILION:
World Exhibits

PROJECT:
A Personal Aspect on the History of Tokyo / Norihiko Dan Recent Works: 4 contextures in East Asia

DESCRIPTION:
Part I: In a film, the author expressed a personal brief history of Tokyo, a city among its growth and changes, always had to deal with calamities including earthquakes, fires, and bombing, and its connections with Metabolism.
Part II: Four Recent projects in Tokyo and Taiwan revealed the author's perspectives towards context.

EXHIBITOR:
Norihiko Dan and Associates

Norihiko Dan was born in 1956 in Kanagawa, Japan. He received his BA from Tokyo University and master's degrees from Tokyo University and Yale University. He has completed projects in Japan and Taiwan.

ORIGIN:
Japan

WORLD EXHIBITS

300 WORLD EXHIBITS

Hong Kong is a great city and was a very pleasant place to visit. Best was hiking to the top of Lantau Peak.

EXH 047

PAVILION:

World Exhibits

PROJECT:

Storage

DESCRIPTION:

The bunk bed in the context of Hong Kong does not merely provide the minimal space for inhabitance, but often also serves as storage space. Storage was the materialization of a design methodology within a compact environment. It was a statement on the observation of density and the efficient use of space through improvisation within the city.

EXHIBITOR:

Office for Metropolitan Architecture (OMA)

OMA is a leading partnership practicing architecture, urbanism, and cultural analysis. Our buildings and master plans around the world insist on intelligent forms while inventing new possibilities for content and everyday use. OMA sustains an international practice with offices in Rotterdam, New York, Beijing, and Hong Kong.

ORIGIN:

Hong Kong / The Netherlands

OMA | 藏
OMA | Storage

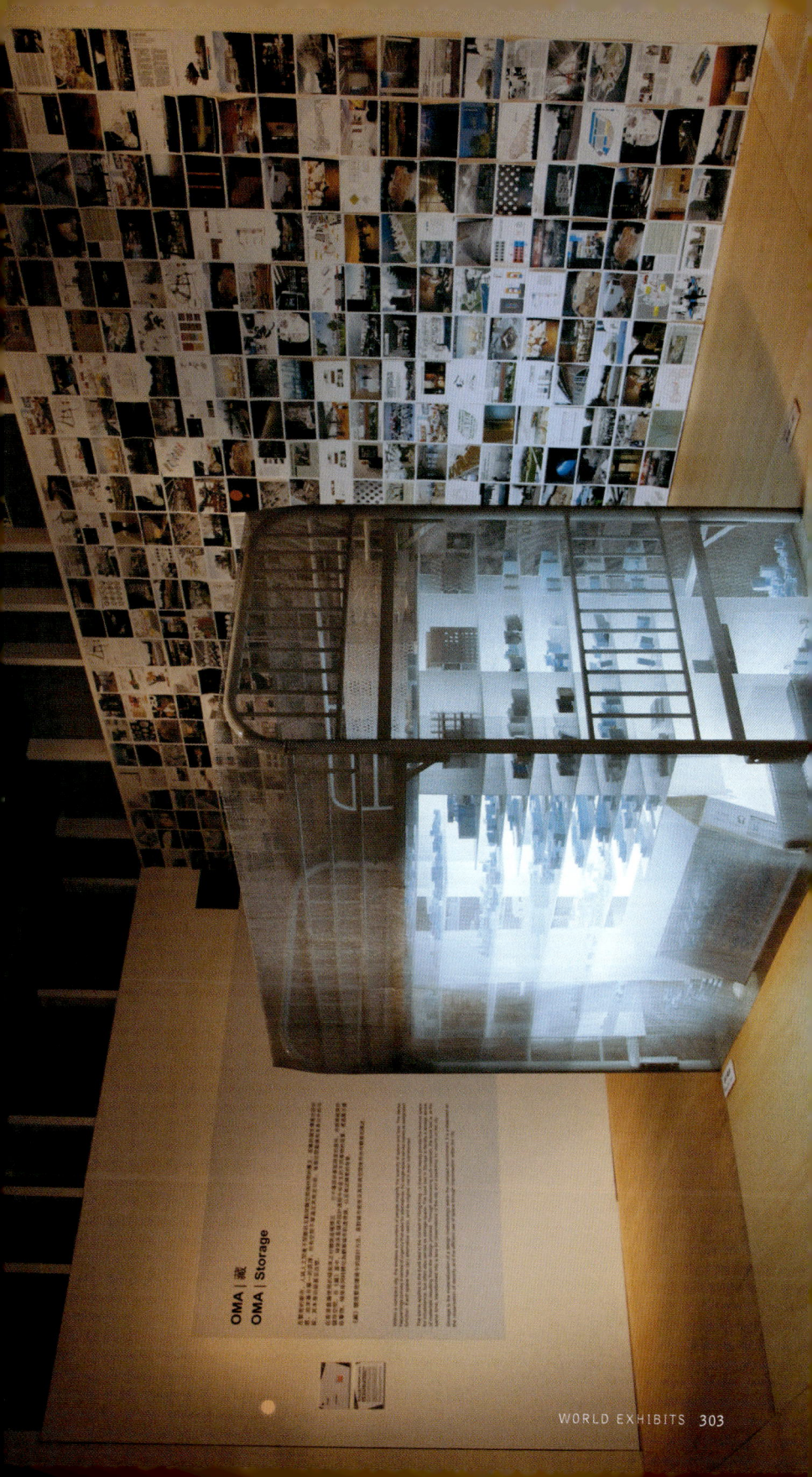

WORLD EXHIBITS 303

304 WORLD EXHIBITS

亲爱的朋友：

今年平安夜

祝你快乐！

EXH 048

PAVILION:

World Exhibits

PROJECT:

A Cord of Rail History

DESCRIPTION:

Railway history commenced officially in Singapore in 1903, connecting Malaya and has played a vital role in economy, culture, and landscape. In 2010, Singapore and Malaysia agreed to return the railway land to Singapore. This land's development represents a new opportunity for state agencies, civil society groups for nature and heritage, and the public at large to jointly reimagine this former umbilical cord to the Asian continent.

EXHIBITOR:

Dr. Chee Kien LAI, Mr. Darren SOH

Kayngee Tan is an architect and writer. He has established offices in London, Singapore, and Istanbul. Chee Kien Lai is a registered architect in Singapore and a lecturer at the Department of Architecture at the National University of Singapore. Darren Soh is an independent photographer in Singapore. The exhibition received support and assistance from the National Museum of Singapore.

ORIGIN:

Singapore

A Cord of Rail History
浪文的陥带

This exhibit documents and summarises this long-drawn history in photographs and in words, providing snapshots of an enduring past that will now translate into a meaningful programme to redevelop the new KTM Corridor green belt. This is an initiative between the Singapore government, the academia, civic society groups as well as the public at large, over the next few years, which now sees the coming together of collaborative efforts to develop the island nation.

The line, like a cord that connected physically and functionally, linked southern Peninsular Malaysia, commenced in the mid-19th century. The connections were fully expressed when a land bridge, the Causeway, was commissioned in 1923 to tie both ends of the linked colonies across the Straits of Johore and led to towns on the western coast of the Malaya Peninsula.

In 2011, Singaporeans witnessed the closure of the iconic Tanjong Pagar Railway Station as well as train services that had been run. People both saw about "exiting" the island in trains. From July last year, trains started from the northernmost point in Singapore, known as Woodlands, and marked the end of a century-old legacy that had seen the country endure the colonial era to the post-independence period and industrialization.

308 WORLD EXHIBITS

心里 please !!!
no money
no talk
by 卫小馋 ♀

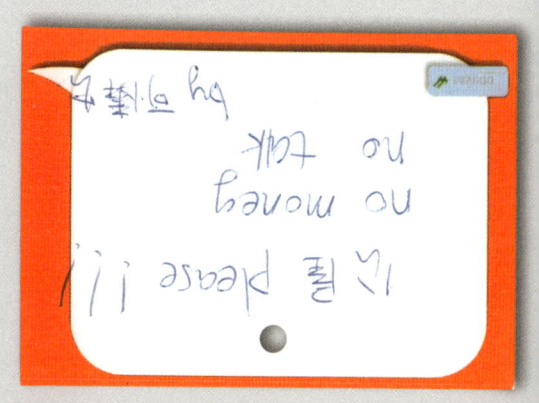

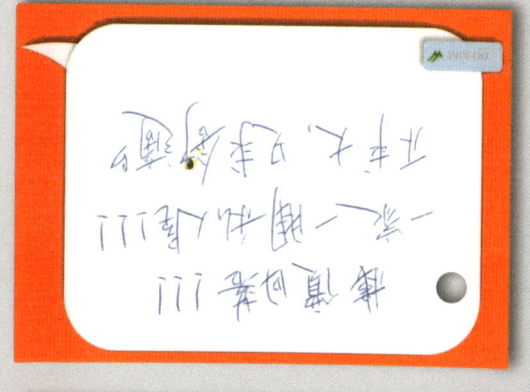

情真的美 !!!
一 起一起来玩吧 !!!
生下人, 月亮好漂亮 a

culture in recent Hong Kong. Since your project spans across two separate administrations of the HKSAR, do you see any change in how the new HKSAR government is dealing with issues regarding the resettlement of village people in the name of (mostly) public housing development or infrastructural work? And how you would like us, as architects, to respond to that?

Looking forward.

TO: Weijen
FROM: Gene

That sounds great. There is actually a sequel. Am I going to see you on Saturday?

Q&A 014

DIALOGUE WITH

Kacey Wong

TO: Kacey Wong
FROM: Anderson Lee, Gene King

You have two very interesting pieces of installation 'Sleepwalker' and 'Doomsday' at two of the most populated spots in our Biennale. Basically visitors have no choice but to confront your pieces since they were sited right at the entrance and exit of the World Pavilion located inside the Heritage Discovery Centre.

Doomsday is a reflection on nuclear disaster of 311 earthquake, which we had intentionally coupled your piece with Hitoshi Abe's installation which also dealt with the aftermath of 311. You seem to be saying that this lead-made object may become a daily equipment that we need to drag along all the time. What was your first reaction when you saw Abe's piece? and how, or if, it triggered your further postulation of the Lead-made Armour? What is the present status of this installation since we had gone through quite a number of natural disasters since our biennale (e.g. Hurricane Sandy, continuous detection of nuclear seepage at the Japan coastlines)? Will there be a 2.1 version of the Armour coming out from your 'line'?

Sleepwalker is a poetic representation of bunk bed, which is an almost utilitarian furniture for crammed living condition. It was also the point of departure of rest of the exhibition unit in this biennale. As the 'grandfather' of the bunk-bed idea, would you like to share your thoughts on the notion of using the bunkbed as a 'storage/display' unit in this exhibition, after you have seen so many transformed bunk beds?

Also, both of your work border on the utilitarian and the poetic, ordinary and extraordinary. Has that always been your focus and how would you 're-contextualize' both pieces if they were to be exhibited today, i.e. Does the 'time' factor affect these piece at all?

TO: Anderson, Gene
FROM: Kacey

thanks for the questions regarding my sleepwalker project, i am currently in Nagoya, Japan now participating in the Aichi Triennale, will send you further reply in the next two days.

TO: Anderson, Gene
FROM: Kacey

hi all. here is my reply.

Living peacefully with nature and all its beauty and power including disasters seems to be part of life for the Japanese. It is easy to forget we are part of nature as the development of the city grows larger and larger until disasters such as earthquakes and Tsunami strikes, then the man from the city finally awaken. In the Japanese hardware store one

311

312

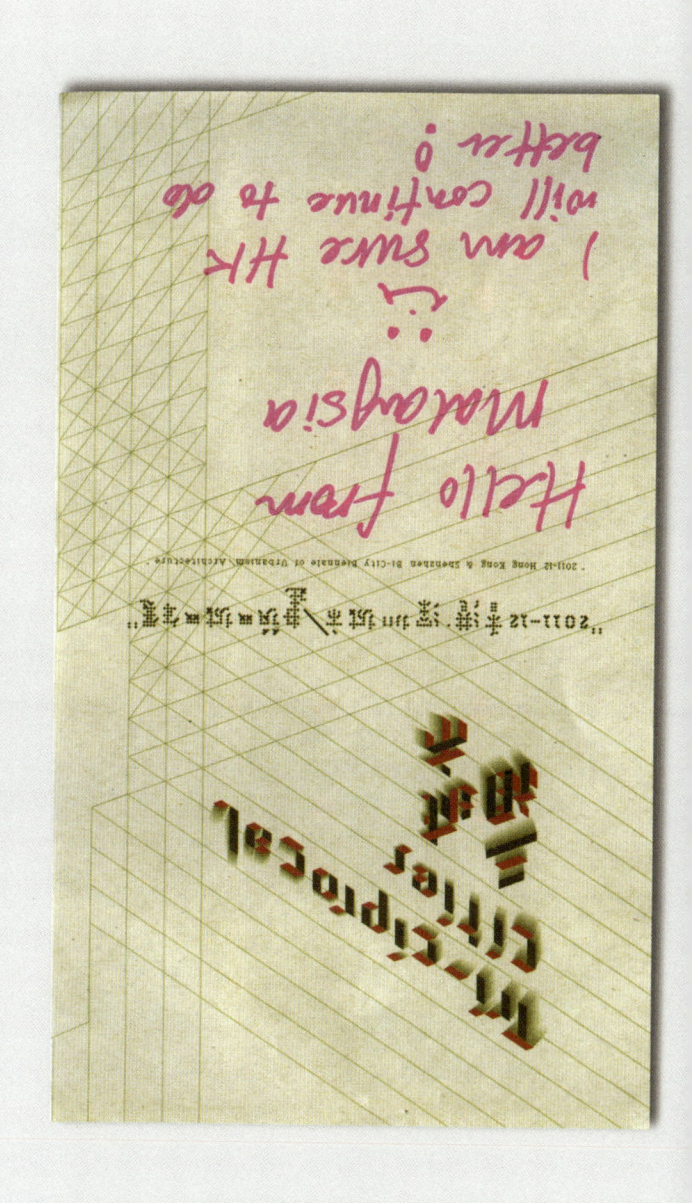

Hello from Malaysia :)
I am sure HK will continue to do better :)

EXH 049

PAVILION:

World Exhibits

PROJECT:

2011–12 Hong Kong & Shenzhen Bi-City Biennale of Urbanism \ Architecture: A Film

DESCRIPTION:

The film was based on the central theme of the exhibition. It introduced all the works by each exhibitor for about one minute each, and also included behind-the-scenes footage on the making of the Biennale. The result was a lively and powerful film that illustrated the many facets of the Biennale.

EXHIBITOR:

Kal NG

Born in Hong Kong, Kal Ng is a film producer with a background in architectural design. He has a B.Arch from the University of Oregon, an M.Phil in Comparative Literature and a PhD in Architecture from the University of Hong Kong. He is a founding member of the Hong Kong Independent Filmmaker Co-Op Ying E Chi. In 2005, he started KGE LAB, a studio specializing in creating architectural media.

ORIGIN:

Hong Kong

WORLD EXHIBITS 315

請勿觸摸
Please don't touch

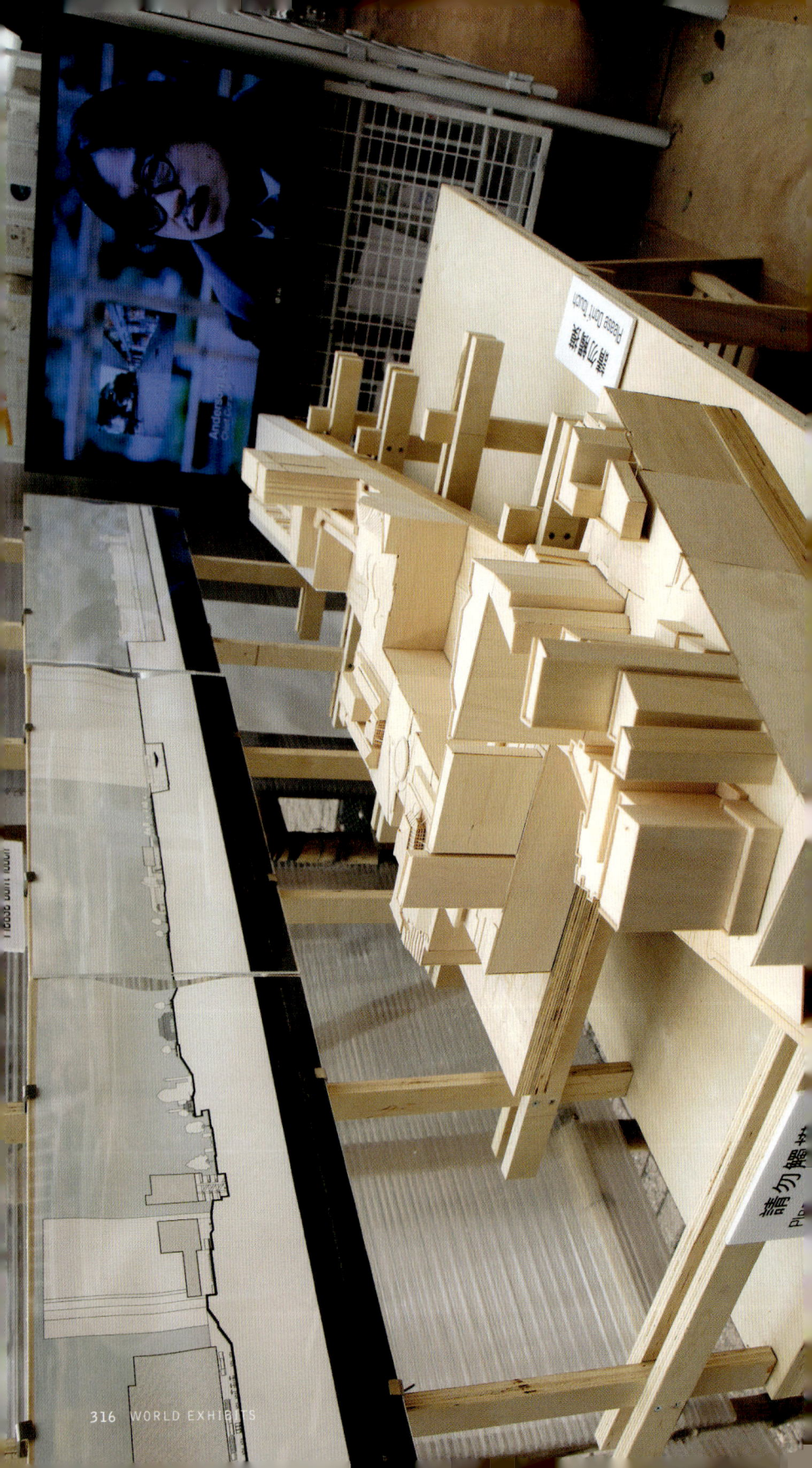

- 徐小平(?)

- I ❤ Hong Kong

- A bientôt.

- de Hong Kong

- Gros bisous

EXH 050

PAVILION:

World Exhibits

PROJECT:

The Story of Living in Sendai, March 11th

DESCRIPTION:

The Story of Living in Sendai researched the transformation of habitation after the Great East Japan Earthquake. People who lost their homes had to relocate to shelters, temporary housing, and recovery housing, and in a short period of time they used urban and interpersonal relationships to create an independent definition of 'home.'

EXHIBITOR:

Atelier Hitoshi Abe; Tohoku University Motoe Lab; Kazuki ENDO; Yuzuru ISODA

Hitoshi ABE has taught in universities in Japan and the United States, and is currently Professor and Chair, Department of Architecture and Urban Design, School of Arts and Architecture, UCLA. Masashige MOTOE is Professor and Principal of Sendai School of Design. Kazuki ENDO is a designer for Design Matoka and a lecturer at Fukushima Collage. Yuzuru ISODA is an Associate Professor of the Graduate School of Science, Tohoku University.

ORIGIN:

Japan

WORLD EXHIBITS 319

320 WORLD EXHIBITS

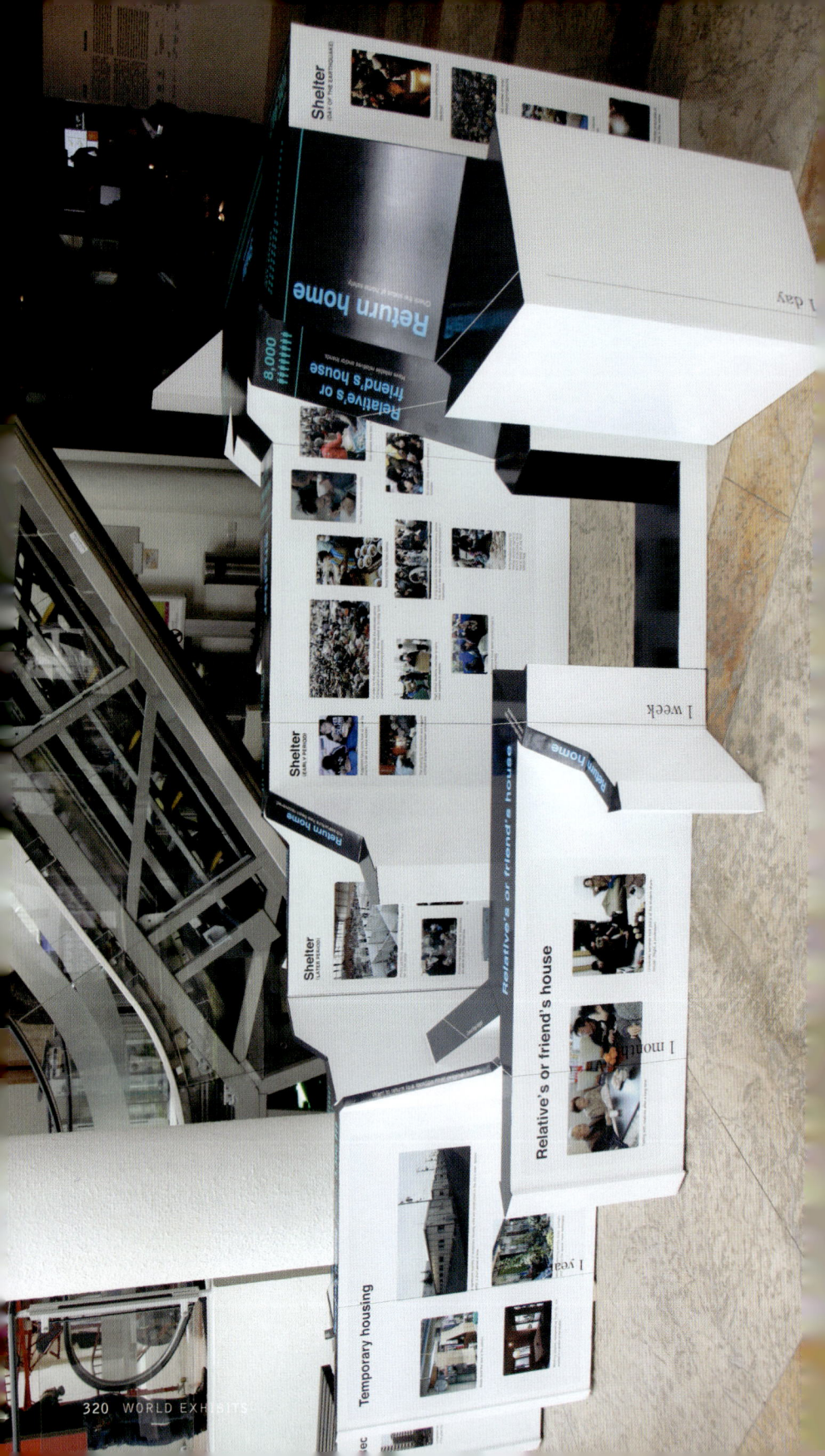

四月十日

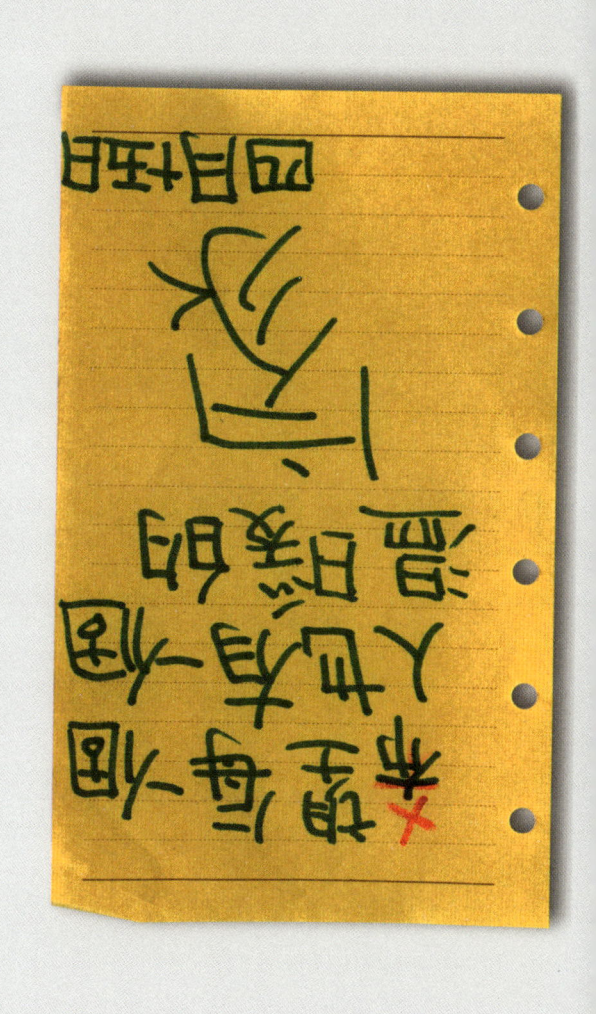

誰組美的
人有有個
大每天個 ✗

EXH 051

PAVILION:

World Exhibits

PROJECT:

Doomsday

DESCRIPTION:

As events of the past year have made clear, it is time to reflect on the potential hazards of nuclear energy. Doomsday was an anti-nuclear-radiation mobile living unit for one person, made of lead panels. When laid flat on the ground, its solar panels could generate 15 volts of electricity.

EXHIBITOR:

Kacey WONG

Kacey Wong was born in Hong Kong in 1970. He studied architecture at Cornell University and later received his Master of Fine Arts degree from Chelsea School of Art and Design and Doctor of Fine Arts degree from the Royal Melbourne Institute of Technology. He is now an Assistant Professor at Hong Kong Polytechnic University. His experimental art projects investigate the poetics of the human living environment.

ORIGIN:

Hong Kong

WORLD EXHIBITS 323

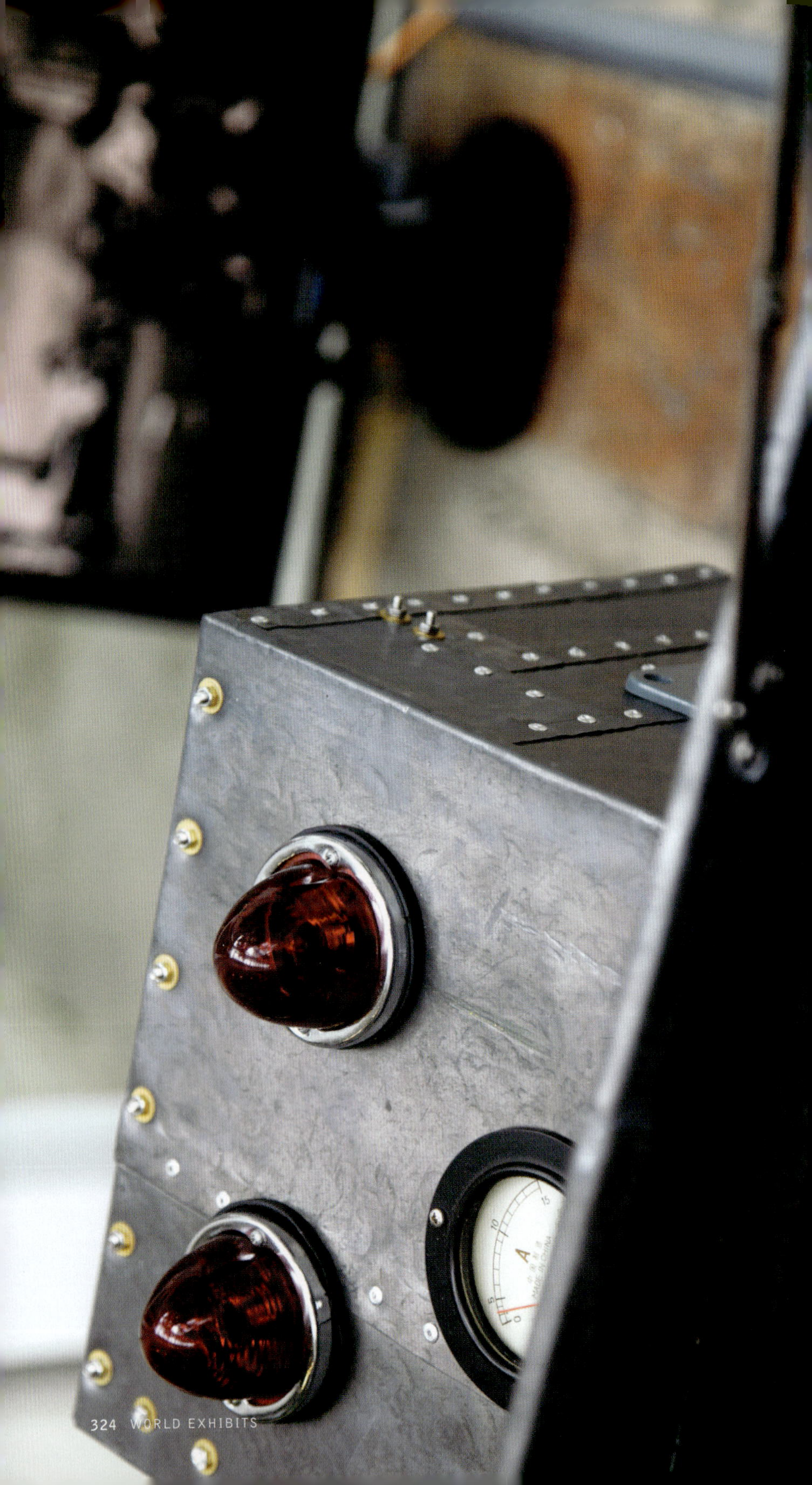
15
10
A
5
0

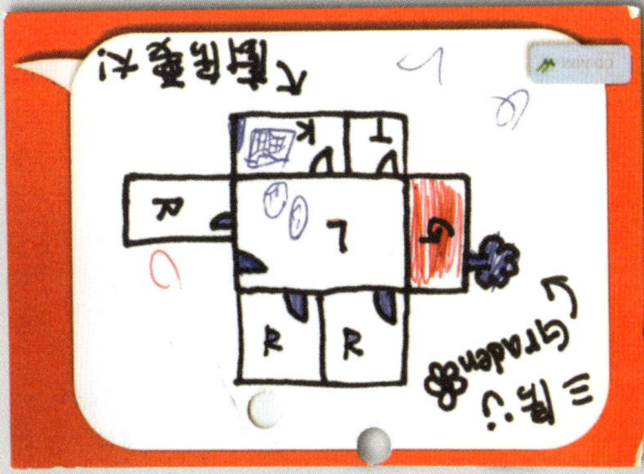
三房
Graden
廚房要大!

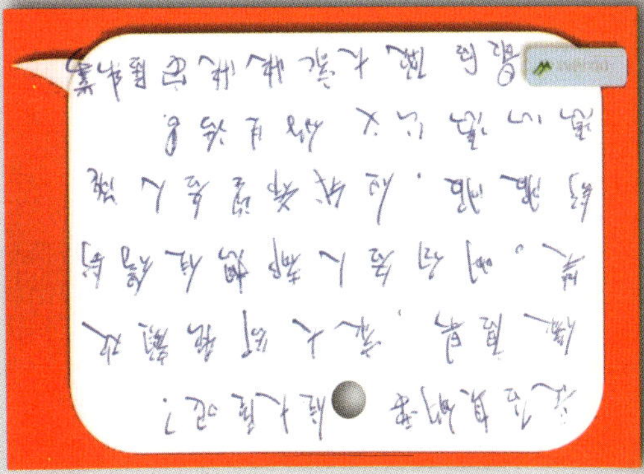

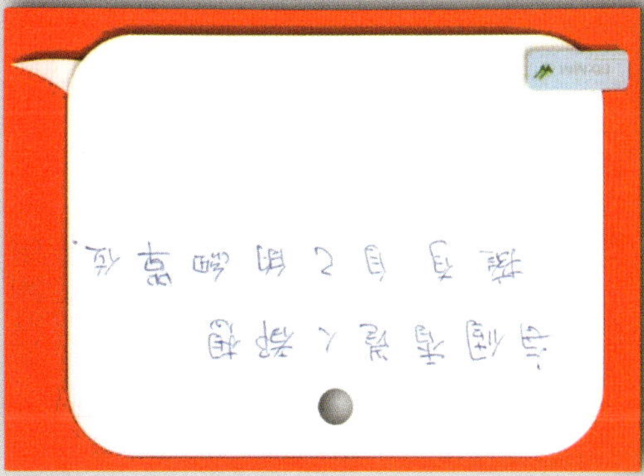
每個香港人都想
擁有自己的細單位.

can find earthquake related specialty packages such as medic kits, face mask, etc. for sale. I once even had seen a portable solar power convertor in the form of a small suitcase for sale converting the sun energy into electricity for everyday's electronics. These items reminded us that disasters are very real and part of the everyday Japanese experience.

Hitoshi Abe's work reminded me of a blind spot architects often ignored – the logistics of disaster. Often we see architects are only focusing on temporary housing and redevelopment related construction. Abe's survey style work clearly outlined how the individual handle the aftermath of disaster, the immediate post-disaster afterlife before temporary housing was erected. In other words, how to deal with life in limbo or forced exile by nature, I am sure there are plenty of design opportunity there waiting for us to explore.

Indeed after 311 we have gone through plenty of other disasters. Fortunately Hong Kong was blessed from natural disasters such as earthquake and Tsunami. However, on the unfortunately side, the recent political Tsunami from mainland China is affecting everyone living here in Hong Kong now hits critical level. Unlike the physical Tsunami the damage is not apparent but the damage will sure be very long lasting. 'Everything is art, everything is politics' renown mainland visual artists Ai Weiwei once said, no one can escape. To re-contextualized my work Doomsday in the currently moment of Hong Kong, if there is a 2.1 version I think what we need today is to create a shelter that can free and protect us from politics, that will be very nice. But like physical disaster, once the earth is shaken, the man will be awake and he cannot go back.

I think my other work Sleepwalker being transformed into the concept of storage/display during the biennale is quite accurately reflecting the rite of passage as one growing up here in Hong Kong. Due to the lack of space in our domestic environment the bunk bed often becomes the first storage/exhibition space inside one's home. It is the most sacred area where we store our comic books, hide treasured photos, and kept our favorite dolls, etc. A place that defines our identity within our home and a safe space that is most truthful to us. It is fascinating to see teams of international architects/designers transforming the bunk beds creatively to suit their purpose for the biennale exhibition. What I enjoy the most is to see these international designers rethinking the bunk bed, in a way like it is like we the people of Hong Kong inviting them to go through our process of living, that's great cultural exchange.

'Poetics' and 'spirituality' are the two words I think deeply about when I create artwork. In order to see clearly of the present I sometimes pretend I am an archeologist from the future looking curiously at the ordinary objects that surround us. Pretending I am looking at these objects for the first time in my life and to rethink about what they really represent. From that standpoint the concept of 'timelessness' really doesn't exist since every object man created can be traced back to a certain time period. For example, Doomsday can be traced back to the runaway robots in the 1940s and Sleepwalker can be traced back to Hong Kong living in the 1960s. What is timeless about the two works is the struggle of man and his environment, be it society, politics, technology, or nature. It is a struggle to survive or to live in harmony. Now, that's timelessness.

Q&A 015

DIALOGUE WITH

Kim Yao

TO: Kim Yao
FROM: Anderson Lee

Half a year after the Biennale, Hurricane Sandy hit New York, it almost collapsed the infrastructure of the City, destroyed Fire Island neighborhood. How would you 're-evaluate' your proposal now it almost seemed 'eerie,' if not inappropriate, to assess the true implication of your installation as purely hypothetical? We would like to find out if

327

328

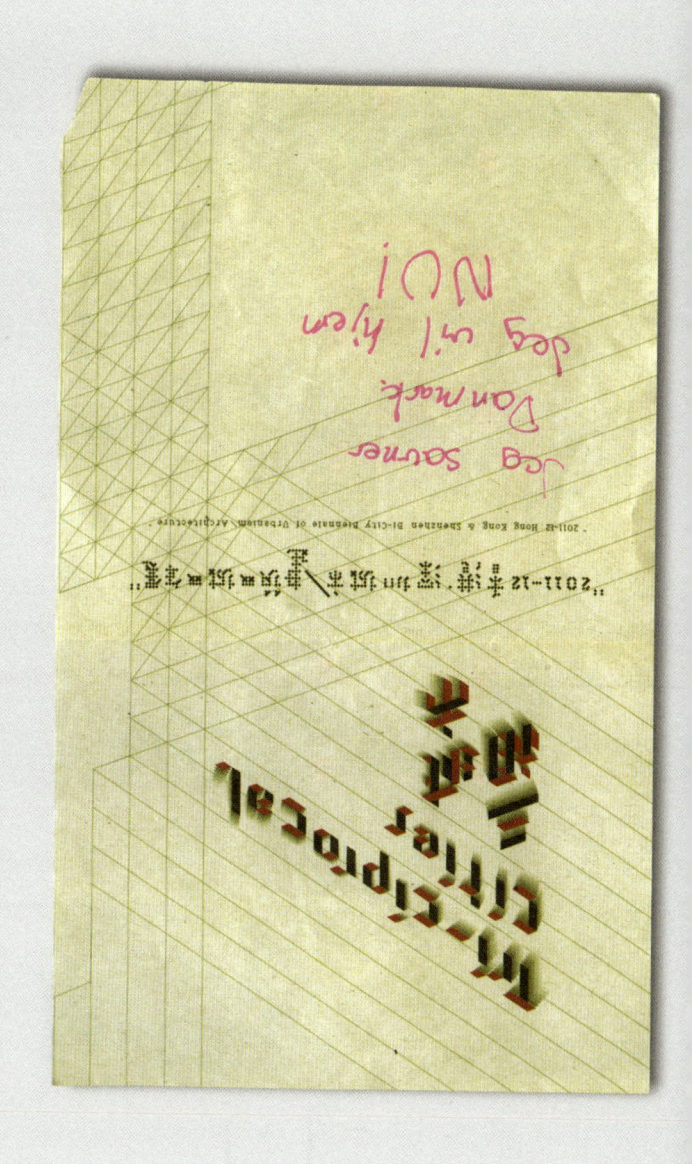

"2011-12 香港・深圳城市\建筑双城双年展"
2011-12 Hong Kong & Shenzhen Bi-city Biennale of Urbanism\Architecture

城市
边缘
Inter-
cities
边缘

Jeg savner
Danmark
jeg vil hjem
NU!

EXH 052

PAVILION:

World Exhibits

PROJECT:

Sleepwalker

DESCRIPTION:

Every morning when I open my eyes, it is a new beginning. The bed is my point of appearance. One day when it is time to depart, my body will be resting on a bed, my point of disappearance. Sleepwalker is a metal bunk bed similar to one I dreamt on as a child.

EXHIBITOR:

Kacey WONG

Kacey Wong was born in Hong Kong in 1970. He studied architecture at Cornell University and later received his Master of Fine Arts degree from Chelsea School of Art and Design and Doctor of Fine Arts degree from the Royal Melbourne Institute of Technology. He is now an Assistant Professor at Hong Kong Polytechnic University. His experimental art projects investigate the poetics of the human living environment.

ORIGIN:

Hong Kong

WORLD EXHIBITS 331

332 WORLD EXHIBITS

要通告世界，請自由、希望、民主、公正、尊嚴、我爱你！

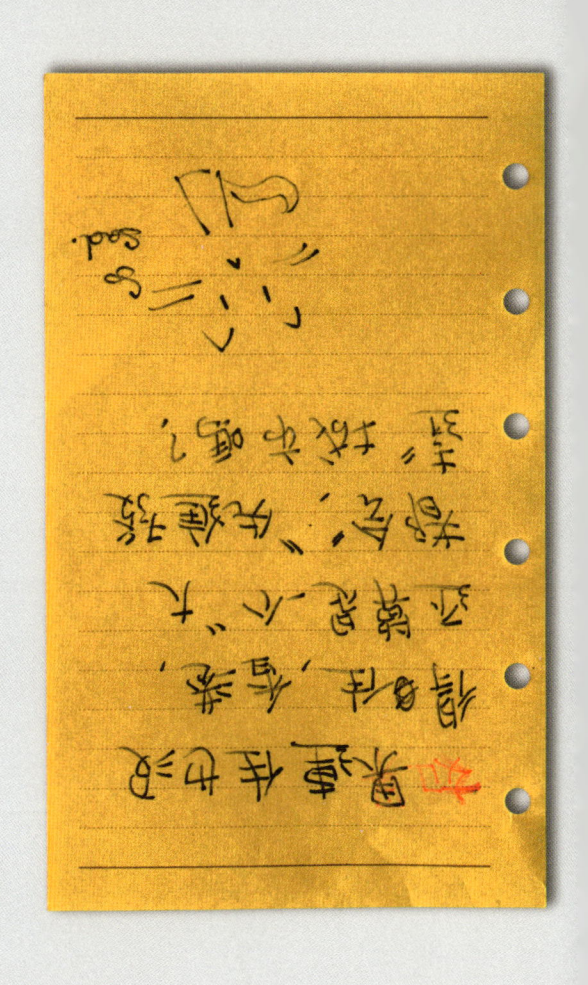

EXH 053

PAVILION:

World Exhibits

PROJECT:

City Memory: A Digital Dialogue Across Time, Place & People

DESCRIPTION:

The virtual sculpture City Memory invited visitors to respond to the thoughts of the past and add their own feelings of the present. This dialogue across time, place and people was made possible using QR codes, online forums and text messaging. It allowed visitors to use their own digital devices to interact with the exhibition display to enrich the meaning of the city itself.

EXHIBITOR:

Ming Wai WONG, Karmin TONG, Sze Man CHAN, Ka Lo KAN

All four practitioners Ming Wai Wong, Karmin Tong, Sze Man Chan, and Ka Lo Kan, are based in Hong Kong with diverse backgrounds – architect, planner, urban designer and social entrepreneur – and have been actively involved in various development projects in Hong Kong and elsewhere in East and Southeast Asia.

ORIGIN:

Hong Kong

WORLD EXHIBITS 335

...oncrete jungle. It is a human zoo.

~Desmond Morris

都市化發展

理性共存、信仰自由及基本財產權保障，包括法律正義軌道，以此融合多種文化及不同移民，在這個基礎上發展出自己一套獨特的都市化模式。

香港是沿著

城市裡的樹木一樣，越來越少發展盛長的空間 ～陶傑

場所

是地理環境的一種重要記號，它有自己的觀點和方向。絕對在這場地應該了解場地的歷史，了解它的方向走。它的根。

現在拆了是一次機會，還有一樣。怎麼建也是一次機會，是拆建又好看文化，是這個建築能不能繼續延後，延後成為一個它的地方。第一就是眼文化有關係。原來找回來？還是其。這是怎麼投回來？

~張永和

Planning bring

is like an ...ry little, but all of ... architecture, history, ... anthropology, ... sociology.

336 WORLD EXHIBITS

何嘗不是藝術家一枚

EXH 054

PAVILION:

World Exhibits

PROJECT:

Interpreting the Asian Street

DESCRIPTION:

The urban street in Asian cities does not necessarily have the formalist configuration of spaces and the highly defined public realm bequeathed to most western cities. The exhibit was intended to expand on both traditional and modern dimensions, illustrating the diversity of the street realm in Asian cities to provide a creative frame of reference for planning and design.

EXHIBITOR:

Peter Cookson SMITH

Peter Cookson Smith is an architect, planner and urban designer. He founded Urbis, a planning and design consultancy, in 1977 and is now the president of the Hong Kong Institute of Planners and the vice president of the Hong Kong Institute of Urban Design. He is also the author of The Urban Design of Impermanence and The Urban Design of Concession.

ORIGIN:

United Kingdom / Hong Kong

WORLD EXHIBITS 339

Gateways" delineate points of spatial transition along important routes. The gateway assists in orientation and legibility acting as both an urban marker and a physical entrance or exit point. In Hong Kong these are known as pāilou, in Japan as torri. The probable origin of pāilou was India where decorative lintols supported by columns were placed at the entrance to temples. Later pāilous in China adopted elaborate wooden structures with manifold roofs, sometimes as a memorial or in honour of nearby temples of alters. Towered decorative gateways to sacred places can be marked by a narrative of tiered niches and statues, and a sequence of stepped approaches establishing an elusive link between spirituality and 'place'. The use of banners, flags, signage displays and lanterns create peripheral characteristics and atmospheric emphasis where animation overwhelms the actual setting. Processional routes to sacred shrines are delineated by physical elements such as gateways, spirit shrines and stone lanterns that emphasise transition rather than spatial demarcation in a compositional sense.
Hong Kong
Beijing
Shanghai
Shanghai
Nanjing
Nanjing
Guangzhou
Guangzhou
Tianjing

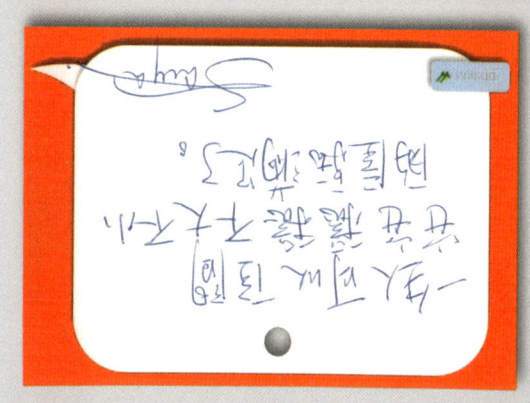

love, comfort, clean & simple design, open space, beautiful view, open room, creature comforts, a wonderful mean to show if with 5

一每個人都有自己
共同建造我子子一
因困難而退了。

My Dream house ←

there is an 'after-life' of your investigations since this whole question of flooding, disaster prevention, water versus land discussions must had been permeated throughout the City after the Sandy incident.

In Taipei and Hong Kong, since we have pretty high mountains and strong typhoons and sub-tropical storms bring in sudden flooding, there are walls built but also block the City from flood plains that is the only sizable open space in the area. Do you see any possibilities other than this device to both prevent/metigate flooding as well as utilize a possible new found open space?

TO: Anderson
FROM: Kim

As a resident of lower Manhattan, in a neighborhood directly impacted by Hurricane Sandy, our work on A New Urban Ground seemed unfortunately prescient. Architecture Research Office's proposal included a number of features that, if implemented, would improve conditions following an event like Hurricane Sandy. I believe the after-life of the Rising Currents exhibition, combined with the actual event of Hurricane Sandy, includes a number of initiatives, such as research by NYC Housing Recovery Planning, and competitions like FAR-ROC and HUD's for the northeast region.

In our collaboration with dLand Studio for A New Urban Ground, we specifically propose techniques for absorbing and redirecting water, rather than attempting to just block its entry. Flood barriers and gates are problematic for large swaths of NYC water frontage (over all five boroughs). In addition, they are extremely costly infrastructural projects that are challenging to implement from an economic and political standpoint. Instead, we proposed softening the edges of lower Manhattan, creating a more porous and absorbent terrain for water – in some cases even creating larger channels for its circulation into Manhattan. These projects are still infrastructural and costly, but can simultaneously provide an amenity (in the form of parks and outdoor space) for immediate enjoyment.

Q&A 016

DIALOGUE WITH

Rocco Yim

TO: Rocco Yim
FROM: Gene King

It was good seeing you, the book for the last Biennale is finally on the way. Ande has an idea that since it is so long after the actual exhibition, we should have a part to have a dialogue with participants. The following is our questions, which we hope you come back with your input.

1. You made the suggestion that we should have an exhibit about the development of schools in Hong Kong. There is a Chinese saying – 'It takes 10 years to nurture a tree while 100 for people' – in which time is the essence. Looking back, school is a building type that probably fits our theme 'Tri-ciprocal city: the time, the place, the people.' Is that why you thought of the idea?

2. You once mentioned that when you design a building in Hong Kong, you may never see the whole building after it is built since it is surrounded by others so tightly. You also mentioned that connections with the surrounding urban elements are more important than building elevations, which are usually very important to architects. I think that is a typical example that separates the missions of Asian architects from western counterparts. Your thoughts on that?

3. You recently published the book 'Reconnecting Cultures,' and during the book launch in Taipei, you mentioned that architecture is the art of problem solving. I think that is quite true, especially in Asian environment since our problems are dynamic, complex,

344

3. 抽風系統聲 Sound of exhaust fan
仁安大廈後巷牛頭角道
back alley Y. Bldg, Ngau Tau Kok Road

78 dB

觀塘聲音地圖
Kwun Tong Sound Map

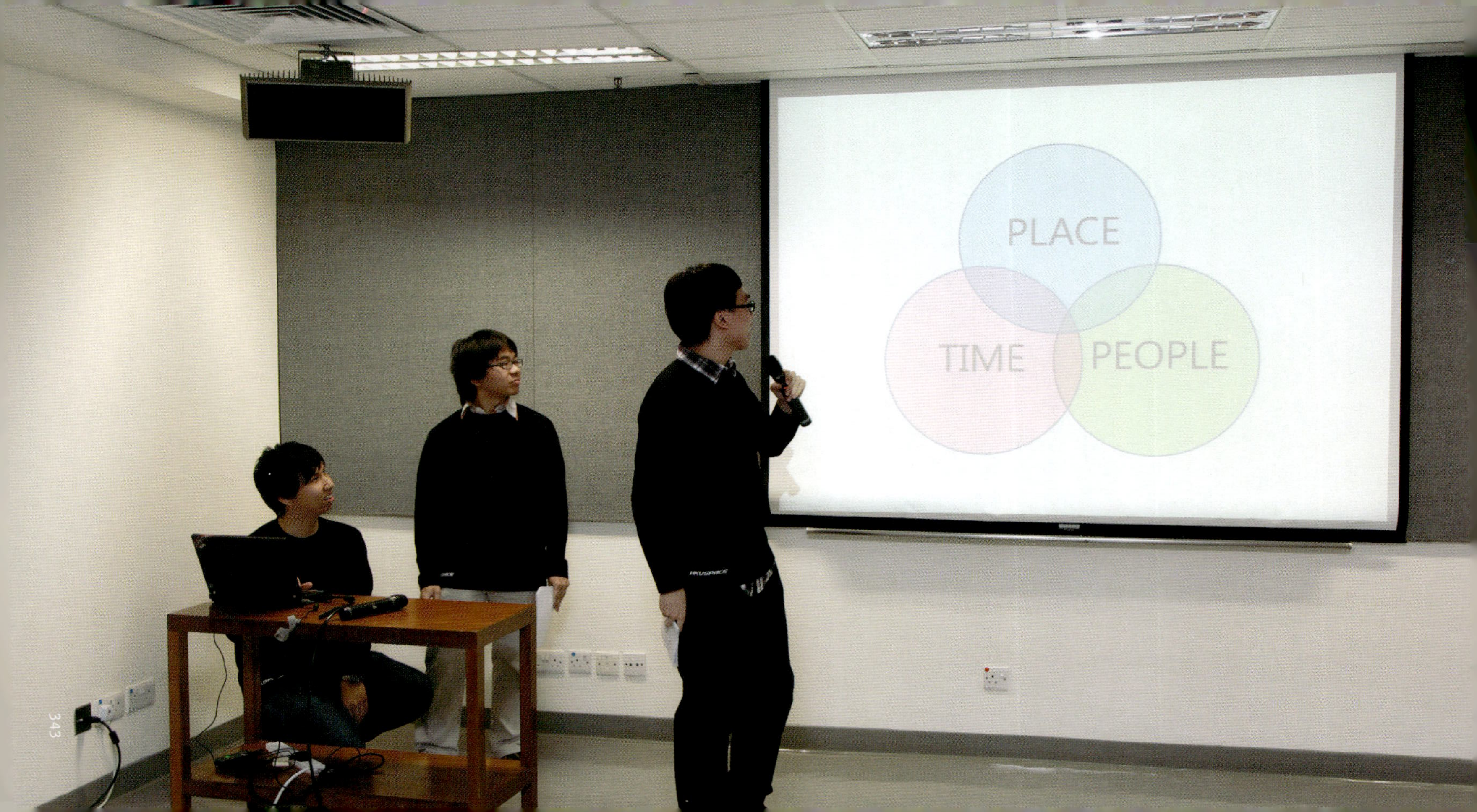
PLACE
TIME
PEOPLE

Vojta + Pavel
from the Czech
REPUBLIC

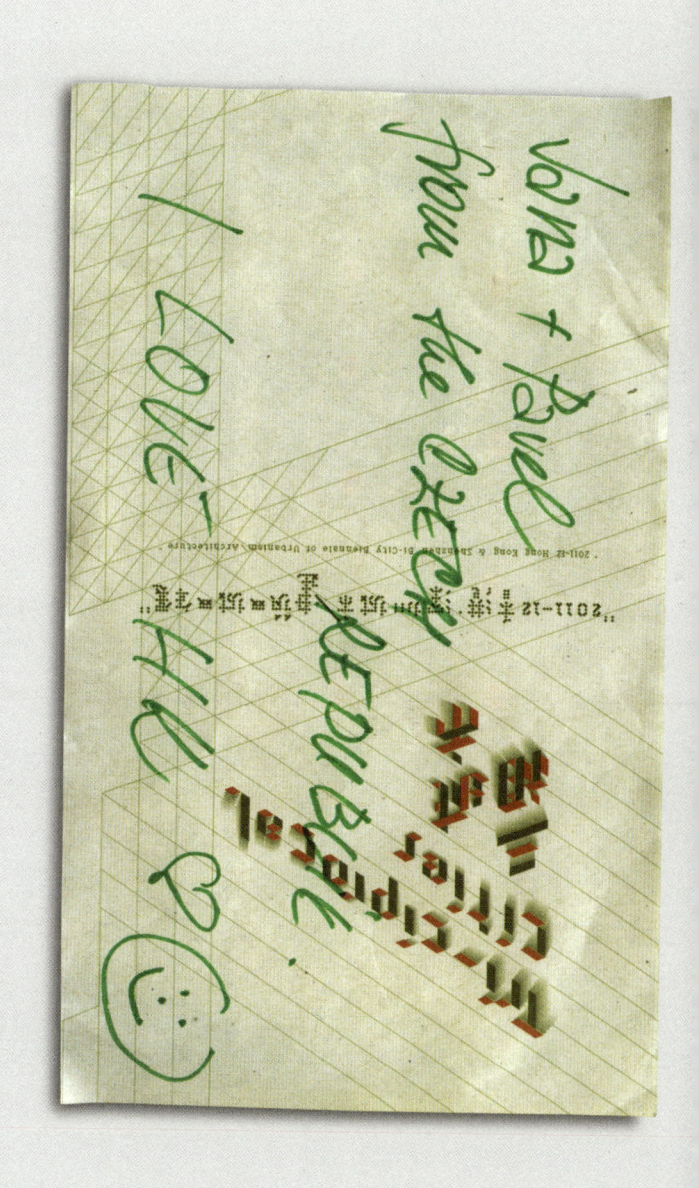

I LOVE
HK ♡ ☺

OUTDOOR INSTALLATIONS
Kowloon Park and Beyond

Besides the main exhibition pavilions, there were five large-scale outdoor installations in Kowloon Park and one site-specific installation on the rooftop of the nearby Wanchai Visual Archive. The sculptural installations in the park acted as anchors to visually connect the pavilions, providing a coherent and enhanced experience for the Biennale visitors. For local residents and regular park-goers, these interactive installations reframed inconspicuous details of familiar surroundings and encouraged the public to experience the park differently as they passed through it in their daily life.

INSTALLATIONS 347

348 INSTALLATIONS

我的整珍 My Sharing

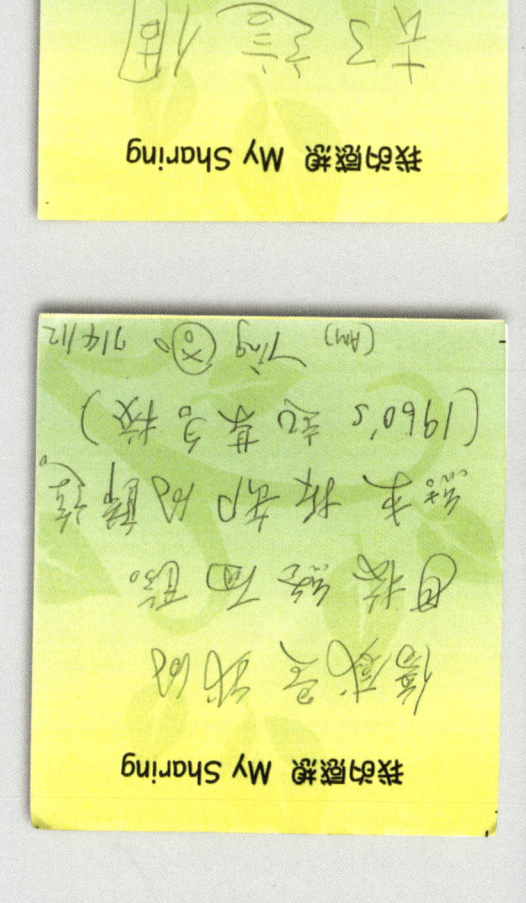

信表哥 分阳
目樣 鉛 颜色
筆 代形 的 顏色
(1960's 約 華方格)
Ying ☺ 9/4/12
(Amy)

我的整珍 My Sharing

豐 小彬 還有 好聞
扎了3次還 好痛
我才痛
扎了好幾個
(痛!)

EXH 055

INSTALLATIONS:

Kowloon Park

PROJECT:

Aqua Industry

DESCRIPTION:

Aqua Industry explored the transformation of culturally significant sites into new prototypes for built form. The installation related to the curatorial theme of 'in-between times, spaces, and peoples' by rethinking the role of water ecologies, fishing communities, and maritime dynamics for a socially sustainable future housing strategy for high-density living. Combining traditional social networks with a specific local sensibility, this soft and fluid urban infrastructure strategy would transform Hong Kong, the Pearl River Delta, and Mainland China by forming both tangible and conceptual links between our past and future.

EXHIBITOR:

ESKYIU (Eric SCHULDENFREI and Marisa YIU)

ESKYIU is an interdisciplinary design studio that explores how architecture intersects with transformative cultural landscapes, mediascapes, products, print and experimental fabrication systems. The office is currently designing a house in Hong Kong, a museum in northern China, and an urban masterplan in central China.

ORIGIN:

Hong Kong

INSTALLATIONS 351

352 INSTALLATIONS

※個個人
我認為自
乙各有
我們方向
一路一路
互相签地

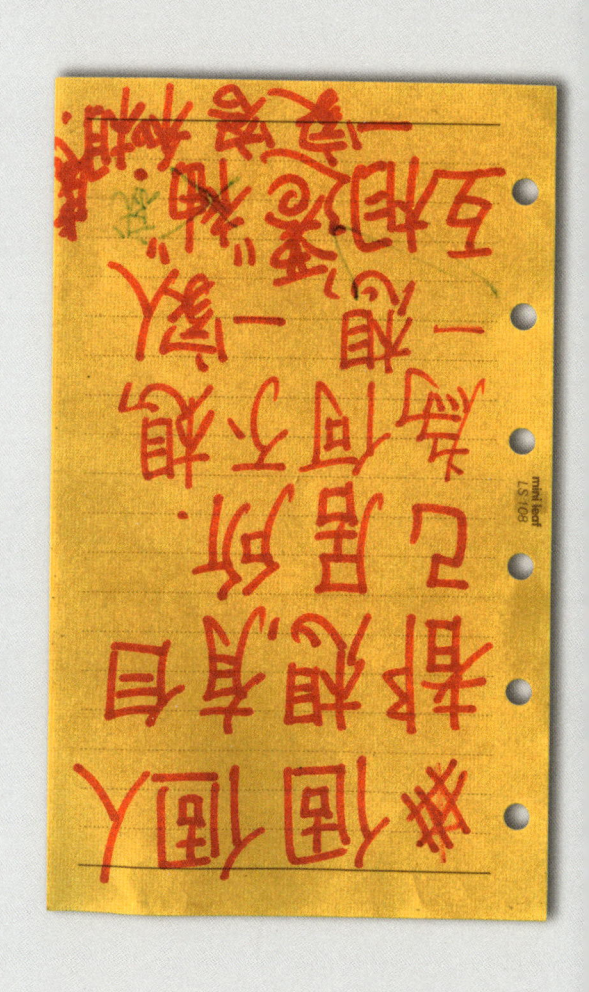

INSTALLATIONS:

Kowloon Park

PROJECT:

The City of Exchange

DESCRIPTION:

The City of Exchange originated from an architectural thesis that studied the use of representational tools to reveal the dynamics of a city. In the midst of globalization, cities have become mere stopping points for citizens who are constantly arriving and departing. With a series of maps, this project revealed the urban geography of tourism in Hong Kong. The installation was a superimposition of informative and sensual devices showcasing the tri-ciprocal relationship between time, place and people.

EXHIBITOR:

Sherry Yik Ping FUNG, Sai Chun YUNG, Sunny Ka Shing CHAN, Chun Hang YIP

The team comprises four young designers who graduated from the Master of Architecture program at the University of Hong Kong. The team has participated in various exhibitions in the field of architecture, art and calligraphy. C.H. Yip was shortlisted for the Hong Kong Institute of Architects Young Architects Award 2010.

ORIGIN:

Hong Kong

INSTALLATIONS · 255

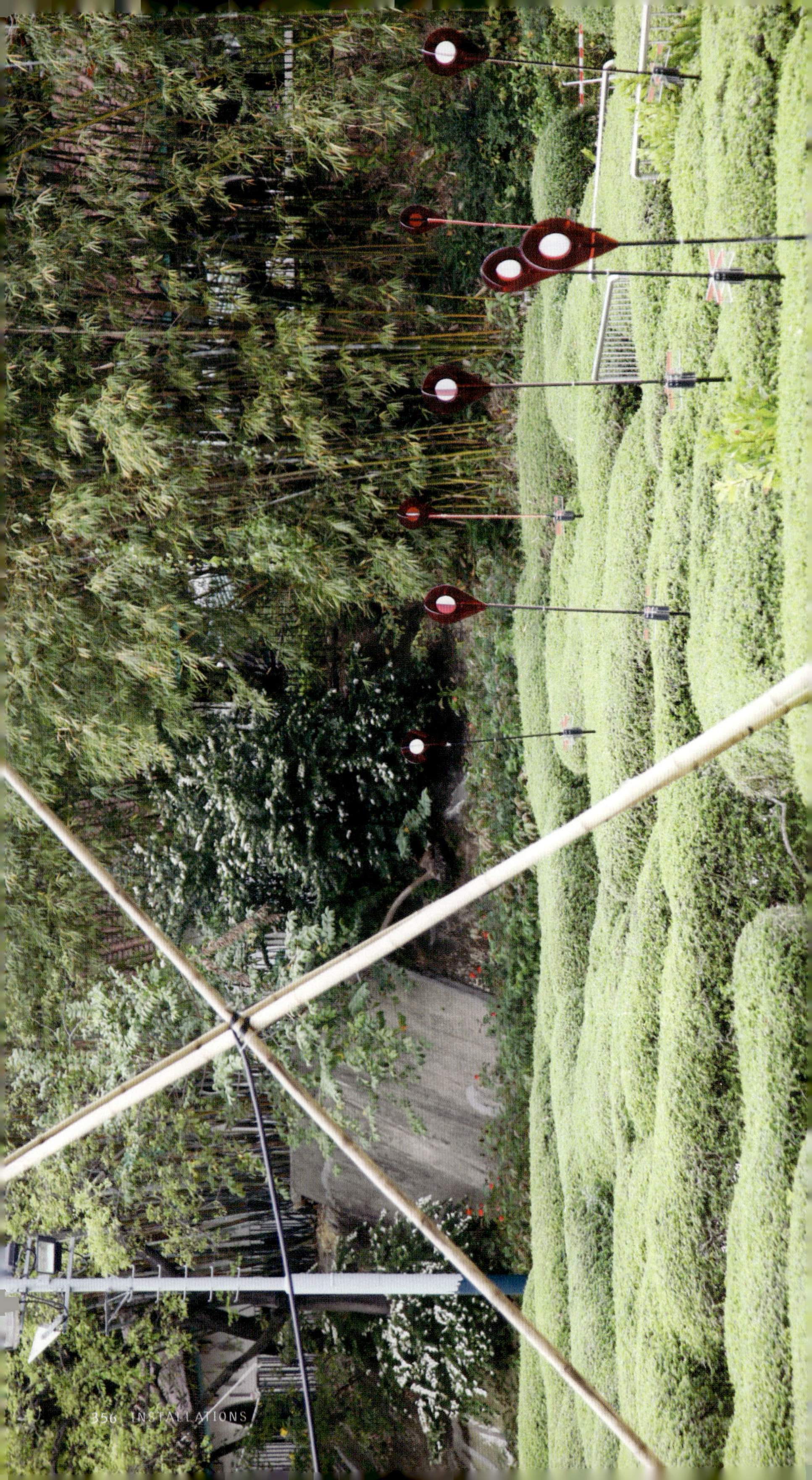

19 April 2012

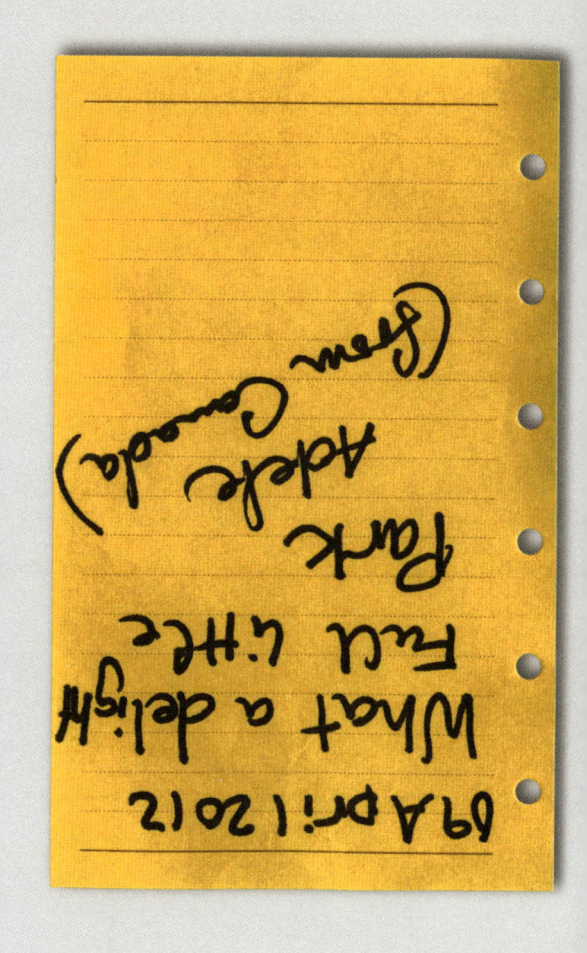

What a delight
Full of the
Park Adele
(from Canada)

EXH 057

INSTALLATIONS:

Kowloon Park

PROJECT:

urbanUPLIFT

DESCRIPTION:

urbanUPLIFT was a piece of urban furniture. urbanUPLIFT was created to provide familiar urban amenities for Hong Kong pedestrians: street stalls, small pagodas, gardens, billboards, newsstands, amongst others. Disseminated in the city, urbanUPLIFT became a collection of mini-towers commemorating the urban scope of the pedestrian embedded within the city of Hong Kong at large. Beginning as identical towers, individual urbanUPLIFT towers absorbed local needs and desires, transforming themselves into local icons. urbanUPLIFT was part of the city.

EXHIBITOR:

openUU ltd. (Kevin LIM, Edward Yujoong KIM, Eddy Man KIM)

openUU ltd. is an award-winning design research laboratory that works at various scales. In 2011, openUU was awarded two Best of Year awards by Interior Design magazine for platform (1x2), a reclaimed space turned gallery, and modelScape, a prototype model-stand. Our work also includes ProjectionOne, an interactive installation exhibited at Harvard Design School, and zzt, a design consultation for a stadium shell.

ORIGIN:

United States / Hong Kong

INSTALLATIONS 359

PATRICK O'NEIL WAS ERE
HAVE A GOOD DAY
NO CLIMBING
GRAFFITI
WELCOME

MIND YOUR HEAD!

House ≠ Home

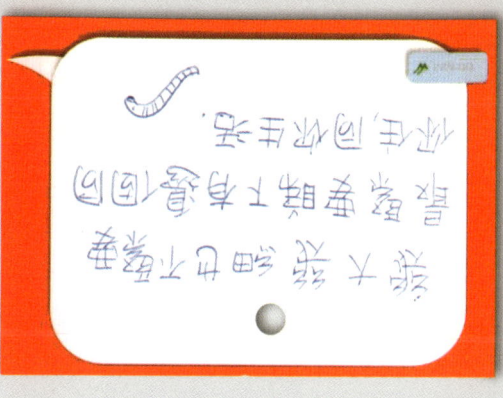

搬 了 新 家 但 不 喜 欢
重 新 布 置 了 卡 看 图 回
使 它, 回 归 本 来 的 家.

and usually unprecedented, and there are no western experiences to apply. Can you elaborate on that?

My last trip to Hong Kong was early June. For the Biennale and HKU teaching, I came to Hong Kong 33 times in the span of less than two years. It is why I am not rushing back. However, I will come again probably for this book and hope to see you then.

TO: Gene
FROM: Rocco

Herewith my attempted answers to your questions:

1. I think the history of development of Hong Kong schools as an exhibit is apt because this is so much interwined with the history of Hong Kong itself. It reflects HK's politics: how and by what mechanism the design of schools are procured. It reflects evolution in our society's structure: how schools are differentiated into types: rural, urban, subvented, direct-subsidied, private and international. And it reflects our architectural/urban culture: how architects grapple with physical constraints and make-do with minimal resources, tackling the design of compact multi-storeyed school premises, usually on difficult terrain. The whole subject ultimately serves to reveal both our follies and our ingenuity as a society.

2. My sayings are actually prompted by my belief that in this age, the city precedes architecture. Instead of giving shape to the city, architecture should in many instances allow itself to be shaped by the city. To put it differently, one should ask the city what it wants its buildings to be. This is as true in the context of Hong Kong, as it is in similarly dense and matured cities like Taipei and Singapore.

3. I promulgate the notion that architecture is the art of problem solving, specifically against the notion that architecture is an art, period. Because the latter position in my mind is actually responsible for so much junk, so much self-centered expression of 'nothingness,' that has sprung up in the last decade, both in the west and in our region. You are correct in saying that our problems are unprecedented, more dynamic and complex beyond western experiences. So it is precisely by addressing the uniqueness of our problems that our architecture could gain such authentic, as against pretentious, identity that we have craved for all these years.

TO: Rocco
FROM: Gene

Thanks a lot for your response. However, it is not so easy to get rid of me. I have further questions as below.

As a foreigner to HK, I was particularly touched by the strive for the basic right to education during difficult times. Compared to that time, current schools look like luxury. However, do you think prototype schools, as hardware for prototype education, produce prototype students? From your understanding, have people growing up during difficult times developed more diversity than young people now?

One thing I am always interested is 'time' factor in architecture. Asian cities are much more dynamic and fluid than Western ones, especially with drastic changes and population growth, when the city changes, how can buildings cope with it? Or how do we design buildings with flexibility to cope with it? Or is it even possible? Do you see the buildings you have designed transform through time?

TO: Gene
FROM: Rocco

While it is absolutely true that prototype education tends to produce prototype students, to say prototype schools are responsible for prototype education might be stretching it a bit. It is perhaps fairer to say that a liberating environment that creative architecture could bring would help students to be more adventurous, diversified and less conforming.

363

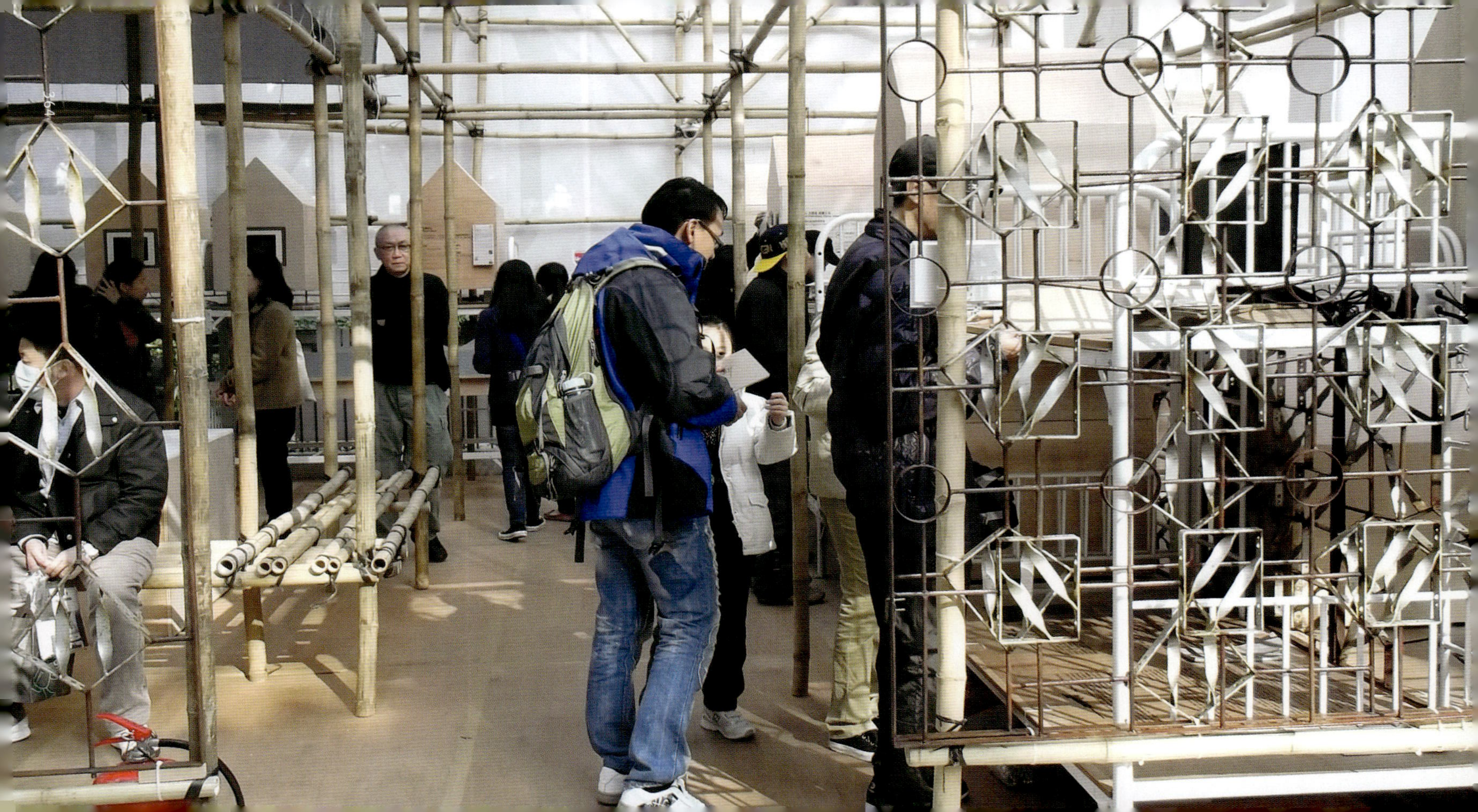

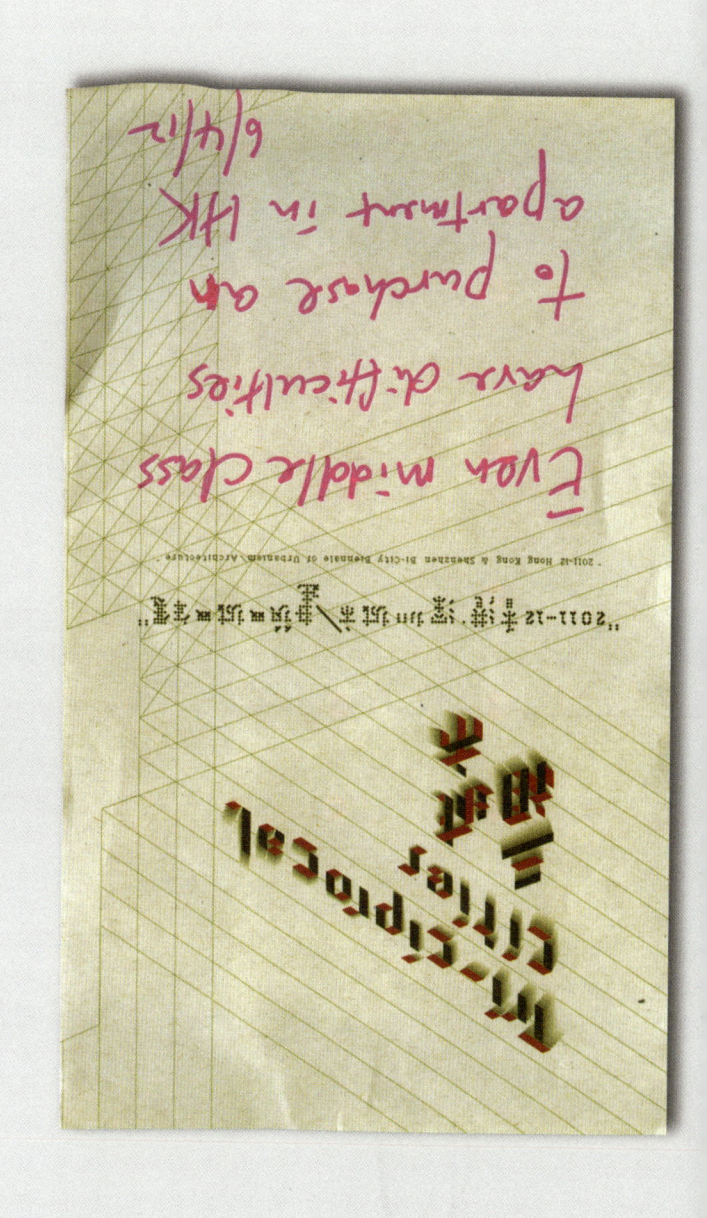

Even middle class have difficulties to purchase an apartment in HK
6/4/12

"2011-12 深圳·香港城市\建筑双城双年展"
- 2011-12 Hong Kong & Shenzhen Bi-City Biennale of Urbanism\Architecture -

EXH 058

INSTALLATIONS:

Kowloon Park

PROJECT:

TETRA

DESCRIPTION:

TETRA was an urban installation using a modular solid-surface system that functions at a variety of scales, from the object all the way up to the city. The basic module of TETRA was inspired by the simple form of a tetrahedron. Each family of tetrahedrons was made up of three different sizes, but all have the same opening at the points of connection. The slight changes in the parameters of these different pieces allowed for variation. The design was based on a fractal logic that opens the possibility for an infinite urban architectural intervention.

EXHIBITOR:

Wendy Wei Yue FOK, Kenneth King Wai TO, Ivan Pui Kin CHEUNG, Kathleen JOHNSON, Michelle Man Sum LOK, Dave Yuen Lok CHEUNG, Marco Kwun Yu CHAN

Team TETRA is a group of creative design practitioners and academics. The project and design teams are: Wendy Fok, Kenneth To, Kathleen Johnson, Dave Cheung, Ivan Cheung, Michelle Lok, and Marco Chan, with the common ground of the Chinese University of Hong Kong and the Relational Modularity Studio.

ORIGIN:

Hong Kong / United States

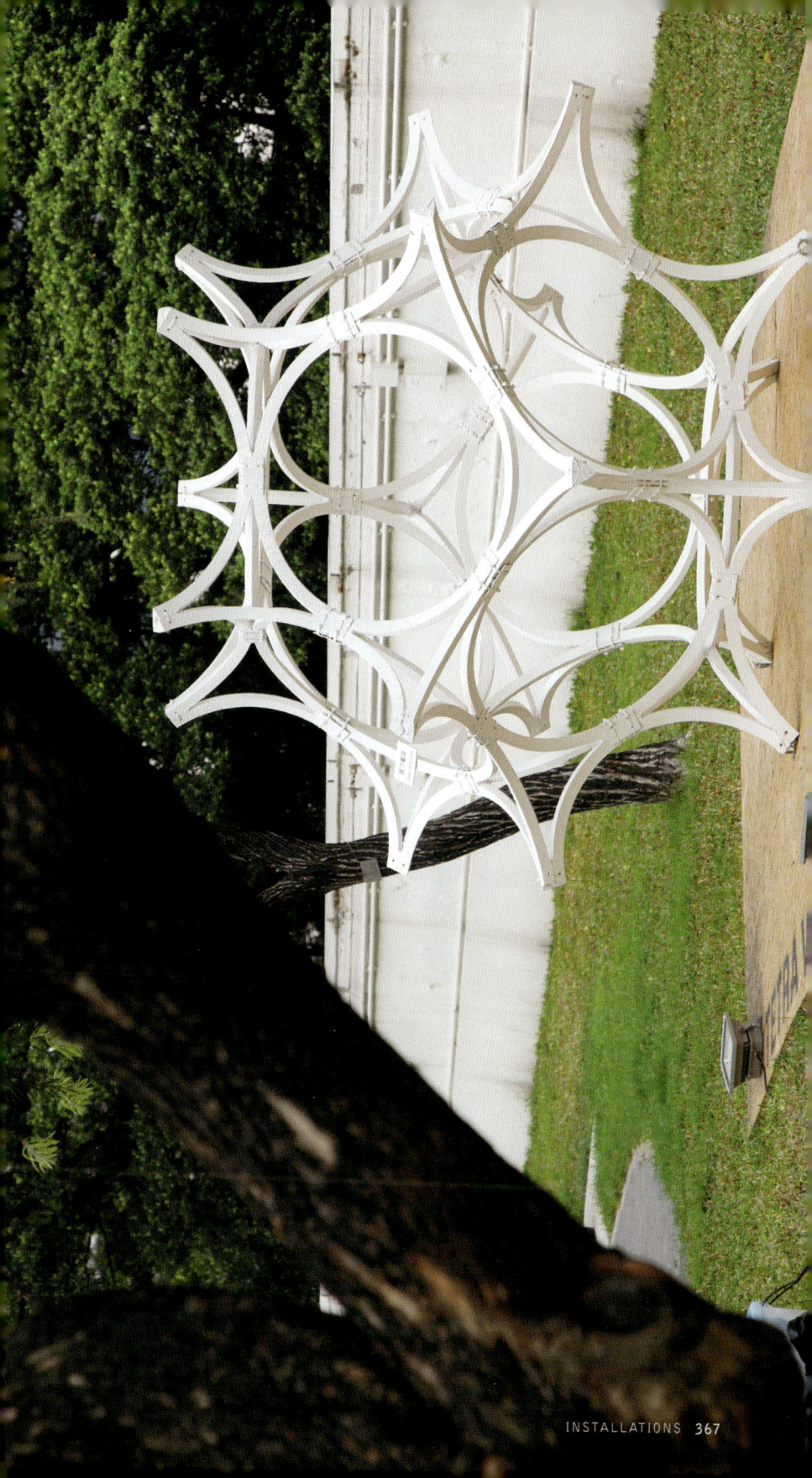

INSTALLATIONS 367

368 INSTALLATIONS

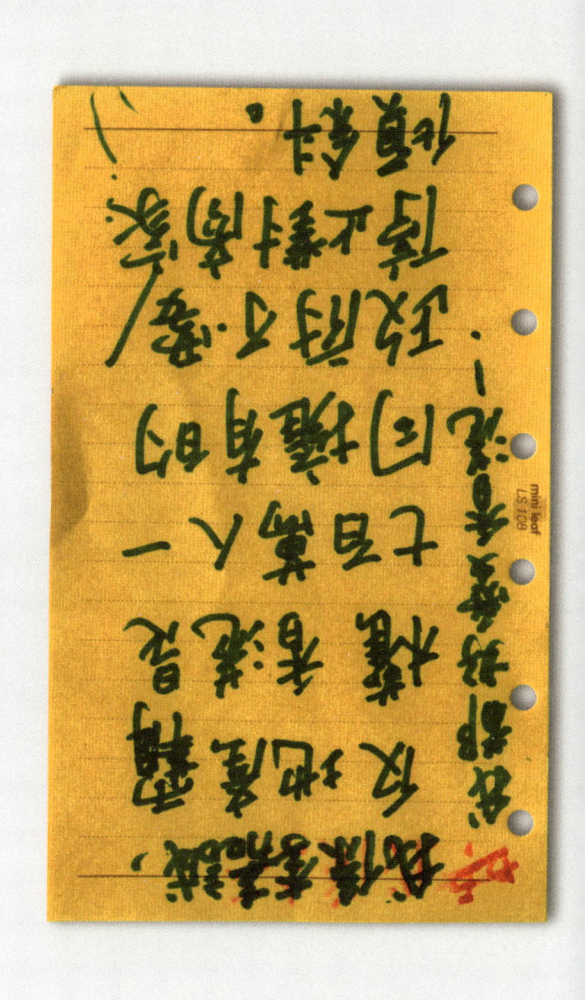

名譽董事長，
您諄諄善誘
諄諄教誨 耳提面命
之恩澤，三十載有
加，沒齒不忘。
順祝闔家康泰，
萬事如意。

EXH 059

INSTALLATIONS:

Kowloon Park

PROJECT:

Super Shelter

DESCRIPTION:

Super Shelter, a collective project of the First Year Design Studio at the University of Hong Kong, offered a unique perspective on the originating idea of architecture – the shelter within Hong Kong's tight or neglected spaces. These twenty-nine full-scale Super Shelter installations that rescued wasted space and promoted a new awareness of public architecture.

EXHIBITOR:

University of Hong Kong, Department of Architecture

The team comprises students from the first year design studio at the Department of Architecture, University of Hong Kong. The studio worked in groups of two to three, collectively forming twenty-nine unique ideas and installation pieces. Teachers: John Lin (BAAS 1 Coordinator), Jean Choi, Chad McKee, Miho Hirayabashi, Alan Smart, Thomas Tsang

ORIGIN:

Hong Kong

he Place, The People
4 2012

372 INSTALLATIONS

我不在意别人说我什么，因为我知道自己是什么样的人。

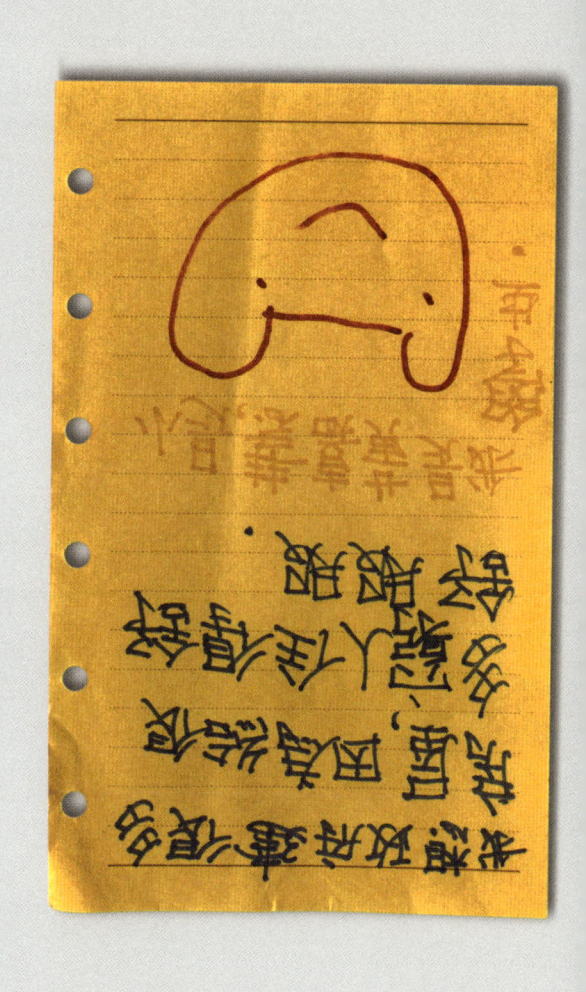

但我没有要嘲笑他的意思。

EXH 060

INSTALLATIONS:

Wanchai Visual Archive

PROJECT:

Observatory / TOFUD # From Shenzhen to Hong Kong

DESCRIPTION:

In Hong Kong, roof shanties have formed a particular urban fabric interweaving multiple levels and spaces. Here the artist was invited to remove the exhibit from Shenzhen Biennale exhibition, and then relocate the work on the open roof at Wanchai Visual Archive, to question what constitutes and locates an (il)legal structure.

EXHIBITOR:

Frank HAVERMANS

Frank Havermans studied architectural design at the Hoge school voor Beeldende Kunsten (Art Academy) St. Joost in Breda. He has won awards including the Houtarchitectuurprijs (a Dutch award for innovative wood architecture) with his artist's studio KAPKAR/TAW-BW-5860.

ORIGIN:

The Netherlands

INSTALLATIONS 375

376 INSTALLATIONS

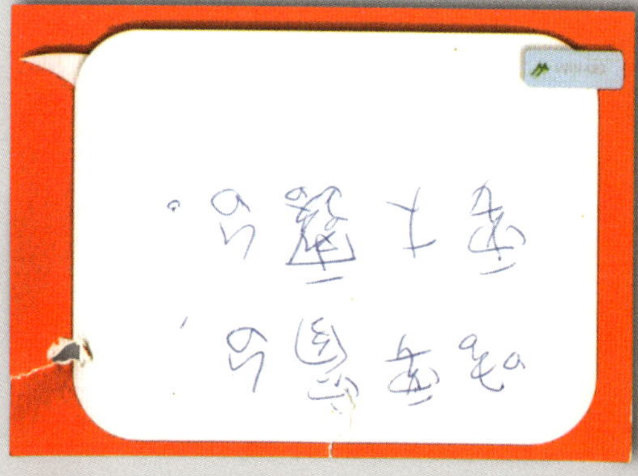

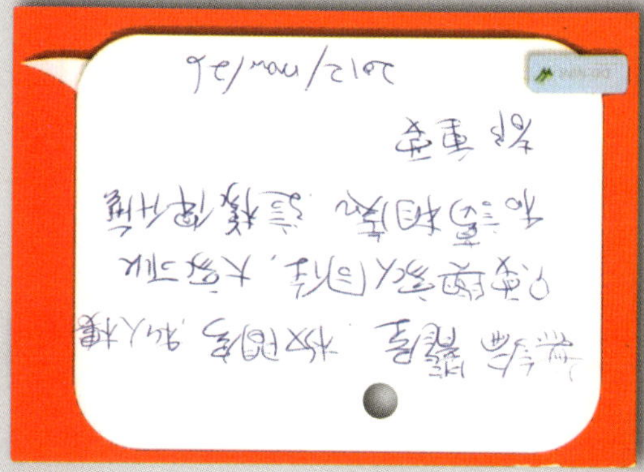

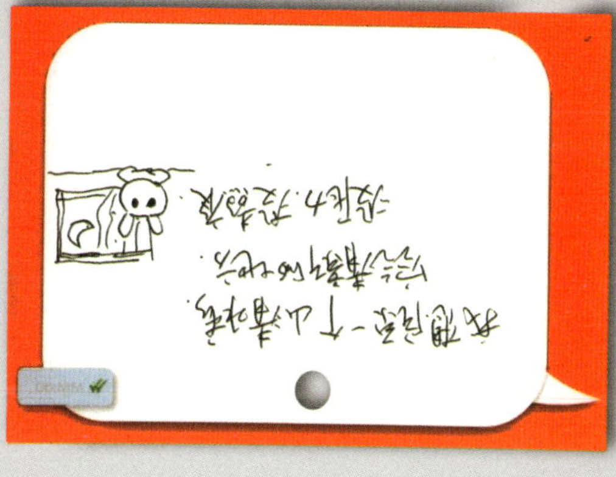

While difficult environments, both at home and in schools (such as roof-top illegal structures) would help to nurture people who are tenacious, persistent, and more endowed with our treasured 'can-do' spirit.

To me, architecture that is flexible enough to adapt to changing times is a myth. It did not really work with any of the metabolists' work, and it certainly is not even attempted in Foster's HK bank building, supposedly a building with inter-changeable parts. My attitude towards changing cities is that we should produce architecture that possesses values and attributes strong enough, timeless enough to absorb change, and inspiring enough to influence how the city changes around it. Cities evolve, slowly or quickly, and I'd like to see my buildings contributing in time to the direction of this evolution, to help shape change and to be engaged in a meaningful dialogue across space/time with old neighbours and new comers.

Q&A / P.S.

DIALOGUE WITH
Binocular Design

TO: Joseph Cho & Stefanie Lew
FROM: Anderson Lee

Stef & Joe, Hope all is well! A small request... Wondering how your schedule's looking like in the next few months... We have this publication on the HK/SZ Biennale and I wanted to see if you will be interested to be the designer. Time is v. tight as usual! I envision the purpose of this book as more than simply a 'document' of the exhibition. The book is divided into three major parts summed up as Past, Present and Future. I was thinking of three columns of information running in parallel, almost independent of each other, so that cross reading is possible and intentional. Hence three parts would co-exist on the same page or same spread. I know it could be hard to read the book but it is not meant to be a catalogue or academic journal. We want it to be FUN to read yet not graphically chaotic! I hope I am making sense... It would be fun to collaborate on this project... Ande

TO: Anderson
FROM: Joe & Stefanie

Hi Ande, Good to catch up with you on Skype last week. There's tons of visual material (2000+ pix!), and a lot of raw data to sort through in those Excel sheets. But we've worked through it all and come up with something, slightly different from your original idea of three parallel columns, still very much respecting the spirit of the original concept of having THREE-ness running throughout. The triangulated relationships between the elements will be obvious when you see the PDFs. There is definitely a bit of 'exquisite corpse' going on here. At the same time, there is a continuity that flows through.

A few key facts: the book is 418 pages, and importantly, it is physically comprised of four-page units – text (present) / image-image (past) / comment card (future). There are 60 exhibits in the book, thus 60 units, plus 21 units for the email dialogues. This creates enough of a rhythm to make their presence felt in the book's 'cross section' (or lasagna) as you flip through it. It has been a New York x Hong Kong style charrette. Total madness! But here it is. Hope you like it. Talk to you later on Skype! j&s

TO: Joe & Stefanie
FROM: Anderson

J&s, Greetings from Tokyo! The book looks... AWESOME & WONDERFUL! thanks for the extra efforts & hearts put into the project. I can almost taste the conceptual 'Lasagna!' Buon appetito. Now I will have Ashley & Karbi look over the Chinese comment cards to be

EVOLVING SCH
學舍春秋

Most of us relate our formative experiences to our school days, and almost everyone has come into contact with schools one way or another, either as students, teachers, parents, grandparents or in other capacities. As with many cities, school designs in Hong Kong evolved with the city's development, reflecting changes in society and politics. Architectural settings for learning embodied shifts in education ideologies, schooling policies as well as economics and demographics.

This exhibition reviews the transformation of school architecture in Hong Kong, from pre-war and roof-top schools, to standard designs driven by education policy shifts and individualized designs oriented to specific school users and stakeholders. By showcasing approaches to standard-campus, special needs, international school and sustainable designs in school architecture, this exhibition recognizes the architects' contribution in working with the education community to shape various school types to meet the needs and aspirations of the community as a whole.

我們大多數人的成長經歷，都與求學的時光有著密切的聯繫。似乎每個人都曾用十多年甚至更多年的時間或學生、或教師、或家長、或師長的身份與學校聯繫在一起。如其它城市一樣，香港的校舍設計隨城市發展而演進，反映著社會政治的變革。而建築作為學習之所，亦體現著教學思維、學校政策、經濟狀況與人口發展的變遷。

是次展覽回顧了香港校舍建築的歷史沿革。內容從戰前小學、天台小學、置至因教育政策改革而衍生的標準化設計，以及為學校使用者和持份者而有的個性化設計，通過展示標準化設計、校園設計、特殊需求設計、國際學校、可持續性設計等案例，展覽為建築師們與教育團體合作塑造多樣的學校環境以達廣大效能的貢獻表示敬意。

策展
香港中文大學建築學院 + 劉旎有限公司

合辦
香港教育博物館、香港教育學院

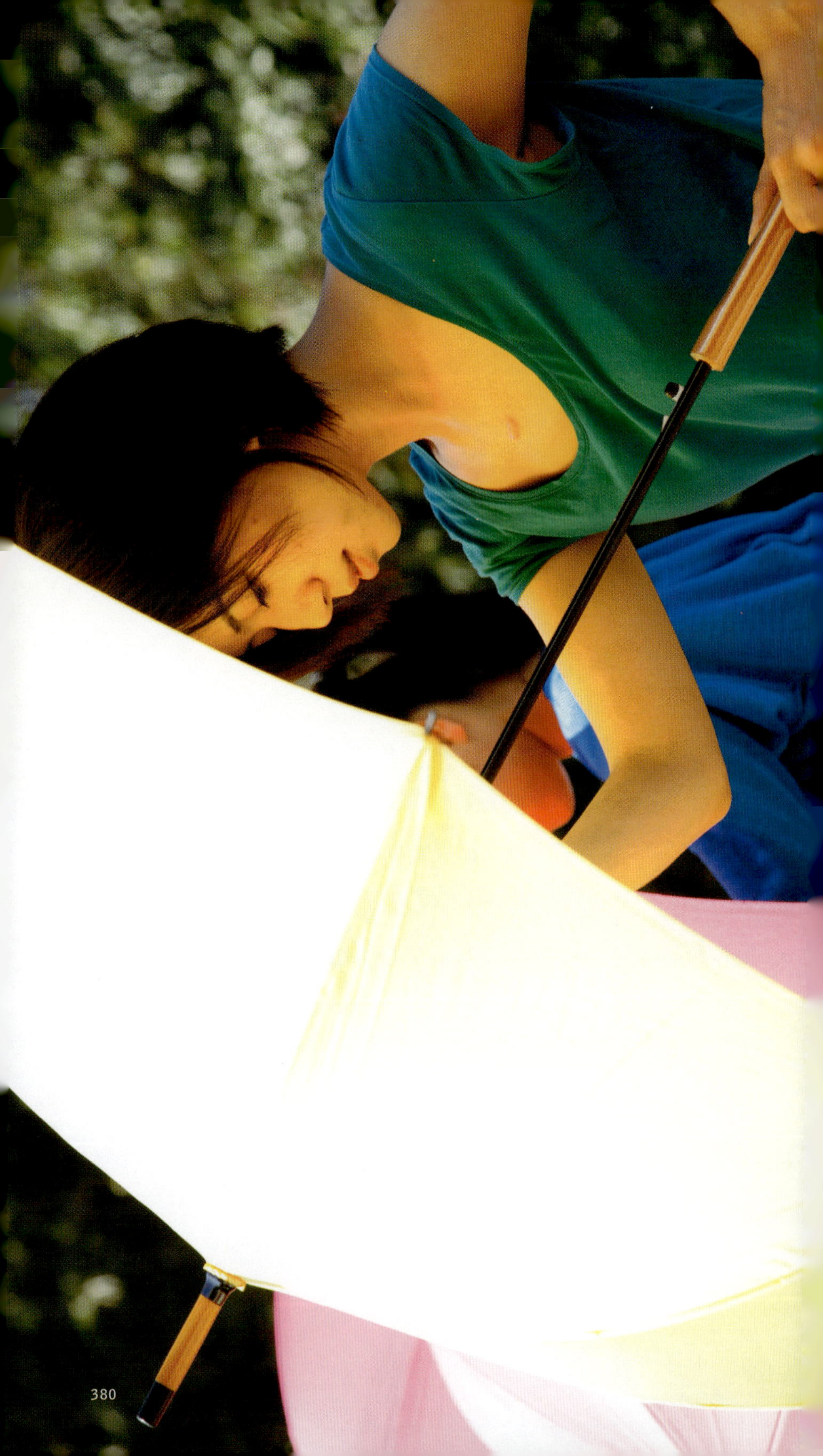

Tri-ciprocal Cities:
The Time, The Place, The People

〈三個城市：時間．空間．人間〉

參展項目：　2011–12香港及深圳城市╲建築雙城雙年展
展覽日期：　2012年2月15日至4月23日
開放時間：　星期一至六（星期四除外）：上午10時至下午6時
　　　　　　星期日及公眾假期：上午10時至下午7時
　　　　　　星期四（公眾假期除外）休館
Venue:　　　Kowloon Park and Hong Kong Heritage Discovery Centre
Date:　　　 15 February to 23 April 2012
Opening Hours:　10am – 8pm, Mondays to Saturdays (except Thursdays)
　　　　　　　　10am – 7pm, Sundays and Public Holidays
　　　　　　　　Closed on Thursdays (except Public Holidays)

"2011–12 Hong Kong & Shenzhen Bi-city Biennale of Urbanism\Architecture"

Public Events & Symposium Excerpts

Recent architectural biennales have acknowledged the increasing importance of providing a platform for public involvement. In many cases, activities and symposia have been organized to engage the general public in dialogues on architecture and urbanism. For the 2011–12 Hong Kong & Shenzhen Biennale, a series of over 30 public happenings took place during the course of the three-month exhibition. Ranging from film screenings to children's workshops and guided tours, these events were a popular way to stimulate progressive thinking, discussions, and the exchange of ideas about cities.

Since the first Hong Kong Biennale, curators have been working to create a space for intellectual debates and to showcase avant-garde architectural creations to both local and overseas audiences. In order to make the process of architectural/cultural production more accessible to the public, the curators of the 2011–12 Biennale sought to be deliberately community-focused and created multiple opportunities for public participation and collaboration. These community programmes became one of the exhibition's main infrastructures for the citizens' engagement with the city.

In response to the curatorial statement, 'triciprocal city – time, place and people,' the organizers developed a significant component for the people with the objective of disseminating professional knowledge to the general public. The curators worked with local cultural organizations such as the Hong Kong Art Center to organize free movie screenings, including '24 City,' a 2008 film directed and co-written by Chinese filmmaker Jia Zhangke; 'Night on Earth' by Jim Jarmusch; and 'PTU,' a local Hong Kong film produced and directed by Johnnie To. Though viewers might not have been aware of any direct curatorial link between the films, they were nonetheless experiencing nuances of architecture, places, people and time while viewing.

Other outreach programmes were specifically planned to attract a wide range of people. Several workshops gave children of different age groups opportunities to explore, invent and interpret their own ideas about cities. For example, 'Building My Ideal City,' planned in partnership with the Hong Kong Architecture Centre, gave local secondary school children the chance to learn model-building techniques using foam and cardboard. These public events were not only rich in content, but also responsive to the concurrent exhibitions.

By diversifying the range of exhibitions, balancing the content of innovative practices, and introducing scholarly content as well as community participation into the activities, the Biennale became the backdrop for creative speculation, bringing forth the critical question of how architects can help to define and share public culture.

PUBLIC EVENTS 383

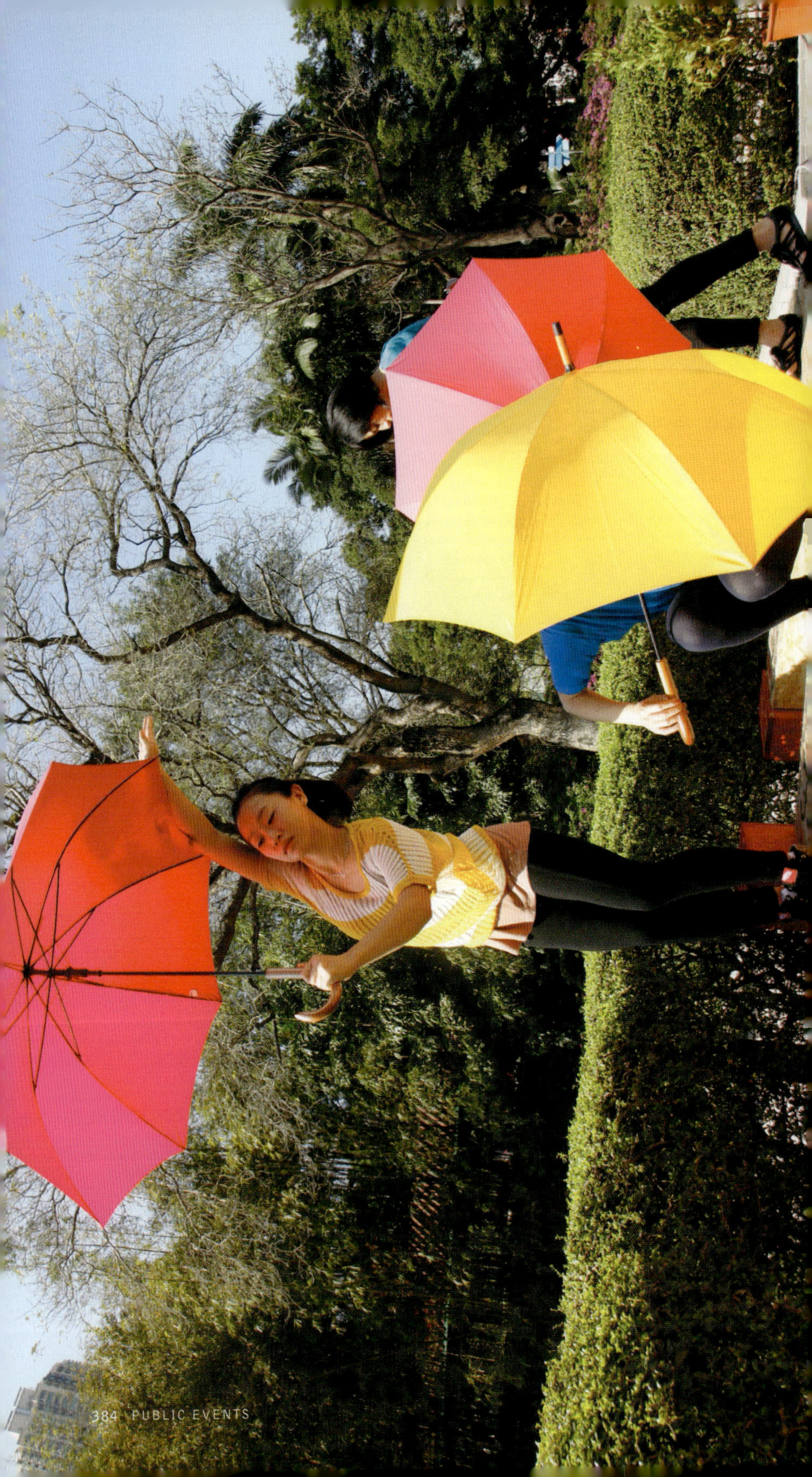

我的感想 My Sharing

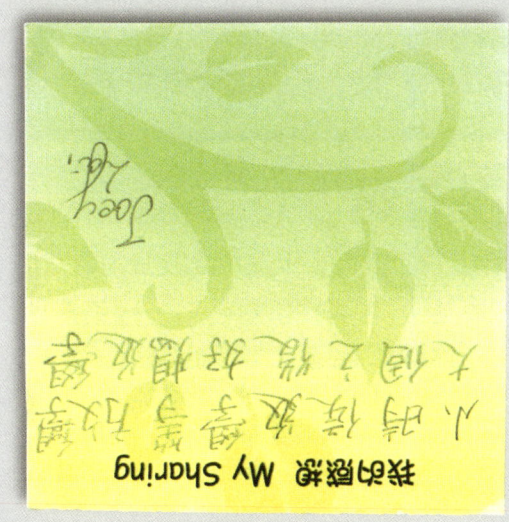

虽然有很大了，但是也記得聽講，
其他是，孩子记得你就是要努力勤奋
记得多参考读书和学习重要
所以到時候，有多点点的朋友
多来看你呢，多相信人，做好事
爱自己，不要放弃了，我也相信你。

我的感想 My Sharing

小朋友你要努力讀書，
大個之後就能賺到錢

Joey Lu,

SYMPOSIUM

Cities for People: Public Space & Public Life in Kowloon East (02 March 2012)

PARTICIPANTS

Mr. David SIM, Director, GEHL Architects; Ms. Ewa WESTERMARK, Associate, GHEK Architects. Dr. Peter Cookson SMITH, President, Hong Kong Institute of Planners; Mr. Vincent NG, Vice-President, Hong Kong Institute of Urban Design; Mr. Edward FARRELLY, Director, Head of Hong Kong Research, CBRE (respondents). Mr. K.K. LING, Head / Pre-Kowloon East Development Office (moderator)

EXCERPTS

David Sim: Every city has a traffic department operated by very professional people. They spend a lot of time making very good decisions, planning well, and always basing their decisions on facts and figures. There is not one street in Hong Kong where they don't have accurate traffic information every weekday and every weekend. But when it comes to people there's almost nothing. There is no department of pedestrians. And actually in Hong Kong, only 7% of the population transports themselves in vehicles. The other 93% of the population uses public transport and walking. It's very interesting that there's no statistic on what is going on there. Of course we know culture is different everywhere in the world. We also know that climate is different everywhere. But the way people basically inhabit the environment is more or less the same everywhere.

Peter Cookson Smith: So really the essential question, sort of underlining all the previous comments, how do we involve all these qualities, not just the sensible qualities of the city, but how do we involve the spirit of Hong Kong? Streets, as you have just seen in others' illustrations, really are the foundation of Hong Kong's urbanism. And we do have to think about them in creating new plans, these become quite fundamental qualities to incorporate and know in terms of our planning. Secondly, what we called the social dimension. I think we need to ensure really that the physical organisation of urban space and its social function actually do go hand in hand. Third, the perception dimension. This combination of sensible values, formal values and symbolic values. And of course all the local signifiers that really make Hong Kong the place it is.

Winston Chu: I love the idea of getting the people into the streets. I would say all of you will agree that Hong Kong is not short of people. If you go into Causeway Bay any time on Saturday or Sunday, Hong Kong is never short of people. You see people all carrying luggage in Causeway Bay.

Audience member: There are some comments on extracting the public from the development process. I think with a lot of these projects, it takes leadership. And it takes leadership on a couple of levels. Obviously within government but also within developers. We studied shopping centres around the world and looked at what makes some successful. And the big idea was to make these shopping centres into the third place. So people will have their homes, they will have their work but we make shopping centres a third place by introducing certain elements that make it more desirable and make it more of a comfortable place, dedicate a little more money to common areas, just to make it a nicer place. All this would go very well until it gets to the accounting. Every time we come up with a new idea, everybody would be in favour but at the end of the process they say, how much is it going to cost?

PUBLIC EVENTS 387

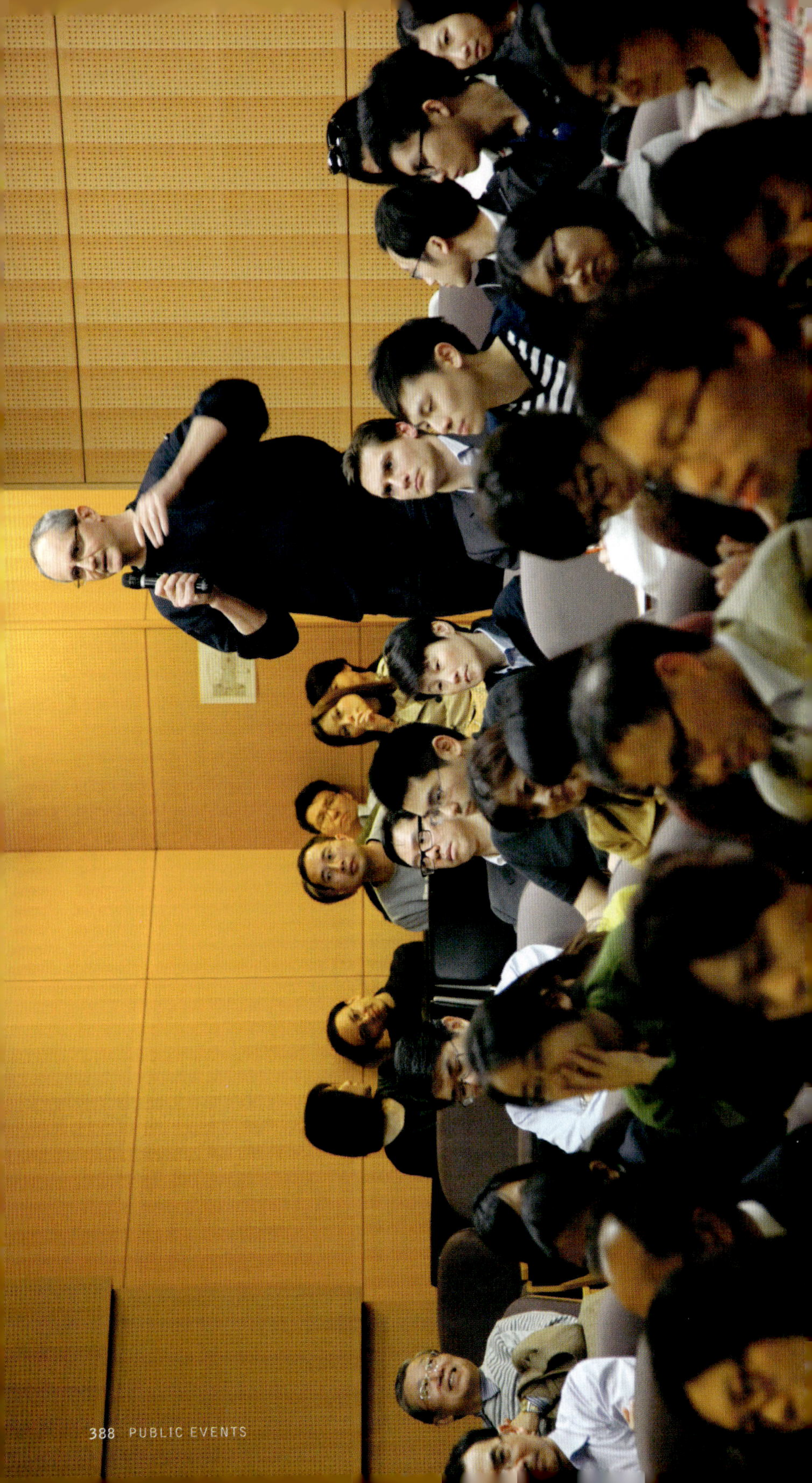

安 有人
那可以
体验到
自己的
Home Sweet
HOME ⌂

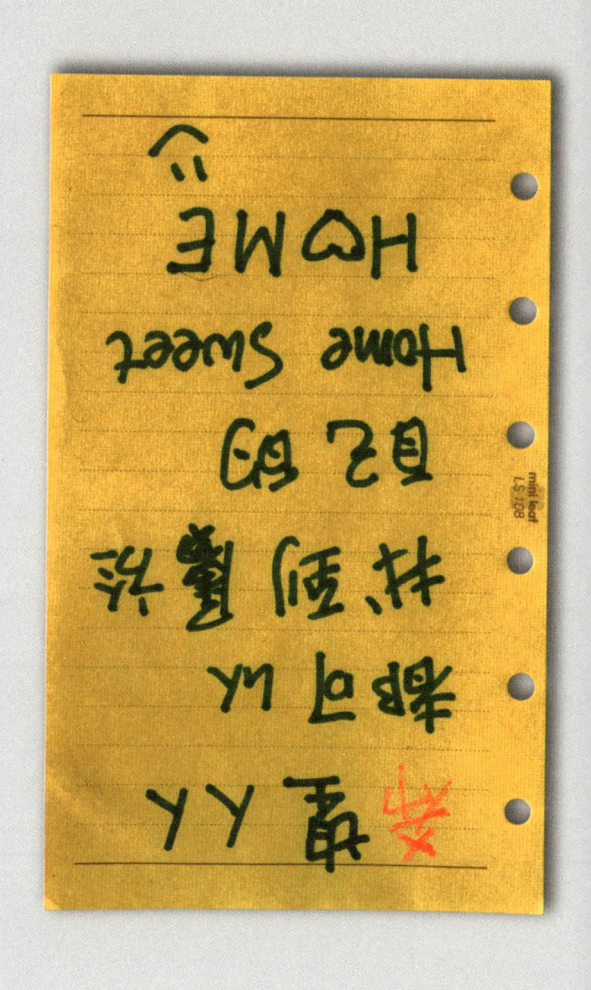

SYMPOSIUM

Community and Development (4 March 2012)

PARTICIPANTS

Mr. Alvin YIP, Poly U; Mr. Weijen WANG, HKU; Dr. Y.C. CHEN, HKBU; Mr. Donald CHOI, Managing Director, Nan Fung Development Limited. Tris KEE, Curator for Community & Media (Moderator and Respondent)

Alvin Yip: I think I will talk more about the relationship between community and development today. This photo was taken at the last biennale in 2009. I like it and have been using it on various occasions over the last few years. If our topic today is community development, you can seen from this photo how interesting Hong Kong is. First, development and community seem to be to separate things in Hong Kong. The photo also shows the tension between community and development. You see at the bottom of the photo, community is weak and small compared to the development at the top of the photo. // Two case studies. Going back to the relationship between community and development, I don't think that's static. I think the relationship evolves. There are also a lot of chances for community and developers to cooperate. I think it's quite like football. So if we can connect more, have strategies, then even the small and weak community can score in this 'football match.'

Donald Choi: You can see I used plural for 'communities.' I believe every community is consisting of many smaller communities. So it is not right to say there is only one community in Hong Kong. So what is a community? I think there are generally two different kinds of communities — voluntary and non-voluntary. Like I am born Chinese but can choose to live in Kowloon, Hong Kong Island etc. Consequently, we can take part in and affect the voluntary communities around us. Ideally everyone within a community should help each other. But that's not what we see in reality. More often than not, community members have conflicts of interest. // From a developer's perspective, what can we do in community development? We take the market risk in development work, which will turn out to be a new community in the future. Very often developers' work is constrained by the environment and other factors. And more should be done by the government. That is to strike a balance of interest between the stake holders. We developers are commercial organisations, obviously we cannot take up charity work. We can try to understand and discuss together what communities need and try to fulfil these needs. For example, if home buyers would like to have clubs in their estates, that's what we can do. We simply follow the market.

Weijen Wang: To me, being an architect, a teacher, all my projects are related to community. This is because an architecture project in most cases will have a site. A site, in most cases, is inhabited. When we make a new development, we move people who originally live there to another place. We need strategies for that. A site has a geography, a landscape, people, trees and water.

Y.C. Chen: In community planning, there is a word that's very important, and that is involvement. I will talk about three principles about involvement. The first principle is bottom-up. I think architects and urban planners have professional knowledge but no local knowledge. The professional knowledge and local knowledge should come together in the participation process. Users are very important. The government listens to the opinions of the users in consultations but does not let them make the decision. The government makes its own decision. Users' opinions are only for reference. But I insist that in good community planning, the users of the community should have the final say on the plan. The decision making process must be democratic. That's exactly the reason why the story of Choi Yuan village has a happy ending.

PUBLIC EVENTS 391

392 PUBLIC EVENTS

大哥再轉
轉會跟會會跟!
會會跟會會
小的跟會跟會小
轉的o

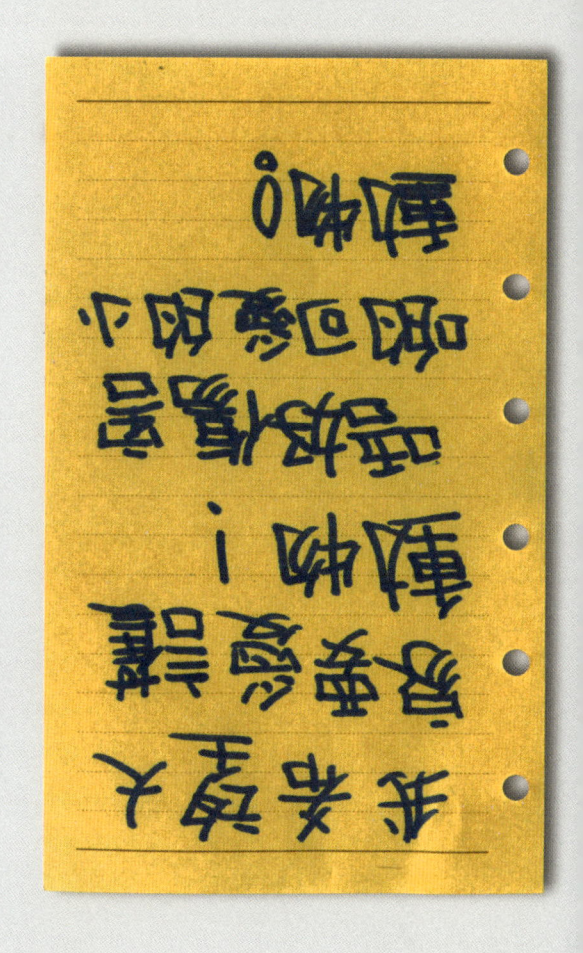

SYMPOSIUM

Industry & Urbanism (16 March 2012)

PARTICIPANTS

Hitoshi ABE, Founder, Atelier Hitoshi Abe Design Inc.; Professor Shinya OKUDA, National University of Singapore; Kristof CROLLA, Founder, LEAD; Weijen WANG, Founder, Wang Weijen Architecture; Eric YIM, Chairperson, Hong Kong Design Council; Xiaodu LIU, Founder, Urbanus. Gene K. KING, Chief Curator; Anderson LEE, Chief Curator (moderators)

Anderson Lee: This is very timely because we just marked the one year anniversary of a disaster that hits everyone's heart, not only Japanese, I believe.... If you get a chance to walk around our Biennale, you can see the projects that specifically deal with – in my mind, in the curators' minds – how fabrication, industrial fabrication specifically, can inform and help disaster relief building types, building methodology, construction methodology. Through this symposium, through the collaboration with industry, this is our hope that there is a stronger dialogue and connections and more exchange of ideas and communication channels between the design and the industry.

Shinya Okuda: Typical lightweight structures are categorized in three types: tent or container or some kind of dome structure. Each has pros and cons. Tent is obviously very materially efficient, container is very space efficient and adaptable, and dome is structurally and materially efficient and adaptable. However, what would have all the benefits together: materially efficient, space efficient and adaptable? That's the concept of the bioshell. The four key features: It's a lightweight structure, only 60 kg. The components are only two types of left and right, so it is completely stackable to reduce transportation and storage fees. It's like a tatami module, so it can be one you need, two you need, both x y z directions [for adaptability]. And it can be quickly assembled and disassembled as you use it, and after several times if we don't need it, we can dispose it to nature without damaging the environment. [...] The recovery process might take tens of years, that's what we learned from the Kobe earthquake, so it's perhaps important to remind people what happened and try to prepare for what happens next.

Kristof Crolla: Our position is that by understanding a material's basic properties and pushing for great performance, while at the same time being aware also of the aesthetic values and those type of effects – we think that the actual design role can be regained for architects. Transforming applications ultimately empowers us to challenge the passive mode of material use that we've been witnessing primarily. So concepts like building complexity with minimal means while trying to see if we can accomplish maximal effect. Bring in personalization, mass personalization, using digital tools that are not only used for ornate production but actually allow a more user-oriented interaction to be brought in. Those are the key elements that I'm working with right now.

Xiaodu Liu: The Chinese are very good at forgetting things, especially [when bad things] happen. It's been a while we haven't talked about things like earthquake or earthquake relief things. Sichuan earthquake was a very serious thing. [...] The situation is very different. Actually, talking about this kind of disaster relief project ... architecture is actually meaningless, the only issue is safety. Everybody is talking about this, saying nothing else. So this is a very special time. And also the speed of construction is very urgent. Then we choose to build some schools so over a year the organization built four schools. [For] many we do the design, we do some management things. At the end of this construction we actually went to the site for the openings and made a movie.

PUBLIC EVENTS 395

396 PUBLIC EVENTS

Small house is OK!

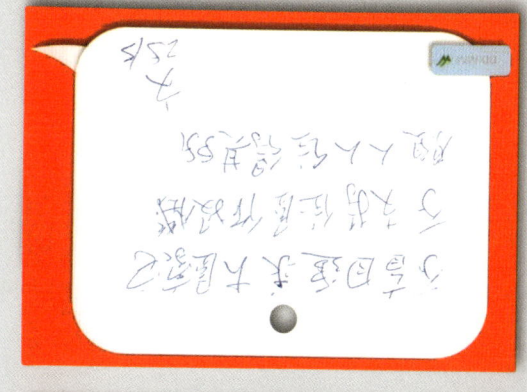

5/25
木

うち田邉夫妻と2?
3次会は井が谷
飯人生送見る。

INDEX OF EXHIBITS AND DIALOGUES

ACHL Architects		EXH 026	p. 182
AR-CH Studio		EXH 026	p. 182
Architecture Research Office (ARO)		EXH 042	p. 274
Artech Architects		EXH 027	p. 186
Artfield		EXH 030	p. 202
Atelier Hitoshi Abe		EXH 050	p. 318
Atelier Seraji Architectes & Associés		EXH 040	p. 266
BASSETT, Shannon		EXH 038	p. 254
BETSKY, Aaron	Q&A 001		p. 034
Bioarchitecture Formosana		EXH 025	p. 178
BOLCHOVER, Joshua	Q&A 002	EXH 018	p. 054 / 134
CABANAS, Cesar		EXH 038	p. 254
CAMPRUBI, Alex		EXH 038	p. 254
CASAGRANDE, Marco		EXH 032	p. 218
CHAN, Sunny Ka Shing		EXH 056	p. 354
CHAN, Marco Kwun Yu		EXH 058	p. 366
CHAN, Sze Man		EXH 053	p. 334
CHAN, Bill Yiu Kwan		EXH 007	p. 074
CHAN, Winnie Yuen Lai		EXH 009	p. 082
CHAU, Athena Kei Yun		EXH 010	p. 090
CHEN, Xian-Hong		EXH 026	p. 182
CHEUNG, Ivan Pui Kin		EXH 058	p. 366
CHEUNG, Dave Yuen Lok		EXH 058	p. 366
CHIANG, Hsing-O		EXH 026	p. 182
Chinese University of Hong Kong, School of Architecture		EXH 005	p. 062
CHIU, Jay W.		EXH 030	p. 202
CHOI, ArChoi Kit Wang		EXH 007	p. 074
Choi Yuen Village Eco-Community Building Studio		EXH 012	p. 098
CHUNG, Howard Chi Ho		EXH 010	p. 090
CLAUS, Felix	Q&A 003	EXH 036	p. 070 / 242
CROLLA, Kristof (LEAD)	Q&A 004	EXH 021	p. 102 / 150
DAN, Norihiko (Norihiko Dan & Associates)	Q&A 005	EXH 046	p. 122 / 298
Department of Architcture, Tamkang University		EXH 030	p. 202
dlandstudio		EXH 042	p. 274
DU, Juan		EXH 017	p. 130
EDGE		EXH 021	p. 150
ENDO, Kazuki		EXH 050	p. 318
ESCH, Hans-Georg		EXH 034	p. 234
ESKYIU (Eric Schuldenfrei, Marisa Yiu)		EXH 055	p. 350
Fei & Cheng Associates		EXH 028	p. 194
FOK, Wendy Wei Yue		EXH 058	p. 366
FUNG, Sherry Yik Ping		EXH 056	p. 354
Grand Hope Architects & Planners		EXH 026	p. 182
HARTOG, Harry den		EXH 024	p. 166
HASDELL, Peter		EXH 018	p. 134
HAVERMANS, Frank		EXH 060	p. 374
HIRAHARA, Hideki		EXH 026	p. 182
Hong Kong Institute of Planners, Young Planners Group Committee		EXH 002	p. 046
Hong Kong SAR Planning Department		EXH 001	p. 042
Höweler + Yoon Architecture LLP		EXH 008	p. 078
HSIEH, Ying-Chun		EXH 031	p. 214
HUANG, Po-Yu		EXH 026	p. 182
Institute of Historical Resources Management, Taiwan		EXH 030	p. 202
ISODA, Yuzuru		EXH 050	p. 318
Jiakun Architects		EXH 023	p. 162
JOHNSON, Kathleen		EXH 058	p. 366
KAN, Ka Lo		EXH 053	p. 334
KEE, Tris	Q&A 006		p. 138
KEI, Juliana Yat Shun		EXH 007	p. 074
KIM, Eddy Man		EXH 057	p. 358
KIM, Edward Yujoong		EXH 057	p. 358
Kohn Pedersen Fox Associates (KPF)		EXH 043	p. 282
KUNG, Shu-Chang	Q&A 007		p. 170
LAI, Chee Kien		EXH 048	p. 306
LAI, Guo-Rui		EXH 026	p. 182
LAI, William Wing Fung		EXH 007	p. 074
LAU, Julia	Q&A 008		p. 190
LAW, Ruby Wai Yue		EXH 007	p. 074
LEAD		EXH 021	p. 150
LEUNG, Calvin Chi Hoi		EXH 009	p. 082

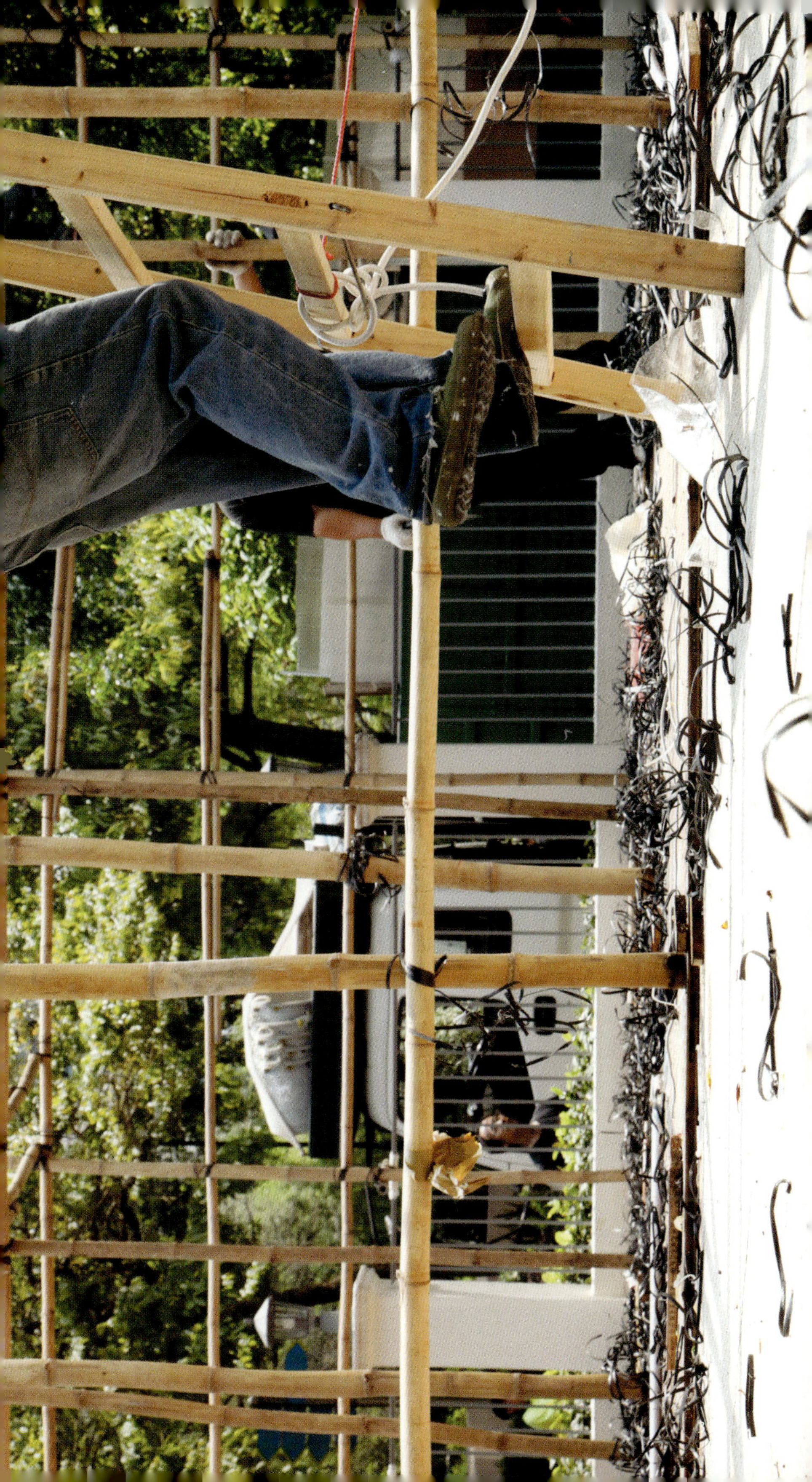

400

9.4.12

Such an amazing area within a city! Well done for conserving the area for future generations

Ella (Australia)

Lewis.Tsurumaki.Lewis Architects (LTL)		EXH 041	p. 270
LI, Xiangning		EXH 024	p. 166
LIM, Kevin		EXH 057	p. 358
LIM, William		EXH 013	p. 110
LIU, Wei-Kung		EXH 029	p. 198
LIU, Yuyang		EXH 024	p. 166
LOK, Michelle Man Sum		EXH 058	p. 366
LWK & Partners (HK) Limited		EXH 006	p. 066
MEYER, Ulf	Q&A 009	EXH 034	p. 206 / 234
MINIWIZ		EXH 025	p. 178
Morphosis		EXH 037	p. 250
MVRDV		EXH 033	p. 222
Neri & Hu Design and Research Office		EXH 019	p. 142
NG, Kal		EXH 049	p. 314
Norihiko Dan & Associates		EXH 046	p. 298
Office for Metropolitan Architecture (OMA)		EXH 027 / 047	p. 186 / 302
Ohno Laboratory, University of Tokyo		EXH 045	p. 290
OKUDA, Shinya		EXH 003	p. 050
openUU Ltd.		EXH 057	p. 358
PO, Chung Yin		EXH 010	p. 090
PUN, Stanley Ka Chun		EXH 010	p. 090
REISER, Jesse (RUR Architecture)	Q&A 010	EXH 028 / 035	p. 226 / 194 / 238
RILEY, Terence	Q&A 011		p. 262
Riptide Creative Collective		EXH 014	p. 114
ROAN, Ching-Yueh		EXH 031	p. 214
Rocker-Lange Architects		EXH 011	p. 094
RUR Architecture		EXH 028 / 035	p. 194 / 238
SCYS ASDD		EXH 026	p. 182
SERAJI, Nasrine (Atelier Seraji Architectes & Associés)	Q&A 012	EXH 040	p. 278 / 266
SHANE, Grahame		EXH 035	p. 238
Shu Chang & Associates Architects		EXH 025	p. 178
SIU, Stanley Kwok Kin		EXH 009	p. 082
SMITH, Peter Cookson		EXH 054	p. 338
SO, Kwok Kin		EXH 009	p. 082
SOH, Darren		EXH 048	p. 306
SOLOMON, Jonathan D.		EXH 020	p. 146
Squared Design Lab		EXH 008	p. 078
Steven Holl Architects		EXH 044	p. 286
TANG, Dorothy		EXH 020	p. 146
TO, Kenneth King Wai		EXH 058	p. 366
Tohoku University Motoe Lab		EXH 050	p. 318
TONG, Karmin		EXH 053	p. 334
Traces Limited		EXH 005	p. 062
TSAI, Chia-Hao		EXH 026	p. 182
TSAI, Wan-Lin		EXH 026	p. 182
TSANG, Thomas		EXH 004	p. 058
TSENG, Pu-Ming		EXH 026	p. 182
University of Hong Kong, Department of Architecture		EXH 059	p. 370
Urban Design Division, Shenzhen Urbanus Architecture and Design		EXH 016	p. 126
Urban Planning, Land & Resources Commission of Shenzhen Municipality		EXH 016	p. 126
Urban Redevelopment Office, Taipei City		EXH 030	p. 202
WANG, Hui-Juan		EXH 026	p. 182
WANG, Jinsong		EXH 022	p. 158
WANG, Shu		EXH 031	p. 214
WANG, Shuzhan		EXH 022	p. 158
WANG, Weijen (Wang Weijen Architecture)	Q&A 013	EXH 012	p. 294 / 098
WANG, Xiangdong		EXH 022	p. 158
Whole+Design Architects & Planners		EXH 026	p. 182
Why Factory		EXH 033	p. 222
WOLF Michael		EXH 039	p. 258
WONG, Chi Yung		EXH 015	p. 118
WONG, Kacey	Q&A 014	EXH 051 / 052	p. 310 / 322 / 330
WONG, Ming Wai		EXH 053	p. 334
WONG, Reine		EXH 010	p. 090
YAO, Kim (Architecture Research Office)	Q&A 015	EXH 042	p. 326 / 274
YIM, Rocco	Q&A 016		p. 342
YIP, Chun Hang		EXH 056	p. 354
YUNG, Sai Chun		EXH 056	p. 354
ZHANG, Yan		EXH 022	p. 158
	Q&A/P.S.		p. 378

403

404

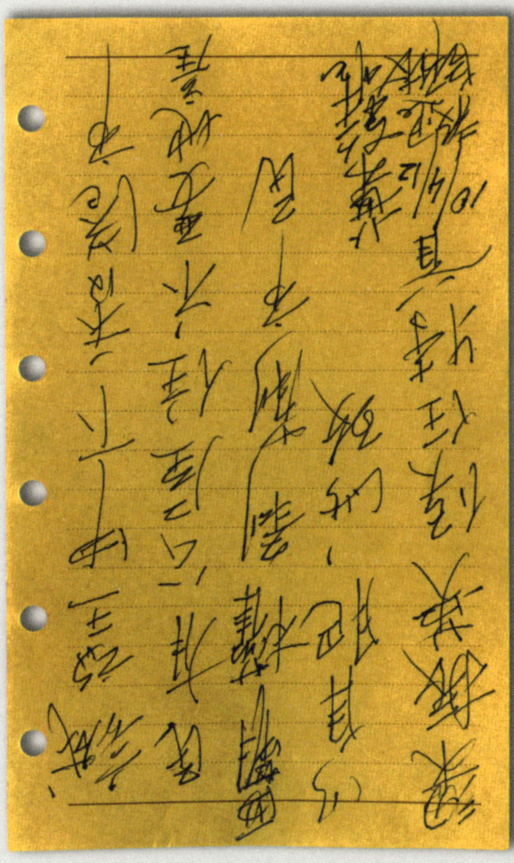

ACKNOWLEDGMENTS

The chief curators would like to thank all of the exhibitors and participants of the 2011–12 Biennale. We would also like to thank specifically our colleagues who contributed to the dialogue portion of this publication: Aaron Betsky, Joshua Bolchover, Felix Claus, Kristof Crolla, Norihiko Dan, Tris Kee, Shu-Chang Kung, Julia Lau, Ulf Meyer, Jesse Reiser, Terence Riley, Nasrine Seraji, Weijen Wang, Kacey Wong, Kim Yao, and Rocco Yim.

Our appreciation goes to to HKIA, HKIP, and HKDA for sponsoring the Biennale and the Tri-ciprocal Cities project. We are grateful to HKADC and HKU for generous grants in support of this publication. And we would like to thank Gordon Goff at ORO Editions for publishing this book at Hong Kong speed.

At Index Architecture Limited, Hong Kong, thanks are owed to Karbi Chan and Ashley Lau for assistance in managing the project. And finally, a special thanks to Joseph Cho & Stefanie Lew of Binocular, New York, for taking our raw materials and 'tri-ciprocal' ideas and transforming them into this book, the final Biennale exhibit.

AL & GK

BIENNALE CREDITS

Curatorial Team: Gene Kwang-Yu KING and Anderson LEE (Chief Curators); Julia Lau (Curator for Venue and Programme); Tris KEE (Curator for Community and Media); David TSENG (Curator for Taipei Exhibits); Shu-Chang KUNG and Wei CHANG (Curators for Taipei Pavilion); Aaron LEE (Curator for Asian Urban Portraits).

Administration: Sallie CHAN (Project Manager); Winki CHENG (Project Officer). Fiona LAU, Suki CHAN, Frankie AU, Yuni YIP, Chloe YAU of Index Architecture Limited; Edwin TANG of Traces Limited; Alfred HO, Inaciso CHAN, Calvin CHAN, Norman UNG, Wiki LO, Helen FAN, Mark LIU of the Community Project Workshop, Faculty of Architecture, The University Hong Kong (Coordinators). Lisa LAU (PR Consultant).

Architecture & Planning: Sai Chun YUNG, Angus OR, Kim FUNG, Suki CHAN of Index Architecture Limited; Alfred HO of the Community Project Workshop, Faculty of Architecture, The University Hong Kong; Ever Green Decoration Works Co. Ltd. Conceptual Phase Support: Erin C. SHIH, Penny CHEN, Christine YEH of King Shih Architects.

Translations and Editing: Jessica Niles DEHOFF (English Editor); Gene Kwang-Yu KING, Moon Lin JAU, Winki CHENG (Chinese Translators and Editors).

HKSZ 2011–12 Steering Committee: Bernard LIM, JP (Chairman); Weijen WANG (Vice Chairman); Alice Lai Fong YEUNG (Vice Chairman); Thomas CHUNG; Ivan FU; Stephen HO; Dominic LAM; Joshua LAU; Kar Kan LING, JP; Eunice MAK; Ellen NGAN; Stanley SIU; Kelly SZE; Rocco YIM, BBS, JP; Alvin YIP; Franklin YU.

HKIA Secretariat: Rita CHEUNG (Registrar); Vivian SIE (Senior Manager); Yvonne GOD (Project Officer).

407

408

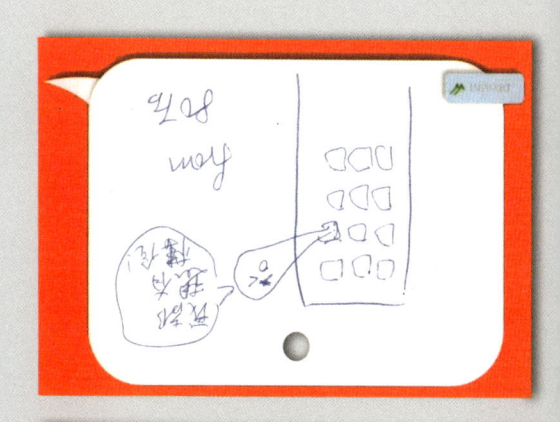

FRIENDLY NEIGHBOURS
++++
Small House
vegetable patch
CHICKENS

ABOUT THE CURATORS

Anderson LEE, Chief Curator
Assistant Professor, Faculty of Architecture, The University of Hong Kong
Founder, Index Architecture Limited

Anderson Lee received a Master of Architecture from Princeton University. Prior to founding Index Architecture Limited in 2000, he worked at Steven Holl Architects (New York) for eight years. The architectural practice encompasses multidisciplinary services providing conceptual and technical consultancy on urban planning, architecture, interior design and product/furniture design. Anderson has been an assistant professor at the Faculty of Architecture, the University of Hong Kong since 2003. He is a Registered Architect in the State of New York, and a member of the American Institute of Architects (AIA).

Gene Kwang-Yu KING, Chief Curator
Founder, King Shih Architects

Gene King is a Registered Architect in the State of New York and Taiwan. In 1999, he established King Shih Architects (KSA) with Erin C. Shih in Taipei. Also as a writer, he won The Literature Award of China Times and United Daily News (1982) and National Literary Award in Fiction (1989), which are considered important honours for Chinese literature in the region. He has published four collections of short stories and essays.

Tris KEE, Curator for Community and Media
Assistant Professor, Director of Community Project Workshop, Faculty of Architecture, The University of Hong Kong

Tris Kee is a graduate of Master of Architecture, University of Waterloo, Canada. She is a Registered Architect in Hong Kong and Canada, a Professional Member of the Hong Kong Institute of Architects (HKIA), Royal Architectural Institute of Canada (RAIC), the Hong Kong Institute of Architectural Conservationists (HKICON) and an Executive Committee Member of the Hong Kong Interior Design Association (HKIDA). Also she is the Director of Community Project Workshop at HKU.

Julia LAU, Curator for Venue and Programme
Founder, Traces Limited

Julia Lau is a Registered Architect in Hong Kong and an Authorized Person (List 1). She has also obtained PRC Class 1 Registered Architect Qualification. Professionally, she has served the Hong Kong Institute of Architects and the American Institute of Architects, Hong Kong Chapter for a number of years. Currently, she is a Council Member of the Professional Green Building Council. She is a member of the Town Planning Board, Hong Kong Housing Authority, and a Council member of the Academy of Performing Arts. She has also served on The Board of Management of the Chinese Permanent Cemeteries and Hong Kong Arts Centre (HKAC) for many years, and advocates cooperation of Architecture and the Allied Arts.

Speculative Surfaces for the Chinese Eco-city

412

Hong Kong is awesome!

Afterlife

Time, place, and people have all changed, but the objects remain. Possessing new identities and igniting new possibilities and scenarios since the closing of our Biennale, we have recorded the 'afterlife' of 'Tri-ciprocal Cities.'

As in the aftermath of any other events of similar scale, a massive number of banners and exhibition booths were left abandoned after the closing. We have made conscious and active efforts to find new 'hosts' for these items. This is a form of 'upcycling' since the items have not been disintegrated into their original raw material forms. Rather, future users can still see strong traces of these objects, which may even remain completely unaltered, in their original forms. Banners became bookshelves, and bunk beds have been reused in a community center as shelves, storage, beds (back to the real ORIGINAL purpose!), and even props in theatre performances. Most of the bamboo sticks that were used to build the pavilions were recycled naturally.

The idea of this 'object continuum' in a changed time, place, and people fascinated us. It was one of the key messages for our Biennale visitors and perhaps, for the readers of this publication: The sheer number of objects we generated during the Biennale were not unlike the buildings and architecture that we, as professionals, create on a daily basis. We have the responsibility to understand and acknowledge the potentials (good or bad) that our collective acts entail. And we should treat our physical environment with tender care.

415

416

please take one and leave a m

ORO Editions
Publishers of Architecture, Art, and Design
Gordon GOFF: Publisher

www.oroeditions.com
info@oroeditions.com

Copyright © 2014 by Index Architecture Ltd.
All Rights Reserved
ISBN: 978-1-941806-36-4

Chief Curators / Volume Editors:
Anderson LEE & Gene Kwang-Yu KING

Book Design & Assemblage:
Joseph CHO & Stefanie LEW,
Binocular, New York

Project Management:
Karbi Yuet CHAN & Ashley Paak Tik LAU,
Index Architecture Ltd., Hong Kong;
Joseph CHO, Binocular, New York

Production Assistance:
Alexandria NAZAR, ORO Editions

Printing & Binding:
Hang Yau Printing Company

Printed in Hong Kong

All rights reserved. No part of this book may be reproduced, stored in a retrieval system, or transmitted in any form or by any means, including electronic, mechanical, photocopying of microfilming, recording, or otherwise (except that copying permitted by Sections 107 and 108 of the U.S. Copyright Law and except by reviewers for the public press) without written permission from the publisher.

ORO Editions has made every effort to minimize the overall carbon footprint of this project. As part of this goal, ORO Editions, in association with Global ReLeaf, have arranged to plant two trees for each and every tree used in the manufacturing of the paper produced for this book. Global ReLeaf is an international campaign run by American Forests, the nation's oldest nonprofit conservation organization. Global ReLeaf is American Forests' education and action program that helps individuals, organizations, agencies, and corporations improve the local and global environment by planting and caring for trees.

North American Distribution:
Actar Distribution
151 Grand Street, 5th Fl.
New York, New York 10013

International Distribution:
www.oroeditions.com/distribution

Publication Sponsors:

The Hong Kong Institute of Architects

Hong Kong Institute of Planners

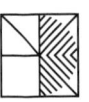

Hong Kong Designers Association

香港藝術發展局
Hong Kong Arts Development Council

Hong Kong Arts Development Council fully supports freedom of artistic expression. The views and opinions expressed in this project do not represent the stand of the Council.

This book is supported by the HKU Knowledge Exchange Fund granted by the University Grants Committee.